Queen
of the
Conqueror

Queen of the Conqueror

THE LIFE OF MATILDA, WIFE OF WILLIAM I

TRACY BORMAN

BANTAM BOOKS

NEW YORK

Published in the United States by Bantam Books, an imprint of
The Random House Publishing Group, a division of Random House, Inc., New York.

BANTAM BOOKS and the rooster colophon are registered trademarks of Random House, Inc.

Originally published in hardcover in Great Britain as *Matilda: Queen of the Conqueror*
by Jonathan Cape, an imprint of the Random House Publishing Group Limited,
London, in 2011.

Library of Congress Cataloging-in-Publication Data

Borman, Tracy.
Queen of the Conqueror : the life of Matilda, wife of William I / Tracy Borman.
p. cm.
Includes bibliographical references and index.
ISBN 978-0-553-80814-8 (acid-free paper)—ISBN 978-0-553-90825-1 (ebook)
1. Matilda, Queen, consort of William I, King of England, d. 1083. 2. Great Britain—
History—William I, 1066–1087—Biography. 3. William I, King of England,
1027 or 8–1087—Marriage. 4. Queens—Great Britain—Biography. I. Title.
DA199.M39B67 2012
942.02'1092—dc23
[B]
2011029689

Printed in the United States of America on acid-free paper

www.bantamdell.com

2 4 6 8 9 7 5 3 1

First U.S. Edition

Book design by Caroline Cunningham

To Eleanor, with love

ACKNOWLEDGMENTS

*I*t is no exaggeration to say that this book could not have been written without the unstinting support of my parents, John and Joan Borman. Between them, they have clocked up so many miles on the East Coast Railway that they deserve shares in the company. My mother in particular has spent many days looking after my daughter in order for me to be able to visit the British Library and other places necessary for research. I am deeply grateful for her kindness, and that of my father, who made regular trips to the London Library on my behalf. I have also been lucky enough to have the support and encouragement of my sister, Jayne, her husband, Rick, and their two lovely daughters, Olivia and Neve.

This book has been greatly enhanced by the dedication and expertise of my publishers. In particular, I would like to thank my editors at Jonathan Cape and Bantam Dell, Alex Bowler, Jessica Waters, and Tracy Devine, for their invaluable insight and meticulous attention to detail. I am also delighted to have been supported by my wonderful publicists Hannah Ross and Lisa Barnes, and I am grateful to Steven Messer for his excellent detective work with the picture research and to Tom Avery for seeing the book through to completion. My agent, Julian Alexander, has—as ever—supported me throughout with his sage advice, patience, and humor.

I have been very fortunate to have had the help and encouragement of my friend and fellow historian Alison Weir, who generously shared her research notes on Matilda with me, as well as her extensive collection of images. I would also like to thank Nicola Tallis for her valuable insights into the castles and abbeys of Normandy that are connected with Matilda's history. Sincere thanks are also due to Julian Humphrys for sharing his expertise on eleventh-century warfare and for assisting with translations.

My colleagues at the Sandford Award have continued to encourage my writing career, and I am particularly grateful to Jean MacIntyre, John Hamer, and Gareth Fitzpatrick. I also owe an enormous debt of gratitude to the staff at Historic Royal Palaces with whom I have been lucky enough to work, notably Michael Day, John Barnes, David Souden, Ruth Gill, Rhiannon Goddard, and Sam Brown. I would also like to express my thanks to Dr. David Musgrove, editor of *BBC History Magazine,* and Hugh Alexander of the National Archives.

In a short acknowledgments section such as this, I cannot possibly do justice to the many kindnesses that I have received from the friends who contributed—in different ways—to the crafting of this book. They include Honor Gay, for her infectious enthusiasm about the book and for being such a wonderful playmate for Eleanor. Likewise, Maura and Howard Davies have continued to provide support with everything from babysitting to publicity. It is thanks to Lucinda and Stuart Eggleton that I was able to do much of the editing in Cyprus, and to Lisa, Rob, Lily, Zoe, Matthew, and Frances Cameron for letting me stay in their beautiful home in northern France while undertaking the research. I have been greatly touched by the kindness and support of my former headmaster Len Clark and his wife, Jeanne. It has also been a delight to become reacquainted with Judi Jones, the teacher who inspired my interest in history to begin with and who has shown great enthusiasm for my writing career.

I would also like to thank the following friends for their kindness, patience, and encouragement during the writing of this book: Rosie Fifield, Carol Scoones, Margot Ducat, Jess Goon, Tina Ingram, Lon Gibbons, Doreen Cullen, Siobhan Clarke, Helen Dawson, Jean Franczyk, Chris Hall, Richard and Lizzie Knight, Nina Newbery, Leora Leboff, Anna Scott, Alice Burton, Philippa Treavett, Helen Durham, Janet

Clarke, Mary Wackerbarth, John Moses, Chris Warwick, Brian and Elinor James, my fellow "History Girls," Sarah Gristwood and Kate Williams, and the "NCT Girls," Liesel Alexander, Paula Alvarez, Louise Groves, Susan Porter, Joanne Tresidder, and Katie Whitmarsh.

Finally, I would like to thank my daughter, Eleanor, for bringing me such joy over the past two years . . . and for going to bed (more or less) on time so that I could get this book written.

TRACY BORMAN
NOVEMBER 2011

CONTENTS

CONTENTS

LIST OF ILLUSTRATIONS

1. A nineteenth-century sketch of Matilda (© National Portrait Gallery, London)
2. An engraving of a fresco showing William and Matilda (Bibliothèque nationale de France)
3. Engraving from frontispiece to Agnes Strickland's Queens of England series (illustration by G. P. Harding, Esq., produced expressly for Strickland, *Lives of the Queens of England from the Norman Conquest*, vol. 1 © Cambridge University Press)
4. Abbey of La Trinité (© Olivier Petit)
5. Abbey of St.-Etienne
6. The castle at Falaise (Getty Images)
7. The remains of Bonneville-sur-Touques castle (courtesy of www.bzho.com)
8. Illustration showing the descendants of William and Matilda (British Library Board)
9. Harold Godwinson swears an oath recognizing William's claim to the English throne (Musée de la Tapisserie, Bayeux, France / with special authorization of the city of Bayeux / Giraudon / The Bridgeman Art Library)
10. *The Mora* (Musée de la Tapisserie, Bayeux, France / with special authorization of the city of Bayeux / Giraudon / The Bridgeman Art Library)
11. Matilda and her ladies working on the Bayeux Tapestry (Musée Baron Gérard)

GENEALOGICAL TABLES

MATILDA'S ANCESTRY, SHOWING HER DESCENT FROM THE HOLY ROMAN EMPERORS, KINGS OF FRANCE, AND THE ENGLISH ROYAL FAMILY

CHARLEMAGNE, Holy Roman Emperor
and King of the Franks (768–814)
|
LOUIS THE PIOUS, Holy Roman Emperor
and King of the Franks (814–40)
|
CHARLES "THE BALD,"
King of West Franks (840–77)
|
KING LOUIS "THE STAMMERER"
(877–79)
|
Judith = BALDWIN "IRON ARM," Count of Flanders (862–79) — ALFRED "THE GREAT," King of Wessex (871–99)
|
Elfrude = BALDWIN II, Count of Flanders (879–918)
|
Adele of Vermandois = ARNULF I "THE GREAT" (918–65)

Adalof, Count of Boulogne and Ternois (d. 933)

Baldwin Baldzo (d. 973)

Mathilde Billung = BALDWIN III (958–961)

Hildegard

Counts of Holland

Arnulf, Count of Boulogne (d. after 972)

Susanna (Rozala of Italy) = ARNULF II (965–88)

Luitgard

Counts of Guelders

Robert II "the Pious," King of France (966–1031)

1) Ogiva of Luxembourg =
2) Eleanor, daughter of Richard II, Duke of Normandy = BALDWIN IV (988–1035)

Judith = 1) Tostig Godwineson
       = 2) Welf IV, Duke of Bavaria

Adela, daughter of Robert II "the Pious," King of France = BALDWIN V (1035–67)

MATILDA = William "the Conqueror," King of England (1066–87)

Gertrude, widow of Floris I of Frisia = ROBERT I "THE FRISIAN" (1071–93)

Richilde, widow of Herman I, Count of Hainault = BALDWIN VI "OF MONS" (1067–70)

Baldwin II, Count of Hainault

ARNULF III (1070–71)

WILLIAM AND MATILDA'S SHARED ANCESTRY AND THEIR DESCENDANTS

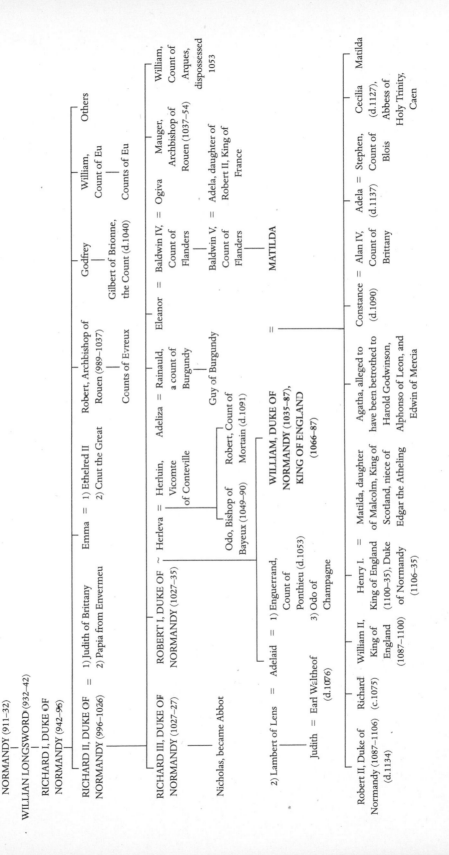

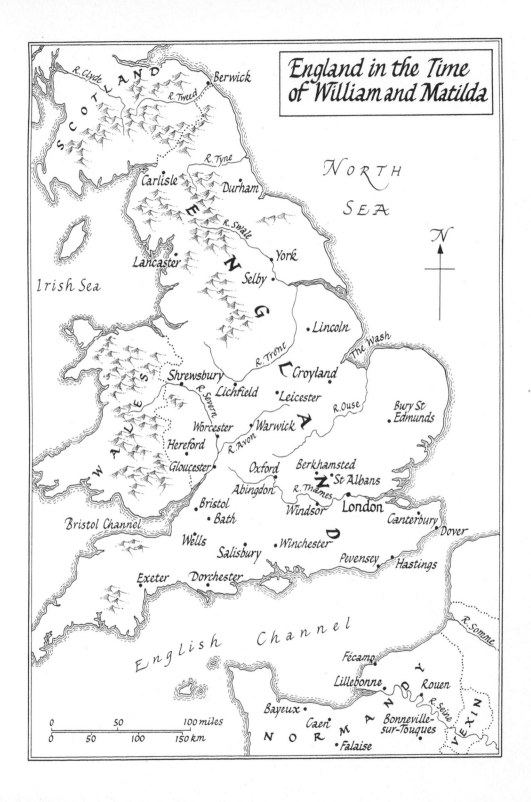

England in the Time
of William and Matilda

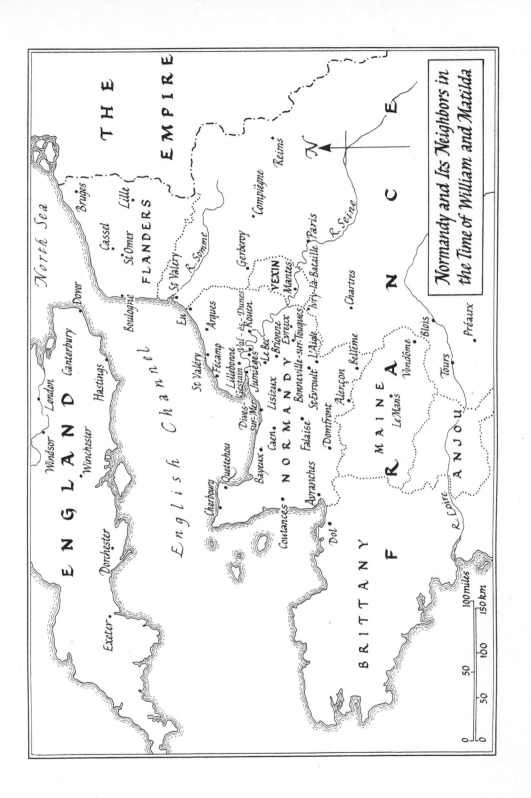

Normandy and Its Neighbors in the Time of William and Matilda

INTRODUCTION

Around the year 1049, William, Duke of Normandy and future conqueror of England, rode furiously to the palace of Baldwin V, Count of Flanders, in Bruges. Upon reaching it, he encountered the object of his rage as she was leaving the palace chapel: Matilda, the count's only daughter. This headstrong girl had dared to refuse his offer of marriage, haughtily declaring that she would not lower herself so far as to accept a mere bastard. Without hesitation, the young duke dragged her to the ground by her hair and beat her mercilessly, rolling her in the mud and ruining her rich gown. Then, without another word, he mounted his horse and rode back to Normandy at full speed. Shaken and humiliated, Matilda was helped to her feet by her terrified ladies and carried home to bed. A few days later, she shocked her family, the court, and most of Europe by declaring that she would marry none but William. Thus began one of the most turbulent marriages in history.

✣ ✣ ✣

Matilda of Flanders was the diminutive yet formidable wife of William the Conqueror. She broke the mold of female consorts and established a model of active queenship that would influence her successors for centuries to come. By wielding immense power in both Normandy and England—not just on behalf of her husband, but at times in direct opposition to him—she confounded the traditional views of women in medieval society. Her remarkable story is played out against one of the most fascinating and transformative periods of European history. Dutiful wife, ambitious consort, doting mother, cold pragmatist, proud scion of a noble race, her character emerges in all its brilliantly contrasting facets.

And yet Matilda has been largely overlooked by historians, and there has never been a full biography of her in English. In the many modern-day accounts of William the Conqueror and the Norman invasion, his wife is accorded little more than an occasional reference. One leading medievalist has dismissed her as "a completely colourless figure," and in a printed collection of contemporary legal documents (in which her name features time and again) she does not even warrant her own place in the index, which lists her instead under the entry for her father, Baldwin V of Flanders.[1]

Such neglect can be blamed partly upon the perceived lack of contemporary sources for Matilda's life. The lives of women in this period are often so scarcely covered that it raises the question of whether it is possible to write a biography of any of them. The Bayeux Tapestry, for example, depicts six hundred men and only three women, and as a leading authority has observed, "the bulk of medieval records were written by men for men."[2] Moreover, even if women had wished to contribute to the historiography of the age, most were illiterate.

Nevertheless, there is a staggering array of contemporary records upon which I have been able to draw for this biography. The eleventh and early twelfth centuries were a time of intense activity among monastic historians. Motivated by a desire to preserve the traditions of their communities, they would spend many hours in the scriptorium recording the history of their own religious house, including the lives of its abbots and lay patrons. This grew to encompass local, national, and even international events that occurred during their lifetime or that could be remembered by the elders of the community in which they lived.

The accounts—or chronicles—that emerged from the labors of monks across England and Normandy span the entire period of Matilda's story. Some were written at the time that the dramatic events of her life unfolded, whereas others were retrospective accounts from the later eleventh and early twelfth centuries. They vary enormously in scope, detail, and accuracy, from the fulsome (and often salacious) early-twelfth-

century narratives of Orderic Vitalis and William of Malmesbury to accounts such as the *Anglo-Saxon Chronicle,* which at times is so concise that
the events of an entire year are covered by a single sentence.

The major chroniclers all drew upon a common pool of earlier
sources, either quoting them verbatim or embellishing them with their
own interpretations. Thus arose a form of historiographical "telephone
game," in which fact intermingled with fiction, real events with legend.
The chroniclers also often wrote their histories as morality tales rather
than strictly factual accounts. Although he claimed that each generation
had a duty to keep a truthful record for the glory of God, Orderic Vitalis
also firmly believed that history provided a record of events that was full
of moral examples profitable to future generations: "Everyone should
daily grow in knowledge of how he ought to live, and follow the noble
examples of famous men now dead to the best of his ability."[3]

The story of Matilda's rejection of William—and its aftermath—is
found in the *Chronicle of Tours,* an extraordinarily lurid and sensational
account written almost two centuries after the events that it describes. It
is accounts such as this that are responsible for the many myths and legends about Matilda that sprang up during the years after her death. They
provide a marked contrast to the official documents that chart her public
duties as duchess of Normandy and queen of England. The emerging
portrait is of a woman of profound contradictions: on the one hand a
model wife and consort, on the other a headstrong, adulterous traitor.

Given that she was the consort of England's most famous conquering
king, the number of established facts about Matilda of Flanders in which
we can rest any confidence is surprisingly small. The years before she
rose to prominence as duchess of Normandy and then as queen of
England are given only the most cursory mention in the contemporary
records. It is nigh on impossible to decipher such fundamental details as
how many children she bore William, and in what order. But by piecing
together the often fragmentary evidence, we can still paint a vivid picture of this most striking medieval queen.

Matilda spent most of her life in Normandy, and it was there that she
enjoyed the greatest political power. The proliferation of Norman
sources has therefore been of considerable value in exploring her history.
But after 1066, her attention was increasingly drawn across the Channel

to her husband's newly conquered kingdom. She would become the first woman to be crowned queen of England and formally recognized as such, and would wield authority so effectively that she proved an inspiration for female consorts for many centuries afterward.

One of the most important sources for the period of Matilda's reign in England is the series of charters to which she put her signature. These were usually written to record the transfer of property or estates, whereby the king and queen would grant lands to a favored subject (or in some cases a religious house) who would manage them on their behalf. Matilda signed these with an elaborate Jerusalem-style cross, which is both symmetrical and made with *"une maine ferme"* (a firm hand)—suggestive of her strength of character—distinguishing hers from the more mundane marks that were made by her fellow attesters.[4] By following the charters, we can trace the itinerary of this most peripatetic of consorts, and the frequency with which she witnessed them helps us grasp her growing influence and enormous importance in William's administration.

Arguably the most famous documentary source for the eleventh century is Domesday Book. Immensely valuable as a testament to the impact of the Norman Conquest upon England, it also tells us of the considerable wealth that Matilda accumulated during her tenure as queen. Moreover, it gives us an insight into her career as chief justiciar of England during William's frequent absences, and the many references to her settling contentious property disputes prove just how active she was in this sphere. Domesday also holds a rare clue to the identity of one of Matilda's daughters, and as such it has shed much-needed light on a subject that still confounds historians today.

As well as the documentary material, there is a rich background of architectural evidence—from the magnificent abbeys that Matilda and William commissioned at Caen and Rouen to their lavish ducal palaces at Falaise, Bayeux, Bonneville-sur-Touques, and Fécamp and the Conqueror's imposing fortresses in England, notably the Tower of London and Windsor Castle. Other physical remains help to bring the narrative to life. These include the statues and frescoes representing Matilda and her husband that adorned the walls of cathedrals and abbeys across France, her remarkably preserved tomb at Caen, and—most famously—

the unique record of the Bayeux Tapestry, which was for many years believed to be the work of Matilda and her ladies.

The making of the tapestry has in some respects served as a model for the compilation of this biography. On their own, the various threads of evidence have at first appeared fragile and insubstantial, but when carefully and painstakingly bound together, they present a rich and illuminating picture of one of the most remarkable women in history.

Queen of the Conqueror

"Of Kingly Line"

From the very beginning, Matilda's life was shrouded in mystery. Even the date of her birth cannot be deduced with any certainty from the surviving sources. At the earliest, it would have been toward the end of the year 1031. Her parents were the future Count Baldwin V of Flanders and Adela, daughter of Robert II "the Pious," King of France, by his third wife, Constance of Arles.[1] Their marriage took place in 1028. The Norman chronicler William of Jumièges, who was a direct contemporary of Matilda, claims that it was not consummated until 1031, and that the long period of waiting was one of the factors that incited Baldwin to rebel against his father that year.[2] In fact, young Baldwin had already rebelled soon after the wedding; it seemed that an alliance with French royal blood had given him an inflated sense of his own importance, and he therefore contested his father's position as count. The two men came to terms in 1030 and a truce was concluded whereby they agreed to rule jointly.

Despite the rumor of its delayed consummation, Baldwin and Adela's marriage was said to have been blessed with "a numerous progeny of gifted sons and daughters."[3] However, the only children we can be certain of are Matilda and her two brothers, Baldwin and Robert, and it is not clear in what order they were born. Matilda is often referred to last in the lists provided by contemporary chroniclers, but this does not necessarily mean that she was the youngest child: daughters were seen as being of secondary importance to sons and were often left out of accounts altogether.

If Matilda's age was uncertain, her pedigree was not. One of the most prominent chroniclers of the age introduces her to his readers as "the highly born Matilda."[4] This was no mere flattery. Born into the ruling family of one of the most important principalities in Europe, she could trace her descent from impressive stock. The Flemish counts had the most distinguished lineage of any nonroyal house in Europe. Her father's male forebears had been counts of Flanders since the ninth century and were descended from the great Charlemagne, founding father of the French and German empires. Count Baldwin II had married the daughter of King Alfred the Great—an alliance with Saxon blood that would prove useful to Matilda. Moreover, as the granddaughter of a French king, she retained strong royal connections. On Robert II's death in 1031, her maternal uncle, Henry, had become king of France, and another uncle, Robert, had inherited the dukedom of Burgundy the following year, and so through her mother's side of the family, Matilda was related to most of the great nobility of France.[5]

Her parents chose a name to emphasize this impressive pedigree. "Matilda" was a highly unusual moniker in Flanders and France at the time of her birth. It came from the old Teutonic "Machtild" and was firmly rooted in Baldwin's German ancestry.[6] With her illustrious lineage, Matilda was a great prize in the international marriage market— even more so given the immense strategic importance of the principality in which she was born. Flanders was situated in the heart of western Europe, embracing parts of modern-day Belgium, northern France, and the Netherlands. Its name derived from the area around Bruges known as the Pagus Flandrensis. It had been dominated by Germanic tribes for several hundred years before becoming part of an empire established by Charlemagne in the ninth century. The first known count, Baldwin I, ensured his family's fortune in late 861 by eloping with Judith, the eldest child of the Carolingian emperor Charles the Bald. His lands were at that time limited to the prosperous town of Ghent in eastern Flanders, but when he finally married Judith in 863, he was granted the Pagus Flandrensis. The marriage greatly enhanced the prestige of the county by uniting it with both the French and English royal families.

Under Baldwin I's leadership and that of his son, Baldwin II, Flanders was made secure against the incursions of the Vikings, who had plagued the province for many years. The latter added other territories to the county so that it comprised a sprawling area of land bordering parts of Normandy, northern France, and the Germanic empire. Baldwin II's marriage to Aelfthryth, the daughter of King Alfred the Great, also strengthened ties with England. In the early part of the tenth century, their grandson, Baldwin III, laid the basis for the future industrial and commercial greatness of the region by establishing the wool and silk industries at Ghent and instituting annual fairs at Bruges and other towns. Prior to this, their son, Arnulf I, who succeeded as count in 918, had embarked upon an ambitious campaign to extend the Flemish territory southward. His attempt to take the strategically important town of Montreuil-sur-Mer led to conflict with William Longsword of Normandy. There followed a prolonged period of hostilities as each tried to gain the upper hand, which culminated with William's murder by Arnulf's men in 942. This rivalry between Flanders and Normandy continued to dominate Flemish foreign policy until the middle of the eleventh century, when Matilda's marriage brought it to an end.

Although it was later to become a thriving center of commerce and culture, in the early eleventh century Flanders was a primitive place. The landscape to the west was dominated by swamps and was barely habitable. The east, which was densely wooded, was comparatively more civilized and had a higher number of inhabitants. But in contrast to neighboring Normandy, there were no bustling urban centers, and the towns that did exist were small, with rudimentary buildings. Language also presented a problem. There was no uniformity, with some areas speaking a Germanic dialect and others French. It was only gradually that Flemish was adopted as the national language. It seems the populace, too, retained a certain primitivism. In 900, for example, Archbishop Fulk of Rheims scorned the inhabitants as being "of barbarous . . . savagery and language."[7] Indeed, the Flemish soon became the butt of jokes among the more civilized nations, such as England and France, where they were derided for their crudity and backwardness. Their reputation had improved little by the late twelfth century, when Richard of Devizes advised a young man who was due to travel to England that he should expect nothing but ignorance and boorishness from Cornishmen, "as we in France consider our Flemings."[8]

Flanders was also a notoriously lawless area, where violence and uprisings were commonplace. "Daily homicides and spilling of human blood had troubled the peace and quiet of the entire area," claimed the twelfth-century *Life of St. Arnulf*. "Thus a great number of nobles, through the force of their prayers, convinced the bishop of the lord to visit the places where this atrocious cruelty especially raged and to instruct the docile and bloody spirit of the Flemings in the interest of peace and concord."[9]

Nevertheless, under the stewardship of Count Baldwin IV (988–1035), Flanders began to show signs of improvement. Its salvation was trade. The textile industry became particularly successful, thanks to imports of wool from England and Spain. Matilda's father, Baldwin V, commissioned the building of new roads and canals to stimulate the growth of trade both within and outside Flanders. Before long, he had amassed more wealth than any of his predecessors. This dramatically improved standards of living among his subjects, particularly within the major urban centers. Handsome stone houses replaced the ramshackle wooden dwellings of former days, and the citizens also benefited from the dazzling array of exotic goods that arrived into the principality from far-flung corners of the globe.

By the time of Baldwin V's reign, then, Flanders was enjoying increasing wealth. Given the new count's overweening pride and ambition, it is likely that he would have built magnificent residences for his family. There are very few contemporary descriptions of the buildings and palaces that Matilda would have known, but a detailed account by the twelfth-century chronicler Lambert of Ardres of the castle there gives a sense of a typical stately residence of the principality. The castle was built of wood and stood atop a large mound, towering over the rest of the town. Its rooms were structured according to a strict hierarchy:

> The first storey was on the surface of the ground, where were cellars and granaries, and great boxes, tuns, casks, and other domestic utensils. In the storey above were the dwelling and common living-rooms

of the residents, in which were the larders, the rooms of the bakers and butlers, and the great chamber in which the lord and his wife slept. Adjoining this was a private room, the dormitory of the wait-ing maids and children. In the inner part of the great chamber was a certain private room, where at early dawn or in the evening or during sickness or at time of blood-letting, or for warming the maids and weaned children, they used to have a fire . . . In the upper storey of the house were garret rooms, in which on the one side the sons (when they wished it), on the other side the daughters (because they were obliged), 5 of the lord of the house used to sleep. In this storey also the watchmen and servants appointed to keep the house took their sleep at some time or other. High up on the east side of the house, in a convenient place, was the chapel, which was made like unto the tabernacle of Solomon in its ceiling and painting. There were stairs and passages from storey to storey, from the house into the kitchen, from room to room, and again from the house into the loggia, where they used to sit in conversation for recreation, and again from the loggia into the oratory.[10]

This castle belonged to the lord of Ardres, so it is likely that, as the daugh-ter of the count of Flanders, Matilda would have known even greater luxury.

As well as encouraging the commercial development of his princi-pality, Matilda's father also capitalized upon Flanders's immense stra-tegic importance. Its situation enabled the counts to hold the balance of power between the kings of France to the south, the dukes of Normandy to the west, and the German rulers to the east. This made Flanders a power to be reckoned with in medieval Europe. Baldwin V made the most of this advantage by negotiating favorable treaty terms and arrang-ing prestigious marriages for each of his children. Keenly aware of his family's distinguished pedigree, he took every opportunity to enhance his own prestige, and became known as "prince of the fatherland" in Flemish texts.[11]

The eleventh-century chronicler William of Poitiers was apparently in some awe of Baldwin V, describing him as "a man of great power who towered above the rest" and "this wisest of men." According to his account, "Counts, marquises, dukes, even archbishops of the highest dignity were struck dumb with admiration whenever the duty of their office earned them the presence of this distinguished guest . . . Kings too revered and stood in awe of his greatness."[12] William of Malmesbury, whose *Gesta Regum Anglorum* (*The Deeds of the Kings of the English*) was completed in around 1125, was no less impressed, but he paints a rather more benevolent picture of "a man admirable alike for loyalty and wisdom, grey-haired yet with the vigour of youth, and of exalted position as husband of the king's sister."[13]

The growth of Flanders's status, and that of Baldwin, ensured that Matilda enjoyed a privileged upbringing. Most of her childhood was spent at the comital palace in Bruges, which was by now the foremost city in the principality, Baldwin V having rebuilt and "greatly beautified" it as an expression of his dynasty's growing status. Bruges was immensely rich, having evolved into a thriving center of commerce.[14] This lent it a cosmopolitan atmosphere, with traders from across the globe converging upon the city. One contemporary visitor observed that it "enjoys very great fame for the number of its merchants and for its affluence in all things upon which mankind places the greatest value."[15] Matilda and her family also regularly stayed at Lille, Ghent, Thérouanne, and the coastal town of St.-Omer, where her father's court met on "special days" such as religious festivals.[16]

Matilda's upbringing was superintended by her mother. As such, she had a powerful female role model from her very earliest days. Even though women were assigned the inferior role in marriage, politics, and society in general, Adela's relationship with Count Baldwin was a marriage of equals. Not for her the traditional duties of a consort, which were confined to producing heirs and leading a godly life. Instead she played an active part in the government of Flanders, and her name appears in more than half of the charters that were issued during her husband's reign. In many of these she was styled as the "sister of the king of France," an indication of the same pride in her ancestry that she would pass on to her daughter. Few of her peers enjoyed such prominence in the political life of their kingdoms, and it is rare to find a consort's name on more than a handful of legal documents: Adela's contemporaries were obviously aware of her connections. The biography of Queen Emma of England, who was well acquainted with Adela, claimed that her name meant "most noble," and it was careful to describe her as the "daughter of Robert, king of the French."[17]

It was by no means unusual that Adela should supervise Matilda's education. The role of the mother was seen as paramount in this respect throughout the medieval period. A ninth-century account praised King Alfred's mother, Osburgh, "a religious woman, noble by birth and nature," who gave her two sons a book of Saxon poetry, saying, "Whichever of you shall the soonest learn this volume shall have it for his own." When Alfred triumphs over his brother, his mother "smiles with satisfaction."[18]

Mothers were expected to attain a high standard of learning themselves so that they might pass this on to their offspring. Despite being rarely praised by contemporary sources, it was in fact common at this time for wives to exceed their husbands in intellect. The early eleventh century was one of the most enlightened periods in the education of women, when it was taken every bit as seriously as—and often more seriously than—that of their male counterparts. Daughters were encouraged to spend their leisure time cultivating their knowledge through reading, while sons would undertake more active pursuits such as hunting and training for warfare. Royal women, in particular, tended to be better educated than men. Even though many others were taught little else but how to read the psalter and sign their name, this was more than most laymen were capable of.

The relative enlightenment of the period is proved by comparing it with the later Middle Ages, when the entire emphasis of a woman's education seemed to be upon how she might best serve her future husband. The influential fourteenth-century manual *The Book of the Knight of the Tower* advocated submissiveness and modesty in young girls in preparation for marriage, and said that women's learning should be limited "to the virtuous things of scripture, wherefore they may better see and know their salvation."[19] In a similar vein, in the following century, Bartholomew Granville urged the importance of serenity in appearance to the well-bred woman's character. She should carry herself erect but with her eyes cast down, and she should be "mannerly in clothing, sober in moving, wary in speaking, chaste in looking, honest in bearing, sad in going, shamefast among the people." Even the inspirational Venetian writer and poet Christine de Pisan (born in 1365), whose works challenged contemporary stereotypes of male dominance, advocated such pursuits as spinning, sewing, and embroidery for girls in order to keep their minds from wandering to sinful subjects.

Adela's ambitions extended far beyond such limited pursuits. She herself had received an excellent education, and was determined to pass the same on to her daughter. She inherited her love of learning from her father, Robert the Pious, who was recognized as a "literate man" by Pope Gregory VII. She had been betrothed to Baldwin as a child and had been raised and educated at the Flemish court. This included receiving instruction from the monks of St. Peter's in Ghent, and Adela may later have sent her own children there for lessons.

That Matilda was praised for her learning is a testament to her mother's efforts.[20] She was almost certainly fluent in Latin, which was widely spoken at the Flemish court, and she later passed this knowledge on to her own daughters. It is unlikely that she was similarly well versed in writing, however, for this pursuit tended to be confined to those in religious orders. Aristocratic laywomen often used a clerk to write their letters, and given that her signature was a cross (albeit in an elaborate Jerusalem style), it is possible that Matilda did the same.

One of the most important elements of Matilda's education was religious instruction. This was one sphere in which women enjoyed equality with, and in some cases superiority over, men. The new monastic movement that swept across Europe between the sixth and the tenth centuries was spearheaded by women, notably those drawn from royal and noble families. It is estimated that some fifty religious houses in England appointed their first abbess from a royal family.[21] These women were not simply retreating; by playing such an active role in the foundation of new abbeys, they were helping to create potent symbols of royal power. As active religious patrons, they were able to utilize—and expand—the considerable landed wealth at their disposal. Their role was therefore just as much political as it was religious.

Even so, the women who were involved in the monastic movement were motivated by a genuine religious fervor. For example, Saxon women played an important role in converting their male kin to Christianity. The eighth-century chronicler known as the Venerable Bede cited several examples of this evangelizing spirit, such as Bertha, wife of the Kentish king Aethelred, and her daughter Aethelburh, who in 625 married and converted King Edwin of Northumbria. This chimed with the teachings of St. Paul, who urged upon women the duty to influence their "unbelieving husbands."[22] At the same time, though, it jarred with the traditional Christian ethos that wives should be meek and passive. Matilda's later history would suggest that she was more inclined to follow the former example.

But in the sphere of religion, she had a role model closer to hand. Her mother Adela was instrumental in Baldwin V's reform of the church in Flanders. She was also responsible for the founding of several colleges, including Aire, Lille, and Harelbeke, as well as the abbeys of Messines and Ename—something that inspired her daughter a great deal. Pope Gregory VII recognized Adela's influence in ecclesiastical matters and wrote to implore that she use this to promote clerical celibacy.[23] And while the active role that Adela played in the religious life of the principality lent her considerable political power, it seems her piety was sincere—so much so that she later became a nun herself.

Matilda's aunt, Judith of Flanders, whom she saw regularly during her childhood and youth, also enjoyed a reputation for devoutness and was an active patron of religious houses. No less renowned was Matilda's grandfather, the appropriately named Robert the Pious, King of France. In praising her distinguished lineage, William of Poitiers draws particular attention to this king, "whose praise for his piety and wise rule of the kingdom will be sung all over the world."[24]

Religion, then, had a profound impact upon Matilda's education, and her interest in it would prove both genuine and enduring. She would have been aware of the revolutionary changes that the monastic movement had wrought across Europe, and the fact that she herself would become one of the most active religious patrons in both England and Normandy suggests that she was inspired by the examples she encountered in her childhood. She also learned to appreciate the earthly influence that such piety could bring.

In this respect, she had a powerful role model in Empress Adelaide of

Italy, an enormously influential female ruler of the tenth century who was praised for that rare ability to combine piety with power. So active was Adelaide's role in government and religion that she came to be seen as her husband's equal—as testified by the fact that coins were struck in Italy bearing jointly the names of Otto and Adelaide. Matilda's mother had commissioned a vita (biography) of the empress, and she may well have included this in her daughter's curriculum. The evidence suggests that she certainly encouraged Matilda to challenge the traditional perceptions of women's place in society.

There were other inspiring examples of female power for the young Matilda to draw upon. The previous century had witnessed an unusually high number of queens regent, and for a brief period during the 980s, almost the whole of western Europe had been ruled by women whose force of character and political acumen had propelled them to the height of international affairs. Among them was Adelaide's daughter-in-law, the formidable Empress Theophanu. As regent for her son, Otto III, she ruled a vast conglomeration of territories and enjoyed a level of power possessed by few of her male contemporaries. She was a fount of patronage, bestowing vast estates and prestigious appointments; she received ambassadors from across Europe; and she could make war and peace as her will dictated.

Little wonder that the late tenth century has been described as the zenith of female power. But it did not last. The eleventh century saw a return to a political climate dominated by men, and women were once more relegated to second place. The fact that Adela should commission a biography of one of the last women to enjoy such power suggests that she had drawn inspiration from Adelaide's story, and that she wished Matilda to do the same.

As the only daughter of the comital family, it was natural that Matilda should also be trained in the accomplishments that would one day make her a fitting bride for a ruler or statesman. As well as learning the art of embroidery—at which she excelled—she may also have practiced the harp and viol, which were popular at the time. In common with other high-born women, she was taught how to manage households and estates. This was an important skill at a time when men were often absent for long periods on military campaigns, and it would have a profound effect upon Matilda's later career. She also learned the arts of deportment: how to present herself in public with a modest demeanor and serenity of countenance, as well as being "mannerly in clothing, sober in moving, wary in speaking, chaste in looking, honest in bearing." She evidently excelled in this, for throughout her life she would be widely praised for her modesty, virtue, and graceful manner, which would prompt Pope Gregory VII to call her "the most serene."[25]

But some of these attributes were little more than skin deep. Although Matilda appeared every bit the modest young woman, as she grew into maturity she became keenly aware of her status. William of Poitiers infers that this was largely due to Adela's influence: "Her wise and blessed mother had nurtured in her daughter a lineage many times greater even than her parental inheritance."[26] The fierce pride that Matilda took in her ancestry would become ever more apparent in the years ahead.

✢ ✢ ✢

As well as the conventional aspects of her education, Matilda's upbringing at the comital court also gave her an unplanned grounding in English politics. This was largely thanks to the exiled queen Emma of England, who arrived in Bruges in 1037. Emma was the daughter of Duke Richard I of Normandy (and thus the great-aunt of the future William the Conqueror), and had married Aethelred of England in 1002. The *Anglo-Saxon Chronicle* records that "in that same spring [of 1002] the Lady, Richard's daughter, came to the land."[27] Upon her arrival in England, she had either adopted or had been given the name Aelfgifu. This was a subtle attempt by the ruling elite to sideline her, for it was the name of her predecessor. But Emma, quick to realize the potential of her queenly status, had insisted upon being called by her proper name. After the death of her mother-in-law, Aelfthryth, around November 1002, she enjoyed a position of virtually unparalleled influence at court, even rivaling the king himself. According to one recent authority, she became "the axis around which English politics turned."[28] Aethelred's death in 1016 did not end her power, for she married his successor, Cnut of Denmark (who had without ceremony "ordered [her] to be fetched to him as wife"), thus becoming the first woman to be made queen twice.[29]

During Cnut's reign, Emma amassed a considerable fortune, making her the richest woman in England. William of Malmesbury depicts her as a profligate wife who encouraged her husband to build up his treasury and then wasted it on jewels and other precious things. "At Winchester especially he [Cnut] exhibited the munificence of his generosity, where his offerings were such that strangers are alarmed by the masses of precious metal and their eyes dazzled as they look at the flashing gems. This was prompted by Emma, who lavished her treasure on such things with holy prodigality."[30] In fact, the English queen had put her riches to far better use than this. Her wealth, which derived from her own inheritance as well as from her position as Cnut's wife, enabled her to become one of the most influential ecclesiastical and literary patrons in western Europe.

In 1035, however, following Cnut's death, Emma was ousted from power by Harold Harefoot, Cnut's son from his first marriage, who "had taken from her all the best treasures which King Cnut had."[31] She remained holed up in her house at Winchester for two years before being "driven out without mercy to face the raging winter."[32] Shortly afterward, she set sail for Flanders.

Although William of Malmesbury claims that Baldwin, "a man of well-tried integrity," offered the beleaguered English queen sanctuary out of kindness and generosity, the wily count was no doubt eager to cultivate this potentially valuable ally for more tactical reasons.[33] He organized a lavish reception, and his daughter was probably among the welcoming committee. At most, Matilda would have been five or six years old when the exiled queen visited her father's court, and she may have been a good deal younger. Given that Emma stayed for some considerable time, it is likely that Matilda became well acquainted with her.

The *Anglo-Saxon Chronicle* notes that Baldwin "received her [Emma] well, and kept her there as long as she had need," and Emma herself attested that she was "honourably received."[34] Baldwin and Adela arranged for a house to be made available for her use in the city. It is a mark of Emma's pride and independence that although she received shelter from Count Baldwin, she lived off her own income and funded her own patronage throughout her stay at his court.

Her visit was recorded in the *Encomium Emmae Reginae*, a very flattering account of her life written during her stay in Bruges, probably by a monk of St.-Omer. The *Encomium* was one of several illuminated manuscripts commissioned by the English queen, which she intended as a means of asserting her power during her enforced absence from England. The book refers to her as queen throughout, and her name is highlighted whenever it appears, leaving the reader in no doubt of her regal status. In the frontispiece, she is depicted crowned and seated on a throne while Edward and Harthacnut, her sons by Aethelred and Cnut respectively, bow deferentially at her side. Meanwhile, the author of the work kneels at her feet in silent supplication. It was extremely rare for anyone other than Christ or another deity to be enthroned in contemporary illustrations such as these, let alone a woman. Moreover, Emma and her sons had been thrown out by Harold Harefoot, and the prospect of their inheriting the English crown was far from certain, so this was an audacious piece of propaganda.

Nevertheless, the illustration proved remarkably prophetic. Emma made good use of her time in Bruges, drawing upon her international contacts to champion the claim of her favorite son, Harthacnut, to the English throne. He joined her in 1039, arriving with an impressive fleet, and spent that winter as the honored guest of Count Baldwin. The following year, news came from England that Harold Harefoot was dead. Thanks in no small part to Emma's campaigning, Harthacnut was now acknowledged as the rightful heir.

Three years after her arrival in Bruges, Emma returned to England in triumph to see her younger son become king of England. Although her departure was under the most auspicious of circumstances, according to Emma's own account it prompted much grieving among the people of Flanders, who had come to view her as one of their own. "They wept, in short, that she, whom during her whole exile they had regarded as a fellow citizen, was leaving them . . . Such was the lamentation on the whole shore, such was the wailing of all the people standing by." Emma proceeded to kiss her hosts goodbye, "after a great abundance of tears had been shed on both sides." It is likely that Matilda was among them, and this touching description (exaggerated though it may be) implies that she and her family had formed a close bond with the powerful exiled queen.[35]

As queen mother, Emma regained the position of power that she had enjoyed during her husbands' reigns. The *Anglo-Saxon Chronicle* records that, accompanied by an impressive retinue, she took up residence in her former home at Winchester, where it was decided that she would "hold all Wessex in hand" for her son.[36] When troubles in Denmark forced Harthacnut to return there, she became regent in all but name, seizing the reins of government in Wessex, the most powerful province in the land. In order to appease Edward (later known as the Confessor), her son by Aethelred, and avoid any rebellion on his part, in 1041 he was awarded dual kingship with Harthacnut. When the latter died suddenly the following year,[37] Emma was forced to adopt a more conciliatory attitude toward Edward, who resented the favor that she had always shown toward his younger half-brother. He was not fooled by her apparent change of heart, however, and "robbed her of all the treasures which she owned, which were untold, because earlier she was very hard on the king her son, in that she did less for him than he wanted before he became king."[38] She died in relative obscurity ten years later. The *Anglo-Saxon Chronicle* dismisses the passing of "the Old Lady" in cursory prose, adding merely that she was buried next to King Cnut in Winchester Cathedral.[39]

Matilda may have been aware of Emma's vacillating fortunes across the Channel. Even though her power had waned during Edward's ascendancy, she had wielded considerable influence in international politics for more than half a century. She had also proved just how much could be achieved by sheer force of personality, and she had had a keen sense of the importance of image to royal authority. As such, she provided a powerful example of what a shrewd and determined woman could achieve in the male-dominated world of international politics. It may have been at this formative period of Matilda's young life that she was inspired with the ambition for power that would become the driving force of her later career.

✢   ✢   ✢

The number of English exiles at Baldwin's court increased dramatically after the accession of Edward the Confessor. In 1051, the king banished his archenemy, Earl Godwine, and his entire family from the kingdom. Given that Godwine's third son, Tostig, was married to Count Baldwin's half-sister Judith, Flanders was a natural refuge, and most of the family made their way to the court at Bruges.[40] Little wonder that the contemporary biographer of Edward the Confessor described Baldwin as "that old friend of the English people."[41]

It was not just English exiles who found their way to Baldwin's court. He also provided sanctuary for some important Norman nobles. They included Richard and Baldwin, sons of Gilbert of Brionne, one of the guardians appointed to protect the young duke William of Normandy, who had succeeded his father, Robert, in 1035. The accession of a minor—and an illegitimate one at that—had led to treacherous times in Normandy, and Gilbert was assassinated, along with various other of William's guardians. Richard and Baldwin fled to Flanders shortly afterward and were accommodated in the ducal residence at Bruges in around 1040. There they were introduced to Matilda, and it is tempting to speculate that they sparked her curiosity in the young Norman duke by telling stories of the dramatic adventures and narrow escapes from death that he encountered on an almost daily basis.[42] But events would prove that Matilda's interest lay elsewhere.

✣   ✣   ✣

According to contemporary chroniclers, as Matilda grew to maturity, she embodied all possible virtues, both in appearance and character. Orderic Vitalis, whose thirteen-volume *Historia Ecclesiastica* (*Ecclesiastical History*) is one of the richest sources for Matilda's life, writes that she was "renowned equally for nobility of blood and character" and "endowed with fairness of face, noble birth, learning, beauty of character, and—what is and ever will be more worthy of praise—strong faith and fervent love of Christ."[43] Malmesbury was just as complimentary, lauding Matilda as "a model of wisdom and exemplar of modesty without parallel in our time."[44] The twelfth-century Anglo-Norman poet and chronicler Canon Wace of Bayeux, whose lively account, *Le Roman de Rou*, was written for Henry II, described her as "very beautiful and noble."[45] Others acclaimed her grace and elegance.[46] Of all the chroniclers, William of Jumièges was

probably the only one who saw Matilda in person, and he attested that
she was "very beautiful."[47] This theme was continued by Fulcoius, archdeacon of Beauvais, a contemporary of Matilda, who wrote two epi-
grams in her honor. As well as lauding her as "courageous, prudent,
sober and just"—qualities that made her superior among her sex—he
gave her the highest accolade possible by declaring: "She was made equal
to blessed Mary in her virtue."[48] According to Fulcoius, it was Matilda's
"noble birth" that made her the "most beautiful" of her time.[49] Nobility
and attractiveness were inextricably linked in the eyes of medieval chroniclers, as were inner purity and outward beauty. The young Matilda apparently encompassed them all.

This praise was typical of sycophantic chroniclers eager to ingratiate
themselves with a woman of such influence as Matilda later enjoyed.
Their accounts were repeated by later commentators—not all of whom
had the same bias as Norman and English writers. In his *Chronicle of the
Kings of Norway,* Snorro Sturleson claimed that Matilda was "one of the
most beautiful women that could be seen."[50] Another thirteenth-century
writer, Philippe Mouskes, bishop of Tours, acclaimed Matilda's virtues in
his extraordinary rhyming chronicle:

> *A girl who knew much*
> *And was very beautiful and worthy*
> *Wise, courtly, eloquent . . .*[51]

In fact, there are few surviving clues to Matilda's appearance in her
youth. Any contemporary portraits or statues have long since been destroyed. The only reliable evidence we have derives from the discovery
of her skeleton in 1961 during excavations at the abbey of La Trinité by
the French archaeologist and historian Michel de Boüard. A detailed
study of her remains suggested that she was an extremely small woman,
for the skeleton measured just four feet two inches high.[52] Doubt has
been cast upon whether these bones were actually Matilda's, because her
tomb had been despoiled during religious riots in 1562. However, there
is good reason to suppose that the remains were genuine, because it is
recorded that Matilda's bones were saved and placed in a small casket
after the original coffin was destroyed in the riots. These were then re-

buried under the original stone slab, which can still be seen in the abbey today.

If the evidence for Matilda's appearance is fragmentary, her character is more clearly defined by the surviving sources. Although these are subject to the same sycophancy that marks the descriptions of her beauty, Matilda's actions throughout her life bear witness to their truth. Her upbringing had served her well, for she was said to embody all of the virtues expected of a young woman of high birth: modesty, piety, and virtue. However, she also had less conventional traits, and these would come increasingly to the fore as she grew into adulthood. Principal among them were her mother's pride and her father's indomitable will.

✣   ✣   ✣

To the outside world, Matilda's apparently faultless character, together with her beauty and pedigree, made her a highly desirable bride, and it is likely that her parents would have begun to consider her marriage prospects soon after her birth. The minimum age at which a girl could be betrothed was not set down in law, but according to the social customs of the day, most noble families tried to marry their daughters off as early as possible. It was not uncommon to see brides as young as twelve, although the general lack of eligible men meant that many women were considerably older than that when they married. But Matilda was apparently eager to settle her own fate at an early age.

As one of the foremost rulers in western Europe, Count Baldwin was well used to receiving envoys and ambassadors from foreign potentates. Among them was a man named Brihtric Mau (or Meaw), who had been sent as an ambassador by King Edward the Confessor. The date of his arrival is not recorded by the sources, but it is likely to have been during the mid- to late 1040s, when Matilda was between fifteen and eighteen years old.

Brihtric was one of the greatest thegns in England, perhaps the wealthiest below the rank of carl in the whole of the kingdom, and he could trace his descent to the royal line of Wessex.[53] His vast lands spanned six western counties, from Cornwall to Worcestershire, and comprised between 338 and 372 hides.[54] The lion's share lay in Gloucestershire and were centered on the prosperous town of Tewkesbury, over which he had lordship. His lands made him immensely rich; some said he was second only to the king in wealth. The Tewkesbury estate alone brought him an annual income of £100, equivalent to around £70,000 today.

With wealth came power. The evidence suggests that Brihtric played an active role in the political life of Edward's kingdom and was among the king's closest associates. He certainly regularly attested charters from the 1040s onward.

As well as being a man of wealth and influence, Brihtric also had more personal charms to recommend him. He was handsome in the Saxon way, being tall and "stalwart," with blond hair.[55] The name "Mau" or "Meaw" may have been a derivative of *snew* (snow), on account of the fair coloring that ran in his family. The fact that he had inherited the manor of Tewkesbury in 1020 and was already politically active by the 1040s suggests that he would have been at least eleven or twelve years older than Matilda. Perhaps this added to his appeal in her eyes, for the *Chronicle of Tewkesbury* claims that she fell passionately in love with him. Even after he had left the Flemish court, her affection did not diminish, and without pausing to seek her father's approval, she sent a messenger to England to offer herself in marriage.[56]

This was an astonishingly audacious act in an age when daughters were expected to meekly accept the fate that was decided for them by their parents. Matilda had not only defied this convention, she had also put her reputation at risk by offering herself in marriage—apparently without encouragement, and with no recourse to the complex etiquette that governed betrothals within royal and aristocratic circles. Little matter that, as Matilda had correctly identified, Brihtric was a suitable match for her in terms of his wealth and pedigree. Her unconventional defiance would have sent shock waves throughout the comital court and noble society at large.

When Brihtric rejected her offer out of hand, Matilda was outraged. She had risked her reputation—not to mention her relationship with her parents—in her pursuit of him. Her status and connections would have meant little if her chastity had been called into question: at a stroke, her prospects of making a good marriage would have been destroyed. What was more, even though he was an eligible suitor, Brihtric was still her inferior in rank and prestige. That he should apparently afford her proposal so little regard was insulting.

Matilda's first act of independence had backfired spectacularly, but there was little that she could do. Suppressing her fury, she seemed to put the humiliating incident behind her. Many years later, however, she would exact a dreadful revenge on the man who had so callously spurned her.

William the Bastard

By 1049, Matilda was still unmarried. She was now about eighteen, and her name had not been connected to any other suitors since the Brihtric scandal. Her father, Baldwin, was no doubt eager to erase the memory of that unfortunate episode by finding her a suitable husband. Ever one to spy an opportunity for strategic advantage, his choice fell upon the leader of the powerful province that bordered his own: the duchy of Normandy.

Normandy had its origins in an early-tenth-century Viking settlement in and around the town of Rouen. The Viking leader, Rollo, had been granted the territory by Charles the Simple, King of the Franks, around 911, and he and his successors had gradually extended its borders through conquest and diplomacy. By the mid-eleventh century, it comprised the regions of Évreux and Alençon to the south, and parts of Brittany to the west, as well as the Channel Islands. It was known by contemporaries as Normandy, or Terra Normannorum—the land of the men from the north.

Although increasingly Frankish in culture and politics, the Normans were proud of their Scandinavian past, for the Nordic people were among the most feared warriors in Europe. They continued to use Scandinavian names and some elements of the language, their legal system was rooted in that of their homeland, and there was a strong tradition of Nordic folklore. On several occasions, Duke Richard II, a formidable

warrior who ruled the province from 996 to 1026, showed himself willing to assist the marauding Scandinavians as they harried parts of
England and France. In 1000, for example, he permitted a Viking fleet to
spend the winter sheltering in Normandy before crossing the Channel to
raid England the following spring. As a result of this identification with
their Viking past, the Normans developed a much stronger sense of national identity than any other Frankish territory.

Richard II was the first ruler to regularly use the title Duke of the
Normans. Until then, the leader of the territory had variously styled
himself count, marquis, prince, or duke. Under Richard's authority,
Rouen, which remained the principal town, became a major trading center, and the territory as a whole was quite prosperous by the standards of
the day. By this time, Normandy had become an independent principality, owing only nominal allegiance to the French king. The same was
true of other major territories, notably Anjou, Brittany, and parts of
neighboring Flanders. In fact, what we know as France today was little
more than a patchwork of territories over which the king exercised only
theoretical control beyond his own immediate domain, a small region
around Paris and Orléans. This, together with the fact that the frontiers
of these principalities were ill-defined, created a highly volatile situation
in which ruthless, power-hungry rulers waged incessant wars.

✢   ✢   ✢

It was into this turbulent, dangerous world that the future conqueror of
England was born, around 1027 or 1028.[1] Known to contemporaries as
Guillaume le Bâtard, William was the illegitimate son of Duke Robert I,
the younger son of Duke Richard II. Robert's elder brother, Richard III,
had been confidently expected to rule for many years. However, he died
barely a year after assuming the duchy in 1026. The suddenness of his
death led many to suspect foul play on the part of his brother—variously
called "the Magnificent" and "the Devil"—who had rebelled against him
and was now quick to seize the reins of power.[2]

It is likely that by this time, William had already been conceived.
Shortly before his death, Robert's father had conferred upon him the title
of Count of Hiésmois, an area in southern Normandy.[3] The principal
town was Falaise, from where Robert had launched his rebellion against

his elder brother in 1027. It was also here that he met and fell in love with a young woman named Herleva,[4] the daughter of Fulbert, a local tradesman. Although Fulbert is most commonly believed to have been a tanner (the tanneries at Falaise were famed throughout the duchy), inconsistent sources and ambiguous translations make it possible that he was an undertaker, furrier, or apothecary.[5]

According to popular legend, Robert first spotted Herleva from the castle at Falaise while she was washing clothes in a stream. Unless he had been gifted with exceptional eyesight, this is unlikely, for the castle was situated some considerable distance above the stream. Writing almost one hundred years after the event, William of Malmesbury took a different stance, claiming that Robert saw Herleva dancing and fell instantly and passionately in love.[6] The truth is that we know little of their relationship: indeed, if not for the son that it produced, it would probably have escaped notice altogether. After all, there was nothing remarkable about a member of the aristocracy taking a local girl to his bed.

At the time of their meeting, Robert was in his mid-twenties. Herleva's age is not recorded, but the date of her death suggests that she was of a similar age to her lover. That there was genuine affection between them is suggested by the fact that Robert did not abandon Herleva when she fell pregnant: indeed, he showed great favor to both her and her relatives, appointing them to prestigious positions in his court.

Legends flourished around the Conqueror's birth. One of the most quoted was by Malmesbury, who claimed that even before William was born, it was clear that he was destined for greatness. According to this account, Herleva had dreamed that her "inward parts" were stretched out to cover Normandy and England—a clear sign that the child she was carrying would rule both domains.[7] As soon as William was born, he made it apparent that he would fulfill the prophecy. Malmesbury described how the infant was left on the floor of Herleva's room while she recovered from the trauma of the birth. To the astonishment of the midwife standing by, the tiny baby grabbed at the rushes covering the floor with such strength that it was obvious he would become a mighty man, ready to acquire everything within his reach, "and that which he acquired he would with a strong hand steadfastly maintain against all challengers . . . The gossiping women received this as a portent with cries of joy, and the midwife, greeting the good omen, acclaimed the boy to be king."[8]

This account owes more to Malmesbury's imagination than to any real evidence. The truth is that William's birth was accorded no mention in reliable contemporary sources. He was, after all, the bastard offspring of an apparently casual liaison between the duke's younger brother and a low-born girl with no connections. At the time, not even the most far-sighted of political observers could have predicted that he would go on to rule Normandy—let alone England. As well as his own illegitimacy, there was the fact that his father was not expected to inherit the duke-dom. Even when Robert did become duke, it was expected that he would marry and beget legitimate heirs. His bastard son would surely soon be forgotten.

But Robert chose not to marry, instead seeming content to remain with his mistress, Herleva. Malmesbury claims that he "loved her above all others, and for some time kept her in the position of a lawful wife."[9] According to the chronicler Robert of Torigny, they had another child, Adeliza (or Adelaide), who went on to make three prestigious mar-riages.[10] Herleva later married one of Robert's favorite noblemen, Her-luin de Conteville. Some accounts claim that her lover arranged this match as a selfless act to ensure her future because she was of too lowly a status to become his own wife.[11] Another theory is that she married Herluin after Robert's death. What is certain is that this marriage pro-duced two sons: Odo and Robert.[12] Both men would play a hugely sig-nificant part in the later history of their half-brother, William.

Duke Robert consistently recognized William as his son through-out his reign and seemed to be immensely proud of the boy, who from a young age showed remarkable military prowess. Shortly before em-barking upon a pilgrimage to Jerusalem in January 1035, Robert showed William the ultimate favor by naming him his heir. This may seem surprising—even shocking—but illegitimacy did not carry quite the same stigma then as it would in later centuries. Christian marriage was still being regularized, and William's grandfather, Duke Richard II, had been the first of his line to make such a formal union. Many rulers con-tented themselves with concubines rather than taking a wife. Although William became widely known as "the Bastard," this was not as insulting as might be supposed. Orderic Vitalis claimed that "as a bastard [he] was despised by the native nobility," but he was writing at a time when social mores had changed significantly.[13] Yet William himself certainly seems to have been sensitive on the subject of his birth; the fact that his "official" chroniclers, Jumièges and Poitiers, omitted to mention his beginnings suggests that he was ashamed of them—but this perhaps owed more to his mother's lowly status than to his illegitimacy per se.[14] By contrast, his origins were seized upon by writers who were more sympathetic to the English, notably William of Malmesbury, who described him rather dismissively as "the child of a mistress."[15]

Nevertheless, Duke Robert knew that he was taking a risk by leaving his domain to a boy whose claim could be called into question, particularly as there were several rival claimants, notably the duke's half-brothers, Archbishop Mauger of Rouen and Count William of Arques, who were untainted by bastardy. In an attempt to negate the threat of civil war while he was on his crusade, Robert "presented" his son William, then just seven or eight years old, to the powerful Norman magnates and "besought them to choose him as their lord in his place and to accept him as military leader."[16] According to Jumièges, "everyone in the town rejoiced in his encouragement and in accordance with the duke's decree readily and unanimously acclaimed him their prince and lord and pledged him fealty with inviolable oaths."[17] But Duke Robert was not satisfied. As a further precaution, he secured formal recognition of his son's new status from Henry I. The French king was pleased to return the favor that Robert had shown him two years earlier when he had been driven out of his domains by rebels and the duke had offered him refuge. Apparently content that he had done everything in his power to protect his young heir, Duke Robert duly took his leave for the Holy Land.

According to Jumièges, Robert succeeded in reaching Jerusalem, and soon afterward embarked upon his return journey. However, he made it only as far as Nicaea in Turkey, where he died suddenly at the beginning of July 1035. As with his brother's demise, foul play was suspected, but nothing was ever proved.[18] His son, William, was genuinely grieved upon hearing the news, and he revered his father's memory throughout his life.[19] But in the immediate aftermath of Robert's death, he was faced with a more urgent matter—namely, the battle to hold on to his inheritance. As Malmesbury recounts: "Soon everyone was fortifying his own towns, building his towers, collecting stores of grain, and on the lookout for pretexts to plan a break with the child as soon as possible."[20]

The fact that William was a minor served to inflame the situation even more, as did his bastard status, which strengthened the claim of the descendants of Dukes Richard I and II—the so-called Richardides. Jumièges tells how one adversary, Roger of Tosny, who could trace his descent back to Rollo, "hearing that the young William had succeeded his father in the duchy . . . became very indignant and arrogantly refused to serve him, saying that as a bastard William should not rule him and the other Normans."[21] It was a familiar cry. Those same power-hungry nobles whom Robert had tried to rein in quickly forgot their oath of allegiance to his young heir and seized the opportunity that the accession of a minor brought in its wake. In this bloodthirsty, lawless land, the race was on to see who could murder the boy first.

William had scant resources to draw upon in this most one-sided of conflicts, and his chances of survival seemed remote indeed. The guardians who had been appointed to protect him soon fell by the wayside. The archbishop of Rouen died in 1037, followed by Count Alan of Brittany in 1040. The latter's replacement, Gilbert of Brionne, was murdered by assassins a few months later as he was out riding, along with another guardian, Lord Turold. Security around the boy was tightened as a result, and he was often concealed in peasants' houses for safety. William himself later recalled: "Many times, for fear of my kinsmen, I was smuggled secretly at night by my uncle Walter out of the chamber in the castle, and taken to cottages and hiding-places of the poor, to save me from discovery by traitors who sought my death."[22] His steward, Lord Osbern, took to sleeping in the same room with him—a precaution that cost him his life. Orderic Vitalis tells how Osbern "unexpectedly had his throat cut one night . . . while he and the Duke were sound asleep in the Duke's chamber at Vaudreuil."[23] The perpetrators had evidently been disturbed or William had awoken in time to escape the same fate.

This was William's education. Instead of reading and writing, he was taught the brutal lessons of murder, violence, and betrayal. Honing his military skills became a question of survival, not merely a nicety of aristocratic upbringing. As Jumièges observed, living in "hardship and deprivation," he had been forever trying to escape from "the snares of his enemies."[24] None of the courtly refinements befitting a duke of one of the most powerful territories in Europe were bestowed upon him. The contrast to the pampered upbringing of his future wife could not have been greater.

✧   ✧   ✧

During his first tempestuous twelve years in power, William's main achievement was to escape the clutches of his rapacious and murderous nobles—which, given the extraordinary number of attempts on his life, was no mean feat. He had been able to do little to assert his control and bring his rebellious subjects to heel. The turning point came in 1047, when he was in his twentieth year. Count Guy of Burgundy was one of his deadliest enemies. As a grandson of Duke Richard II (and thereby a cousin of William), he claimed that he had a stronger right to the duchy than this bastard upstart. By 1047, he had amassed such a dangerous body of support—as many as twenty-five thousand troops—in western Normandy that William had little choice but to take up arms.

The two armies met at Val-ès-Dunes. If William had been forced to rely solely upon his own forces, the day would have been lost. Jumièges describes how the duke was confronted by "an army of innumerable hostile and aggressive warriors with drawn swords ready to join battle."[25] Fortunately, he was able to call upon the support of the French king, Henry I, whose goodwill William's father Robert had been wise enough to cultivate. Malmesbury claims that Henry supported the young duke "most vigorously" during this and other campaigns.[26] Thanks to his backing, William's army was bolstered by an additional ten thousand men. This swung the balance firmly in his favor, and their combined forces won the day. It was a momentous victory, for defeat would have meant deposition. William had emerged as a force to be reckoned with. Gone were the days of being forever on the run from his enemies. Now the twenty-year-old duke was on the offensive. Jumièges proudly described "how valiantly he crushed their reckless necks under his feet."[27]

By vanquishing his enemies at Val-ès-Dunes, William had proved that he had the one quality that was prized above all others when it came to governing medieval states: eleventh-century rulers were military leaders first, politicians second. It was not just Normandy that saw exceptional violence in this period; across whole swaths of western Europe, leaders had to be more than mere figureheads to survive. They had to fight every bit as ferociously as their subjects—if not more so—in order to justify their position. There were few constitutional or legal limitations to their power. Although in theory they were responsible for upholding and enforcing the law, they did not have to abide by it themselves. The fact that they had to exercise some degree of conciliation toward their nobles in order to avoid rebellion did not detract from their immense arbitrary power. They ensured the stability of their kingdom through the sheer force of their personality. Ruthlessness, not diplomacy, won the day.

Duke William of Normandy flourished in such an atmosphere. His military prowess was matched by his unbending will and "superb self-confidence," and he never flinched from imposing his authority by force.[28] Val-ès-Dunes was just the first in a series of bloody conflicts that secured his predominance within the province and repelled the threats from outside. Those whom he conquered were shown no mercy. The savagery of his regime was notorious. According to one chronicler: "Nations foreign and far-distant feared nothing so much as his name."[29] By the age of twenty-two, he had become one of the most respected—and feared—rulers in western Europe.

He was also one of the most hated. His cruelty and brutality were not tempered by conciliation or compromise. His will was the only one that mattered, as anyone who stood in his way found out to his cost. The *Anglo-Saxon Chronicle* describes him as "a very stern man, and violent, so that no one dared do anything against his will."[30] Eadmer, another contemporary, claimed that he was "stiff and terrifying to almost everyone because of his great power."[31] Intolerant and self-righteous to the extreme, William scorned weakness in others—perhaps driven by the deep-seated insecurity that he harbored about his own illegitimacy. Although he was praised for his justice, when blinded by fury his vengeance could be swift and terrible. According to several reliable contemporary accounts, while he was besieging Alençon in 1051, the inhabitants "had beaten pelts and furs in order to insult the duke," a clear allusion to his menial origins as the grandson of a tanner.[32] When the town fell, William ordered that the hands and feet of every man who had participated in the siege should be cut off. The sources contain no further references to the duke's being insulted for his bastard status by the citizens of Alençon.[33]

William was not a subtle man, and his attitude to most matters was conventional, as Matilda would find out to her cost. Domineering and direct, he bulldozed opponents into submission and was merciless in pursuit of his ambitions. But he would not have achieved such staggering success if he had not also had a degree of animal cunning, gained from the hazardous period of his childhood. At its worst, this manifested itself in corruption and avarice, particularly in his later years, but it also made him a match for the most brilliant political strategists. The *Anglo-Saxon Chronicle* describes him as "a very wise man," and Henry of Huntingdon concurred that he was "wise, but crafty."[34]

The duke was also pious. Jumièges claims that "while in his flowering youth, [William] began to devote himself wholeheartedly to the worship of God." In typically sycophantic style, William of Poitiers, who as well as being William's apologist was also his chaplain, praises the "utmost zeal" with which he protected the Norman church.[35] The duke's piety apparently stayed with him for life: "He was a holy and devout worshipper of the Christian religion in which he had been brought up in childhood. And if health permitted him he assiduously [sic] attended church at morning and evening and at mass."[36] In 1071, Pope Alexander II would praise him for his "outstanding reputation for piety among the rulers and princes of the world."[37] This manifested itself topographically, and during his reign, a far greater number of religious buildings were founded across Normandy than ever before. The duke was also a keen reformer, determined to root out corrupt ecclesiastical practices. According to Orderic Vitalis, in appointing high-ranking churchmen, he paid more heed to "wisdom and a good life" than to wealth and power.[38] Although it was common for military leaders to justify any number of brutalities in the name of religion, it seems that William's dedication to the church was more than mere lip service. His "devout and eager" belief bordered on the puritanical, and he protected the church every bit as fiercely as he did his dominions. Even the *Anglo-Saxon Chronicle,* which mostly depicts him as a cruel tyrant, admits that he was "kind to those good men who loved God."[39]

The young duke was also capable of intense loyalty, particularly toward the relatives of his mother, to whom he seems to have been close. Malmesbury observes that he treated Herleva "with distinguished generosity" throughout her life.[40] He promoted her two sons by Herluin de Conteville, Odo and Robert, to the prestigious positions of bishop of Bayeux and count of Mortain respectively.[41] He also made Herluin himself a rich man by granting him vast swaths of land across Normandy. When Herleva died in 1050, William made careful provisions for her final resting place, ordering that she should be buried at the abbey of Grestain, founded by Herluin in a beautiful setting near the river Seine.

If William had a softer side, it surfaced most often in his relations with women. Matilda herself would benefit from it, although she would also learn that if crossed, William's tender feelings would give way to terrifying fury. The duke also believed in fidelity and was known to be chaste.[42] This was viewed with some suspicion by contemporaries and "gave occasion for his manhood to be called into question," for it was positively expected of a young nobleman to sow his wild oats and father a number of illegitimate children before (and indeed after) taking a wife.[43] Perhaps William eschewed such behavior because of his intense shame about his own illegitimacy. William of Malmesbury provides another explanation by referring to reports that the duke was impotent.[44] His marriage to Matilda would prove how ill-founded these were.

The duke's apparent abstemiousness extended to his dietary habits. "Moderate in eating and drinking, especially the latter; he abhorred drunkenness in any man, most of all in himself or at his court," claims Jumièges. "He was so sparing in wine and other drink that after a meal he seldom drank more than three times."[45] This was another trait that would have set him apart from many of his military colleagues.

As with Matilda, there are no surviving contemporary portraits of William, except those found in the Bayeux Tapestry, which are all heavily stylized. They suggest that William adopted the typical Norman style of cropped hair (which may have been of a reddish color) and clean-shaven face. This is corroborated by the images found on the duke's seals and coins, as well as in illuminated manuscripts.

It seems, though, that he was definitely a well-built man. William's tomb, which was first opened in 1522, was said to have contained the skeleton of a large man with exceptionally long arms and legs.[46] However, like Matilda's, it was despoiled during the Calvinist riots later in that century, and the only surviving remnant is a single thigh bone, which might or might not have belonged to William. Still, this was measured during the same 1961 excavations that unearthed Matilda's tomb, and the conclusion was that William would have been about five feet ten inches tall. He would have towered over most of his contemporaries—not least his diminutive future wife.

That William had an impressive physique is also borne out by the descriptions found in contemporary accounts. "He was great and strong, in body, tall of stature, yet not ungainly," according to his apologist.[47] Malmesbury claims that the duke's arms and shoulders were so strong that he could draw a bow that other men could not even bend—and that while he was spurring on a horse.[48]

According to the contemporary narrative *De Obitu Willelmi*, William's physical vigor was matched by his voice, which was harsh and rough.[49] Jumièges agrees that "he could express everything he wished to say very clearly in a rasping voice," but adds, rather confusingly, that this "did not suit his appearance."[50] He was apparently fond of uttering loud oaths "so that the mere roar from his open mouth might somehow strike terror into the minds of his audience."[51] Coupled with his "ferocious expression," this would have intimidated anyone who encountered him.[52]

This terrifying spectacle of a man—at once both domineering and devout, brutal and faithful—was about to take center stage in the life of Matilda of Flanders.

The Rough Wooing

s a potential bride, Matilda of Flanders was not the only appealing prospect for leading potentates across Europe; other noble families possessed beautiful, accomplished daughters. Of course, the prestige of her lineage and the strategic importance of her father's principality increased Matilda's value, as did the fact that any alliance with Flanders would effectively also mean alliance with France. But what set her apart was the fact that she herself was not as politically sheltered as many other eligible daughters. The years that she had spent in the comital court had given her a keen understanding of international affairs, particularly those relating to England.

None of this escaped the notice of Duke William of Normandy. His pride and arrogance bolstered by his recent military success at Val-ès-Dunes, he resolved to establish his dynasty by taking a wife. According to Jumièges, he was prompted to do so by his magnates, who "urgently drew his attention to the problem of his offspring and succession."[1] William of Poitiers agreed that he was "given divergent counsels about his marriage" by the many advisers who occupied his "crowded court."[2] Society dictated that a "youth" became an adult only when he established for himself an independent household with a wife and children. Having proved his masculinity on the battlefield, it was now time for William to do so in the marriage bed.

It was essential that William's bride should be of impeccable pedigree, in order to help erase the stain of his own birth. No less vital was the need to strengthen Normandy's position by forging an advantageous alliance with a foreign potentate. Matilda was ideal in both respects. The fact that she was the niece of the French king was particularly valuable, for even though Val-ès-Dunes had helped to establish William's authority, his hold upon Normandy had been lately threatened by the count of Anjou's capture of Maine, which had brought a hostile power dangerously close to his borders. He knew, therefore, that this authority was still dependent upon the notoriously fickle loyalty of his magnates, and moreover on the support of the king of France as his overlord.

William of Poitiers claims that the young duke need not have confined his marital ambitions to a bride from a neighboring province, for "Kings from far away would gladly have given him their very dearest daughters in marriage." But he admitted that his protagonist had "many weighty reasons" for choosing Count Baldwin's daughter.[3] Not all of them were political. Although there were rumors that he was impotent, William was apparently drawn to Matilda as much for the accounts of her beauty as for her lineage. Jumièges claims that upon hearing that Count Baldwin of Flanders "had a daughter called Matilda, a very beautiful and noble girl of royal stock," William immediately sent envoys to ask for her hand in marriage.[4] Personal desire seemed to have merged with political strategy. The negotiations may have begun around May 1048, when Duke William and Count Baldwin attested a charter by the French king at the city of Senlis, a favored royal residence some thirty miles north of Paris.[5]

The Flemish count, who had no doubt considered (and rejected) various suitors for his daughter in the past, was said to be "very pleased" with William's proposal. Normandy was as useful an ally to him as his own principality was to Duke William. A union with his powerful Norman neighbor would greatly enhance Flanders's growing status in western Europe. Moreover, he was particularly in need of support at this time because the Holy Roman Emperor, Henry III, was threatening his frontiers, and King Edward of England had assembled a fleet to help serve against Flanders if necessary. In such circumstances, it was vital for Baldwin to make a friend of the Norman duke rather than add him to the already dangerous coalition of adversaries. Furthermore, he already had firsthand experience of how obstructive a hostile duke of Normandy could be—when he had attempted to seize power from his father in the early 1030s, he had been thwarted by William's father, Robert I. He therefore eagerly grasped the opportunity to put relations between the two countries on a better footing.

The records attest that Count Baldwin gave the young Norman duke's envoys a courteous reception when they arrived at the Flemish court, probably in late 1048 or early 1049.[6] Only now, however, was Matilda herself consulted. Far from sharing her father's enthusiasm, she flatly refused to lower herself so far as to marry a mere bastard. Worse still, she made no secret of her rejection, and it was soon being gossiped about throughout the court. Count Baldwin was mortified, and admonished his daughter for such outrageous defiance: women were expected to obey their male superiors in all matters. He was determined that Matilda would not jeopardize the alliance. But in vain he urged her to remember her filial duty to obey him in all things. She remained implacable—a telling indication of the same force of character that would bring a conqueror to heel.

Matilda's refusal caused such a stir that it was not long before the news reached her rejected suitor. According to the *Chronicle of Tours*, William was outraged at being rejected so publicly and with so little ceremony, and he rode with all speed to Baldwin's palace at Bruges. He encountered Matilda as she was leaving church. Without hesitation, he dragged her to the ground by her long hair and beat the diminutive girl almost to death "with his fists, heels, and spurs," rolling her in the mud and ruining her rich gown. The young duke then, without a word, strode back to his waiting horse, "sprang to the saddle, and setting spurs to the good steed, distanced all pursuit."[7] Shocked and humiliated, Matilda was helped to her feet by her terrified gentlewomen and conveyed to her bedchamber.[8]

Considering that Matilda had already made her distaste for the young duke clear, it is reasonable to assume that his behavior would have strengthened her resolve to have nothing to do with him. But according to these accounts, just a short while later she announced—astonishingly—that she would marry none but William, since "he must be a man of great courage and high daring" to have ventured to "come and beat me in my own father's palace."[9] Her father, who had immediately declared war on the duke, was left utterly bewildered. In the very brief interim, he and his wife had already chosen another husband for their daughter—the duke of Saxony. But their attempts to reason with Matilda were again in vain: her mind was set. "I will have no other husband but my fiancé, the incomparable Duke William," she told them.[10] The count therefore gave his consent to the match—no doubt consoled by the significant advantages that it would bring to his own position and that of his domain. A cease-fire was declared with Normandy, and the two principalities were brought to terms. The duke formally renewed his proposal at the peace talks, and this time Matilda declared that "it pleased her well."[11] She and William were betrothed a short while later.

How much of this tale is true cannot be known for certain, but the sources are highly suspect. They were written almost two hundred years after William and Matilda's betrothal, and there is no known origin for the story among the contemporary chronicles. Moreover, the *Chronicle of Tours* was a satirical tome, full of anti-Norman sentiments, so it can hardly be relied upon. It seems unlikely that a betrothal between two members of the most high-profile families in Europe could begin with something akin to a tavern brawl. Even if some of the details were true, the violence must have been exaggerated, for if William had kicked Matilda with his spurs, she would almost certainly have died from the wounds—eleventh-century spurs had a sharp spear-shaped point.[12] There are also conflicting versions of the tale. Two other thirteenth-century accounts claim that William had forced his way into Matilda's bedroom and soundly beaten her, and that the encounter had taken place at Lille, rather than Bruges.[13]

Although these sources differ in their telling of the story, they agree that Matilda refused the duke on account of his bastardy. From what we know of the strong sense of pride that she felt in her own ancestry, this is not beyond the realm of possibility. Equally, the extreme sensitivity that William harbored about his shady origins was likely to have provoked furious indignation at such a rejection. And given that he was a notoriously violent man, he may well have resolved to punish this impudent woman as if she had been a recalcitrant servant.

But what of Matilda? Can we really believe that she was so impressed

by the "rough wooing" on the part of a man for whom she had hitherto
shown the utmost disdain that she instantly changed her mind and resolved to marry him at any cost? This would hardly have been consistent
with the pride and strength of will that had already become evident in
her character. Neither is it feasible that, as one nineteenth-century historian has surmised, she was so terrified of "encountering a second beating" that she gave her consent immediately.[14] Matilda had enough
protection at the Flemish court to guard against that. It is therefore likely
that either the accounts were exaggerated, or, if Matilda had initially rejected William's proposal, there was some other explanation for her subsequent change of heart. Such an explanation could lie in Matilda's
earlier relationship with Brihtric of England. Had this scandalous encounter sufficiently tarnished her reputation that she was now obliged to
accept proposals that she would otherwise have disdained? Unless new
evidence comes to light, the story of Matilda's betrothal to William will
remain forever subject to the vagaries of myth and legend. But this
should not obscure the real drama of their betrothal, which was just
about to unfold.

✛ ✛ ✛

Although the papacy was a weak institution in the first half of the eleventh century and rarely intervened in matters beyond Rome, its sanction
was still desirable for a betrothal of the importance of that between William and Matilda. The young duke was particularly keen to secure it in
order to help erase the stain of his bastard status. He did not have long to
wait until the matter was under review. It was decided that it would be
discussed at an ecclesiastical council to be held by Pope Leo IX at Rheims
in October 1049. This was the first time in many years that a pope had
made such a journey, and William might have been forgiven for thinking
that it was a mark of respect. He could not have been more wrong. To
his utter dismay, he learned that the council had summarily condemned
his betrothal to Count Baldwin's daughter.[15] This sent shock waves across
Western society: William had not been alone in assuming that the papacy's sanction would be easily given. It would prove a turning point in the
history of papal authority, creating a volatile situation in which the Pope
vied with secular leaders for supremacy over ecclesiastical matters.

Surprising though the council's decision was, the evidence suggests that it was not entirely unexpected by William. His proposed marriage to Matilda of Flanders had already been debated by high-ranking members of the Norman church, who expressed misgivings about its legitimacy. Although for centuries marriage had been a civil institution that was only loosely regulated, in the eleventh century the papacy began to take an interest in the custom as a means of asserting its growing authority over ecclesiastical matters throughout western Europe. It therefore set down—and was determined to enforce—a series of laws to govern it. Among these was that the individuals concerned must not be connected within seven degrees of kinship.

The origin of such extreme strictures regarding consanguinity lay in the fifth and sixth centuries, when the Western church had first prohibited the marriage of cousins. The reasons are not altogether clear, although within the religious community there seems to have been a general horror of incest. There may also have been a financial imperative, because by limiting marriage—and thereby the inheritance of estates—within families, the church itself could secure large landed endowments. However, it was not until the eleventh century, when the papacy and its satellites embarked upon a program of zealous reform, that the laws regarding kinship were tightened up as part of the creation of a clear, uniform, and enforceable definition of marriage. By this time, consanguinity was the most commonly invoked impediment in declaring a marriage invalid. It was defined so broadly that it was something of a challenge to find a partner to whom one was not related, particularly within the closeted world of royalty and nobility. Equally, few people in any age or society could confidently name their seventh cousins; some would even struggle to name their first or second. At the same time, though, the consanguinity rules presented an opportunity for those wishing to escape from childless or otherwise unsatisfactory marriages. This had been the case with Matilda's grandfather, Robert the Pious, and his second wife, Bertha of Burgundy. Opposition had already been raised during the early days of their union by Robert's father on account of the closeness of their kinship, and when Bertha failed to give Robert the heir he needed, he used this as a convenient excuse to seek an annulment.[16]

No official record of the council's decision was given, and it has been suggested that the reason William had sent a large contingent of Norman bishops to Rheims was not just to influence the outcome but to avoid word of it spreading if that outcome was negative.[17] The fact that the Norman chroniclers afford it scant attention suggests that it caused William some embarrassment in his duchy. According to chroniclers from Le Bec, an interdict was enforced during this period, which may have been intended to prevent further discussion of the matter.[18]

But it was too late: news of the ban spread like wildfire, and William's enemies were quick to seize upon it as a means of undermining his power. This fusing of political and religious opposition was extremely threatening to the young duke, and when one of his foremost churchmen became embroiled in the controversy, William was swift to act. Lanfranc, the influential prior of Le Bec, was a staunch reformist who believed that the laws governing marriage should be strictly upheld. He spoke out against William and Matilda's union after the papal ban had been declared, condemning it as uncanonical. He was subsequently banished from the duchy, and his abbey was sacked by the duke's men. But legend has it that on his point of departure he met William by accident and the two men came to terms. The duke must have been either forceful or persuasive, because Lanfranc not only abandoned his former opposition but agreed to negotiate with the Pope on William's behalf.

The narrative of this extraordinary encounter does not make it clear upon what grounds Lanfranc had objected to the marriage in the first place, but it is likely to have been that the couple were related. In his revision of the *Gesta Normannorum Ducum* chronicle, Orderic Vitalis claims that the papacy banned William and Matilda's marriage "after frequent accusations of several religious people that he had married a kinswoman."[19]

The controversy that followed the council of Rheims eclipsed a core question. Just why was it assumed that consanguinity was the reason for the papal ban? It is possible that Matilda's mother, Adela of France, had been married or precontracted to William's uncle, Richard III, the duke of Normandy, before her marriage to Baldwin of Flanders.[20] It is true that Richard did marry a woman named Adela, but it is by no means certain that this was Matilda's mother. Adela of France had been a young girl when she had been brought to the Flemish court for her betrothal to

Baldwin V. She had been kept there until she was old enough for the marriage to be consummated, which probably took place around 1031. Richard III was duke of Normandy from 1026 to 1027, so even if Adela had been betrothed to him before marrying Baldwin, she would have been much too young for any union to be consummated, rendering questions of consanguinity null.

More convincing is the fact that the two families were related through Matilda's grandfather, Baldwin IV. After the death of Matilda's grandmother, Ogiva, Baldwin had married Eleanor, a daughter of Duke Richard II of Normandy. Another possibility is that Matilda, like William, was descended from Rollo, the first duke of Normandy, which made them fifth cousins.[21] However, this descent is questionable to say the least, and even if it did exist, it would still have made the couple so distantly related that it would hardly have been sufficient cause for the papal ban.

There remains a rather more scandalous explanation for Pope Leo's decision, which was put forward in the nineteenth century and has been the subject of intense speculation among historians ever since. According to this theory, Matilda was already married at the time of her betrothal to William.[22] Her supposed husband was Gerbod, the advocate of St.-Bertin Abbey near St.-Omer, by whom she had a daughter, Gundreda,[23] and possibly also two sons, Gerbod and Frederic.[24] This bizarre claim rests upon the evidence of a collection of charters from Lewes Priory, which was founded by Gundreda's husband, William de Warenne, the first earl of Surrey. Principal among them is the foundation charter itself, in which Warenne refers to *Matildis reginae matris uxoris meae* (Queen Matilda mother of my wife).[25] However, the fact that neither charter states who Gundreda's father was suggests that it was not Duke William, because otherwise he would surely have been named.

Other historians dismissed the idea that Matilda had been married before, asserting instead that Gundreda was her daughter by Duke William. Much was made of the duke's confirmation of the Lewes charter in around 1083. This mentions Gundreda, but there is an erasure after her name and the words *filia mea* (my daughter) have been added. The twelfth-century inscription on Gundreda's tomb adds weight to this theory, because it refers to her as being of ducal descent. The fact that William later assented to—or perhaps even arranged—her marriage to one of the foremost earls of the kingdom has also been viewed as significant.

The monks of Lewes were understandably supportive of the idea that their founder, Gundreda, was of such distinguished pedigree, so they perpetuated the theory that she was William's daughter, and the priory records were still repeating it four centuries later.[26] However, upon closer examination, the evidence soon begins to crumble. All of the documentary sources were compiled many years after Gundreda's death, and the foundation charter for Lewes—which dates from the fifteenth century—may even be a fake. Equally revealing is the fact that none of the contemporary chroniclers even hint that Gundreda was in any way related to Matilda (or, for that matter, to William). If this had been the reason behind the papal ban, then they would have cited it as such, whereas they agree that it was due to consanguinity. Besides, there is compelling evidence to suggest that Gerbod was married to a lady named Ada at the time of Matilda's betrothal to William, and in all of the contemporary accounts, Matilda is consistently referred to as a maid—that is, a virgin.[27] The idea that Gundreda was in some way a bar to Matilda's union with the duke is therefore highly implausible.

In fact, it is more likely that the Pope was motivated by political rather than doctrinal concerns. Like the other potentates of Europe, he was uneasy about the power that this upstart Norman duke was acquiring and had no wish to see him strengthen his dominions still further by forging an alliance with Flanders. There was nothing subtle about William's aggrandizement: he was determined to flaunt it for all to see, as Orderic Vitalis attests: "William duke of Normandy was growing in power and influence, and surpassing all his neighbours in the magnificence and display of his new way of life."[28] The prospect of a coalition between William and the king of France through the proposed marriage to the latter's niece was an alarming possibility.

Leo IX may also have been influenced by the German emperor, Henry III, to whom he owed his position. Henry was at war with Count Baldwin V, who had been systematically distancing his small but strategically important principality from the German-controlled Holy Roman Empire and forging stronger links with France. Not only had he himself married a French princess, Adela, but in 1051 he had allied his eldest son, Baldwin, to Richildis, widow of the Count of Hainault.[29] This had sparked a conflict with Henry III over Richildis's inheritance, and there had been constant skirmishing along the Flemish-German border ever since. The emperor had no wish to see powerful Norman troops joining these clashes on his enemy's behalf. He might therefore have called upon Leo to return the favor that he had shown him and oppose the marriage . between William and Matilda.

The Pope's ban threw the couple's betrothal into uncertainty. Although the duke might well have been inclined to sweep it aside with the same disregard that he showed to his enemies on the battlefield, it was much more complicated than that. As a pious leader, William always surrounded himself with ecclesiastical advisers, who in effect acted as his conscience when he was planning strategies and campaigns. He took seriously the need to do penance for the bloodshed that he caused, and made many generous benefactions to the church. The fact that the most senior pontiff in the Christian world had forbidden his proposed match was therefore not something that he could dismiss lightly. Moreover, if William chose to flout the Pope's sanction, it could provide his recalcitrant nobles with a religious justification for rebelling against him.

Little wonder that his first recourse was to try to persuade Leo to change his mind. He sent a contingent of Norman bishops, including his closest adviser, Lanfranc, to the Pope in order to obtain his sanction. But it was in vain. The latter was evidently just as determined to retain the stranglehold that he had over one of the most dangerous potentates in western Europe. There followed at least two years of frustrated negotiations, all of which came to nothing.

Pious he may have been, but William was also every bit as strongwilled as his prospective bride. He had set his sights on Matilda and was determined to have her at any cost. Count Baldwin was no less determined, and between them they agreed that the marriage should go ahead, regardless of the papal ban.

The date of the wedding is not known for certain. There is some contemporary evidence to suggest that it had already taken place by the time the council of Rheims met in 1049, in which case the decree was condemning a marriage rather than a betrothal. More reliable sources place it at around 1050. They include a charter to the abbey of St.-Wandrille in Normandy that Matilda witnessed that year. It was also in 1050 that her father put his signature to a charter drawn up on William's orders to the monastery of St.-Pierre-de-Préaux, which may have been to mark the occasion of the marriage.[30] The union had certainly been forged before the end of 1053, when Matilda is referred to as the duke's consort in a charter given to Holy Trinity, Rouen.

If Matilda did marry William around 1050, she would have been nineteen or twenty years of age, while her husband would have been around twenty-three. We are told that the count and countess brought their daughter "with all honour" and "together with many gifts" to the town of Eu. As well as being a convenient location on the border between Normandy and Flanders, the town was also a symbol of Duke William's power, as he had wrested the castle from a contingent of rebellious nobles in 1049 and it was still garrisoned by his soldiers. Matilda and her parents were met at Eu by William and a retinue of his soldiers.[31] William's mother, Herleva, and her husband, Herluin de Conteville, were also there, along with a great host of magnates and churchmen.[32] Matilda and William were probably married a day or so later. The precise location of the wedding ceremony is uncertain. While some sources place it at the cathedral church of Nôtre Dame d'Eu, others claim that it was celebrated in the chapel of the castle. Another theory is that it did not take place in Eu at all, but in Rouen.[33] The doubt over its location suggests that it may have taken place in some secrecy—or at least with a good deal less fanfare than might have been expected of the first ducal marriage in thirty years.

An inventory of the treasures of Bayeux Cathedral taken in 1476 by Louis de Harcourt, a member of its clergy, describes two gowns of "incomparable richness" that were believed to be the wedding clothes of William and Matilda. The pair of matching cloaks owed more to a desire to flaunt their wealth than to exhibit good taste. William's garment was covered with small golden crosses to emphasize his piety, as well as flowers, cameos, and precious stones. On the back was a band of cloth of gold with richly embroidered images. But he did not entirely give himself over to extravagant dress for the occasion, because among the treasury of the cathedral was a helmet that he had worn during the ceremony.

It seems that even on his wedding day, he was determined to maintain his warrior reputation.[34]

The wedding ceremony would have contained many of the elements that we would recognize today, including the giving away of the bride, the exchange of promises, and the blessing of the ring. There was also a formal blessing of the bridal chamber, emphasizing that the primary purpose of marriage was to produce heirs, and the bride and groom would each have been led there in great state. William and Matilda would no doubt have adhered to all of the due formalities, hoping that such strict observance of the protocol might help to legitimize their marriage in the eyes of the papacy and their subjects. According to a lively but unreliable account written in the thirteenth century, Count Baldwin had not been able to resist asking his daughter during the wedding feast what had made her change her mind about the man whose advances she had at first so scornfully rejected. To this, Matilda made no reference to his illegitimacy, but replied evenly: "I did not know the duke so well then as I do now."[35]

Mindful of the controversy that had surrounded it, Jumièges took care to stress the validity of the marriage, stating that William "married her legally as his wife."[36] His account, and later that of Orderic Vitalis, claims that it would be many years before the papacy finally sanctioned William and Matilda's union. But recent research suggests that the Pope relented at a much earlier date, probably not very long after the council of Rheims. According to this theory, the whole controversy was exaggerated by Lanfranc's biographer in order to enhance that prelate's role in resolving the matter. The sources that support the latter's account are dismissed as "late and untrustworthy," and the foundation charters for the two abbeys that William and Matilda later built in recompense for their defiance of the papal ban do not mention anything about it. This recent argument attempts to further bolster itself by claiming that relations between William and the papacy were otherwise consistently good during the 1050s, as evidenced by the visit to Rome of two prominent Norman churchmen, Lanfranc and Geoffrey, Bishop of Coutances, in 1050.[37]

But this hardly proves that relations were good: indeed, the two prelates visited the Pope to negotiate on William's behalf. We know that at least two other high-ranking churchmen from Normandy had traveled to Rome during the early 1050s for this purpose.[38] Lanfranc's biographer tells how the influential churchman spoke forcefully to Pope Nicholas II on his master's behalf, urging that William was determined not to give up his wife, so the pontiff would do well to yield. Lanfranc added that Count Baldwin's pride would not suffer his daughter to be returned to him, particularly as by that time she had a brood of children whose legitimacy would be considered doubtful.[39]

That the sources describing the lifting of the papal ban were "late and untrustworthy" cannot be wholly accepted, either. Although it is possible that Lanfranc's biographer used a degree of poetic license in order to make his subject appear more heroic, the same cannot be said of Orderic Vitalis, who had no such interests to promote. Moreover, as will be seen, later events would also suggest that William and Matilda had had to battle against the ban for at least a decade.

Regardless of its longevity, the controversy over the papal ban proves that from its inception, William and Matilda's marriage was affected by, and would reflect, the shifting political climate of Europe. As such, it sheds light on the inception of a new balance of power in the medieval world, with the rise of the papacy as a force to be reckoned with by secular rulers. Uniquely, Matilda's life bridged these two stages, and the story of her marriage to William would be played out against the transition from the old to the new Europe.

As well as adjusting to papal ascendancy, the duke and duchess also faced opposition closer to home, as William's uncle, Archbishop Mauger of Rouen, also objected to the match on grounds of consanguinity. He was promptly dismissed by his nephew. The official reason for Mauger's removal was his "devoting himself more often than was right to hunting and cockfighting and spending the treasures of his church on over-lavish hospitality." But Malmesbury claimed to know the truth: "Some say that there was a secret reason for his deposition: Matilda, whom William had taken as wife, was a near relation, and in his zeal for the Christian faith Mauger had found it intolerable that two blood-relations should share the marriage-bed, and had aimed the weapon of excommunication against his nephew and that nephew's consort."

Matilda apparently played just as active a part in Mauger's removal as did her new husband: "The young man was furious, his wife added her protests, and so (it was said) they had been looking for opportunities to drive from his see the man who had denounced their sin."[40] However, the fact that Mauger was removed with the consent of a papal legate suggests that it had nothing to do with his objection to William and Matilda's betrothal. More likely is that William was eager to be rid of a man who had long coveted his duchy and whose blood claim was not tainted by bastardy like his own. But Matilda had made it clear that she was not content to play the passive wife: from the very beginning of their marriage, her role in the government of Normandy was pivotal.

Birth of a Dynasty

ollowing her marriage, Matilda and her new husband traveled together to the ducal palace of Rouen "with the greatest ceremony and honour."[1] William of Poitiers reported that the city "gave itself over to rejoicing at the entry of this spouse."[2] The duke was no doubt keen to impress his new bride, for Rouen was the foremost city of the province and the source of great admiration among contemporaries. Orderic was dazzled by the obvious wealth that resulted from its flourishing trade, and he described the rich variety of foods and other goods that the burgeoning populace benefited from.[3] Surrounded on all sides by hills and forests, and flanked by the river Seine, Rouen was also a beautiful city, and certainly a fitting place to receive the new duchess of Normandy.

Matilda was not the only one whom William was seeking to impress, for he and his bride were accompanied by her parents, who stayed with the couple until all of the pageantry and festivities were concluded several days later. Afterward, the newlyweds made a leisurely progress throughout the domain over which Matilda was now duchess. William was surely keen to show off his new bride, a "magnificent match" whose esteemed lineage diluted considerably the shame of his birth.[4] Everywhere she went, Matilda was greeted with enthusiasm and tokens of affection by her new subjects and was "very well served and honoured."[5] The Normans had not had a duchess since Duke Richard II's reign (996–

1026), as both of his sons had been content to live with their mistresses, and they were determined to celebrate the new arrival.

Matilda had evidently also enhanced her new husband's international profile. According to Norman sources, shortly after their wedding an extraordinary message arrived from Edward the Confessor, the king of England, promising the throne to William. The message was probably conveyed to William by the Norman Robert of Jumièges,[6] whom Edward had recently appointed archbishop of Canterbury as part of a consciously pro-Norman policy. Jumièges was passing through Normandy on his way to Rome, and he brought two hostages—Wulfnoth and Haakon, son and grandson respectively of Earl Godwine of Wessex, the most powerful man in England after the king—to prove the integrity of Edward's promise.[7] The practice of using hostages as a guarantee of good faith, usually when concluding a treaty, was rooted in ancient times and had been used with great effect by the conquering Romans. In this case, however, Edward had an ulterior motive, for he was only too glad to rid himself of members of the overweening Godwine family.

It may seem perplexing that the English king should promise his crown to a foreign duke with apparently little connection to England and whose origins hardly bore scrutiny. But there had long been an affinity between England and Normandy. For a start, there was their geographical proximity, which made it politic for the rulers of each domain to maintain a close interest in the other. The two lands also shared a Scandinavian heritage, and there had been several marriages between their ruling families, such as the important union between Duke Richard II's sister Emma and the English king, Aethelred the Unready, in the late tenth century. Edward the Confessor, the son of this union, had spent much of his childhood and youth in Normandy, together with his brother and sister. They had been cared for by a succession of northern French rulers, and the dukes of Normandy had played a particularly prominent part. As a result, Edward had grown up with strongly pro-Norman sympathies.

After becoming king, Edward married Edith, daughter of Earl Godwine, in 1045, but they were childless. It was said that he refused to consummate the marriage—or, as Malmesbury put it, "to know her as a

man would"—either from a "love of chastity" or because of his antipathy toward the Godwine family.[8] Indeed, in order to counter their influence, he began to build up a faction of Norman retainers at court. In
1051, the simmering resentment between the king and his wife's family
burst into open conflict. Edward outlawed the Godwine family and sent
Edith to a nunnery. It was this that cast the English succession into doubt
and, according to Norman sources, prompted Edward to name William
his heir.

Malmesbury asserts that William was "well worthy" of being named
heir, "being a young man of high spirit, who had reached his high dignity
by energy and strength of character."[9] The duke also had a hereditary
claim to the throne through the marriage of Aethelred the Unready to
his great-aunt Emma. Malmesbury inaccurately asserts that this made
him "nearest by blood" to Edward, whereas in fact this honor belonged
to the English king's nephew and namesake. But if William's claim was
rather distant, his wife's was not. Matilda's bloodline was far more closely
linked to the English crown, and the fact that she could claim her descent
from Alfred the Great made her an important asset to William in pursu-
ing his ambitions.

Just how seriously William took Edward's promise—or indeed
whether Edward even made such a promise—can never be known for
certain. The accounts of it are mostly Norman and might well have been
written as a retrospective justification of the duke's later invasion. That
said, the foremost English source for the period, the *Anglo-Saxon Chronicle,* claims that William visited England in 1051 in order to make Edward
confirm his promise in person. The English king was said to have presented William with a ring and ceremonial sword to symbolize his sincerity. However, there is reason to doubt this claim. The duke had more
pressing concerns within his own domain at the time of his alleged visit,
for he was preoccupied with a campaign around Domfront, a strategically important town on the border with Brittany.

If Edward's promise was genuine, then William was enough of a
pragmatist to realize that he was unlikely to gain much support within
England should he ever have the opportunity to claim his inheritance.
He also knew that he would be opposed by Earl Godwine of Wessex and

his sons Harold and Tostig, whose lands stretched across the whole of southern England from Kent to Cornwall and who had vast armies at their disposal. Although Edward exiled the Godwine family in the same year that he promised William the crown, the political situation remained volatile, and Edward soon learned that the Godwines were just as formidable a threat away from court as they were within it.

However enticing, the English throne must therefore have seemed more a distant prospect than a distinct possibility to William. Nevertheless, it symbolized the remarkable transformation of his position. It is astonishing that within the space of just sixteen years, he had progressed from being an illegitimate minor with an extremely precarious hold upon the duchy of Normandy to one of the most feared leaders in western Europe and the nominated successor of the king of England.

Even so, William continued to find it difficult to forge closer links with France. He had hoped that his marriage into Matilda's celebrated line might prove useful on this front, but Henry I was no friendlier toward his Norman vassal than he had been before. Shortly after the wedding, he entered into an alliance with the duke's archenemy, Geoffrey, the count of Anjou, the foremost leader in northwestern France. This created an extremely threatening situation for William, whose territory was now sandwiched between two hostile powers.

But Henry did not stop there. In 1053, he struck at the heart of William's power by supporting a rebellion led by the duke's uncles, Archbishop Mauger and William of Arques. William immediately assumed an aggressive stance and besieged the fortress of Arques. In response, the French king led a relief force to aid the duke's enemies. By now, William was used to being on the offensive against hostile forces within his own domain, and thanks largely to his brilliant leadership, Henry's troops were beaten into a retreat. This put paid to Archbishop Mauger and William of Arques' rebellion. Both men fled Normandy shortly afterward, never to return. But the French king was less easy to subdue, and relations remained hostile for some time to come. Henry launched two further campaigns against the duke's territory in 1054 and 1057, supported by Geoffrey of Anjou.

Although William succeeded in keeping Henry of France at bay, the conflict between her husband and her own family must have been a cause of some embarrassment for Matilda. In an age when intermarriage between royal and noble families was a dominant factor of international politics, such conflict was by no means rare. Even so, she would have been painfully aware that her marriage had already failed to deliver one of its most hoped-for outcomes.

In the midst of these hostilities, there was no question where Matilda's own loyalties lay. She was the very model of a dutiful wife—"near-perfect" according to one recent observer, and William's "loyal friend" in the words of the late-twelfth-century chronicler Langtoft.[10] Having been raised in one of the most distinguished courts in Europe, Matilda was well aware of the duties expected of her as a consort. Principal among these was the need for diplomacy. In a society dominated by violence and warfare, medieval women were looked to as peacemakers and media-tors. In the famous Anglo-Saxon poem *Beowulf*, a marriage is arranged between the children of two deadly enemies, Hrothgar and Froda, in order to "settle with the woman a part of his deadly feuds and struggles." The *Exeter Book*, a collection of tenth-century literature, also praises the grace and good manners of aristocratic wives as an antidote to their brutish husbands: "The woman must excel as one cherished among her people and be buoyant of mood, keep confidences, be open-heartedly generous with horses and with treasures, in deliberation over the mead, in the presence of the troop of companions, she must always and every-where greet first the chief of those princes and instantly offer the chalice to her lord's hand, and she must know what is prudent for them both as rulers of the hall."[11]

Matilda's obvious aptitude for the role of duchess quickly won her new husband's admiration and respect. Within a comparatively short space of time, he had come to rely upon and trust her implicitly. More-over, she had already fulfilled the major expectation of her as consort. Soon after marrying William, she had given birth to a son, who was named Robert after William's father as well as Matilda's grandfather, the king of France. Given that the former was known as "the Devil" and the latter as "the Pious," the infant could not have had two more contrasting role models. The date of Robert's birth—like that of most of his siblings—is not recorded by contemporary sources, but is thought to have been around 1053.[12] The fact that there is such uncertainty over the arrival of the duke's son and heir—an event that would usually have been heralded by all of the contemporary chroniclers—suggests that William and Matilda still felt constrained to downplay their union, given that it continued to be outlawed by the papacy. Ironically, although William had desperately wanted to erase his own bastardy by taking a bride of such impeccable pedigree as Matilda, in the eyes of the church their firstborn was illegitimate.

None of this mattered to Matilda. From the start, she doted on the boy. It was a devotion that would last a lifetime. Although William was no doubt pleased to have an heir, he was rather less enamored of Robert, and from the boy's infancy he disdainfully referred to him as "Brevis-ocrea" (short-boot)—usually quoted by the chroniclers in its French form, "Curthose" (or "Courte-Heuse")—on account of his short stature, which he may have inherited from his mother. This was the first obvious point of difference between Matilda and William. It may have seemed a simple matter, the result of an overly indulgent mother and an unduly harsh father, but it would have serious consequences. With Robert's birth, the seeds of eventual discord between Matilda and her husband were sown.

For now, though, the picture was one of marital harmony—and extraordinary fecundity. During the next decade, Matilda was continually pregnant. Of particular significance from her husband's perspective was the fact that she gave birth to two more sons—Richard around 1055 and William (known as "Rufus" for his red hair)[13] around 1060.

All of the chroniclers attest to the success of William and Matilda's marriage in this regard. As Orderic Vitalis observed: "She bore her distinguished husband the offspring he desired, both sons and daughters."[14] However, they are vague about the number, names, and dates of those offspring.[15] Jumièges simply writes that Matilda "bore him [William] sons and daughters, one of whom Robert afterward succeeded to his parents' duchy, performing his father's office."[16]

It says a great deal about the age that the chroniclers give far more prominence to William and Matilda's sons than to their daughters. The latter are so obscure that they are either not mentioned at all or the details are confused. Those chroniclers who do include them in their narratives disagree on the names, birth dates, and even the number of daughters.[17] Piecing together the available evidence, it seems most likely that the eldest was Adeliza (or Adelaide),[18] born around 1057, followed by Cecilia in 1058 or 1059. Orderic claims that there was another daughter, Agatha, although she is not mentioned by any other source, and the history that he ascribes to her suggests that she was in fact the same girl as Adeliza.[19]

Between the birth of Robert around 1053 and that of William Rufus in 1060, the intermission between each of Matilda's children was only one or two years. That such a diminutive woman should prove so fecund and so resilient to the many hard years of childbearing that she endured has been remarked upon with surprise by a number of historians.[20] This is rather perplexing, given that fertility is not generally linked to height. We do not know if Matilda had any miscarriages, or if any of her children died in infancy, but the sheer number of children who survived into adulthood suggests that there cannot have been many such instances.[21] At a time when knowledge of obstetrics was rudimentary and riddled with superstition, and childbirth was fraught with danger for both mother and infant, this success rate defied all the odds.[22] That Matilda herself apparently remained healthy throughout her childbearing years is also remarkable. Women of this period—even those from the upper classes—often suffered from chronic anemia owing to the lack of protein and iron in their diets, which meant that their life expectancy was shorter than that of men. Infant mortality was also high, with between 15 and 20 percent of children dying in the first year and 30 percent by the age of twenty.[23]

Matilda's fertility did a great deal to protect and enhance her position. The prejudice against women was great, and she was by no means immune to criticism—as will be seen later—but by producing the necessary male heirs, she had fulfilled her most important duty as consort. If she had failed to give William a son, he could easily have repudiated her, just as Matilda's maternal grandfather had done to his wife. Many other such cases could be cited. There was no equality in marriage. The woman was the subservient partner, and if she failed to provide her husband with an heir, then all of the blame would be placed upon her. That a man should rid himself of such a wife was not just accepted by society; it was positively encouraged. The church even sanctioned annulments.

That Matilda and William produced such a large family bolstered their dynastic ambitions, and the names they chose for their children were loaded with significance. In the medieval period, female ancestry was just as important as male, and if the wife's family was more distinguished than her husband's (as was the case with William and Matilda), it was usual to give at least equal prominence to the traditional names of her kin. The sons were named for both sides in more or less equal measure. Robert, Richard, and William were all popular names within the duke's family, but the former could also be found among Matilda's forebears. It is interesting that none of the boys was given the name of Matilda's father, Baldwin. This may indicate that while Duke William was keen to publicize his connections with the French royal family, he did not wish to be seen as a vassal of the Flemish counts. The names of the daughters also reflected William and Matilda's ancestry. Cecilia was the name Matilda's cousin, King Philip I of France, had given to one of his daughters. Adeliza, meanwhile, may have commemorated either her father's half-sister or his aunt.[24]

✢   ✢   ✢

The medieval world defined childhood rather differently from our understanding of it. Isidore, the seventh-century archbishop of Seville, gave it a precise duration as part of his "six ages of man," which appeared in his popular encyclopaedia, *Etymologiae*. He claimed that infancy—or *infantia*—was from birth until the age of seven, childhood from eight to fourteen, and adolescence from then until twenty-eight years of age.[25] His theory appears to have had an influence upon the education of children, which followed similar stages.

The role of the mother during the first seven years of her child's life was seen as vital, both for the physical care and nurturing that she gave and for the intellectual stimulation that she provided. Children up to this age were considered to lack moral reasoning, which made such close attention by their mothers indispensable. Matilda seems to have been a paragon of this model. One observer even compared her to a woman in the Bible whose assiduity was legendary: "As a mother, she resembled Martha in her solicitous care."[26] In contrast to later periods, royal and noble children were not immediately farmed out to nursemaids or governesses in separate households of their own. The evidence suggests that all of Matilda's children were raised at court under her direction, at least initially. Certainly her eldest, Robert, remained by her side during his early years.

It is unlikely that Matilda would have breast-fed her children, because this was known to hinder conception. Instead, they would have received their milk from wet nurses—women usually drawn from the noble classes who were breast-feeding babies of their own. But in all other respects, Matilda was an active and committed mother to her many offspring. She had the support of her own mother and her mother-in-law for some of this time, for the records show that Adela and Herleva spent time at the ducal court. The charters suggest that both women knew their first grandchild, Robert, particularly well.[27]

Not surprisingly, as far as the upbringing of his children was concerned, William focused all of his energies on his sons. This was entirely commensurate with the traditions of the day: as a general rule, boys were the responsibility of fathers, and daughters of their mothers. But Matilda must have had some say in her sons' upbringing, because Malmesbury observes that both she and William took "the greatest care" with their education.[28] In the royal household, their three sons were raised alongside those of other Norman aristocrats, sent there by their ambitious parents.[29] They included Matilda's godson and kinsman Simon of Crépy, the future count of Amiens, Valois, and the Vexin.[30] Her influence on his early education seems to have been profound, because it was mentioned many years later by his biographer.[31]

Despite Matilda's influence, all of the boys who were educated at William and Matilda's court would have experienced a very masculine environment in which military prowess and boisterous behavior were encouraged. They would have been taught to ride and hunt from their infancy and would have begun serious military training at the age of twelve. Of the two careers that were open to young men—the military or the church—it was the former that William encouraged more. They were not mutually exclusive, however, as William's half-brother Odo would prove.

It was not an entirely military upbringing, however. Medieval tradition dictated that the children of noble households should be given a literary education, and this would have been taken very seriously by William and Matilda. Both boys and girls were taught the "liberal arts," which included reading, rudimentary Latin, and possibly also writing, though the latter was sometimes neglected and it was common for children to be taught simply to recite poems, psalms, and prayers. It certainly seems that Matilda taught her children to recite nursery rhymes, the Lord's Prayer, and other devotional exercises, and also instructed them in Norman French and perhaps a little Flemish. She was no doubt keen for them to absorb the social and cultural traditions of both sides of their heritage. Young men were also instructed in moral principles and the art of chivalry. According to Malmesbury, William Rufus (who was something of a favorite with his father) spent a great deal of time in "knightly exercises . . . competing with his elders in courtesy, with his contemporaries in courtly duties."[32]

Most noble sons would have been educated in political theory, and this was certainly true for the ducal family. William was keen to involve his sons in political affairs, and the records show that from the time that they were babes in arms, they were regularly witnessing charters—Robert in particular.[33] They were also often in their father's company, no doubt in order that they might learn from his example. But mothers were also expected to advise their offspring on matters of policy, so it is likely that Matilda, whose own upbringing had given her an exceptional grounding in international politics, embraced this task with alacrity.[34]

Marriage was not high up on William's agenda for his boys. His eldest son, Robert, was the subject of a short-lived betrothal when he was about eight or nine years old. Perhaps this experience, which involved a great deal of trouble on William's part, was enough to dissuade him from attempting it with his other sons, or perhaps he did not wish them to have any distractions from what he saw as the far more worthwhile pursuit of military excellence. Either way, there is no evidence of any further attempts to use his sons to forge political alliances. Indeed, neither he nor Matilda seemed concerned with securing the longevity of their dynasty by encouraging their sons to marry and produce heirs at the earliest opportunity. It is interesting to note that none of the boys would marry during their mother's lifetime; William Rufus in fact never married, which was almost certainly due to the fact that he was homosexual. The case would be very different with William and Matilda's daughters, whose value lay in their potential to strengthen Normandy's position through advantageous marriages.[35]

Religious instruction would also have been led by Matilda, whose piety was lauded by all the contemporary chroniclers. According to William of Poitiers, her husband also played a role, for he noted that William was a "pious parent" who taught his sons Christian doctrine.[36] The children would certainly have attended church regularly, both for the daily worship that was an integral part of the courtly routine and for the great assemblies that were staged for the dedication of churches or the confirmation of grants to religious houses. But the evidence suggests that Matilda's efforts in this regard were wasted on two of her sons. Robert was more interested in the pursuit of pleasure than of piety, and William Rufus (whom his parents may have intended for the church) grew up with a contempt for theology and intellectual pursuits.[37] Richard alone was lauded for his virtuous and promising character.

Despite his daughters' worth as currency in the international marriage market, for William it was his sons who counted. Indeed, from the charter evidence, one would be forgiven for thinking that the duke had only sons and no daughters. In a grant addressed to the Abbey of St. Peter, Préaux, he offered several gifts "for the redemption of his soul and those of his wife Mathilidis and his sons."[38]

By contrast, it was upon her daughters that Matilda focused most attention. This may seem odd, given that the career choices available to girls from noble families were limited to marriage or a nunnery. As at least one of her daughters would learn to her cost, the former option was by no means guaranteed. Even for the daughters of a distinguished family, finding a suitable husband was not necessarily a straightforward undertaking. There was an abundance of marriageable girls compared to boys, which meant that many were obliged to follow the celibate life of the cloister, there being no other option.

Despite the limited prospects that faced her daughters, Matilda resolved that they should have aspirations far beyond the desire to please a prospective husband. In her view, learning should not be the privilege of men alone. She knew from her own education that this was one sphere in which women could hold sway. It is a telling indication of her sense of ambition that she wished her daughters to set their sights higher than convention dictated.

The more sophisticated lessons in noble households were usually assigned to tutors, and Matilda conformed to this by appointing Arnulf of Chocques, the son of a priest in south Flanders, as schoolmaster to her daughter Cecilia.[39] Arnulf was a renowned scholar, and Cecilia no doubt benefited from his instruction, which included the arts, Latin grammar, rhetoric, and logic.

All of Matilda's children would be remarkable for their level of education—something that would not have been the case if their upbringing had been left to Duke William. The daughters in particular were a credit to the ducal family, and although the sources are sparse in their descriptions, the few references are all complimentary. They were lauded for their beauty, which they inherited from Matilda, as well as for their honesty and chastity.[40] The evidence suggests that they were close to their mother, and they lived with her at court until they were obliged to enter marriage or the cloister.

Unlike her husband, Matilda did not show a prejudice for either sex. Although she seems to have given greater attention to the education of her daughters, this was by no means to the exclusion of her sons. Her involvement included appointing their tutors.[41] As the eldest, Robert received the greatest attention. He was known to have had at least three tutors during his childhood,[42] and both William and Matilda were anxious to ensure that he was groomed for the role of duke. Meanwhile, William Rufus was later tutored by the influential Lanfranc of Bec—"a man comparable with the Ancients for learning and religious fervour."[43] Lanfranc became prior of the magnificent abbey that William built in Caen, and William Rufus may have been educated there. Rufus grew up with a stammer, which tended to manifest itself when he was angry. Speech defects such as this often result from an excessively strict or repressive childhood. Whether this was at the hands of Lanfranc or his father is not certain. It could well have been both.

Although Matilda's sons benefited from being taught by some of the most renowned scholars of the age, they did not seem to appreciate it. A method of teaching that was common in the eleventh century was the *lectio,* whereby the master would recite passages from selected texts and painstakingly explain their meaning while their pupils were obliged to listen passively and take notes. Robert Curthose later complained of the tedium of such lessons in an argument with his father, exclaiming: "I did not come here to listen to a lecture, for I have had more than enough of those from my schoolmasters."[44]

The contemporary descriptions of Matilda's sons are a good deal less positive than those of her daughters. Only her second son, Richard, is universally praised in the contemporary sources. By contrast, the chroniclers are highly critical of both Robert and William Rufus. Although Robert had initially given every appearance of being a dutiful son and had done "exactly as his father told him," as he and Rufus grew into adulthood it became obvious that their characters were flawed in one way or another.[45] Both were prone to sin and became notorious for their sexual license. They were also short-tempered, greedy, and at times brutal—characteristics that they shared with their father. In common with other children from noble households, they would also have picked up the baser aspects of life from servants.

William Rufus was perhaps the least likable of all the ducal children. He became known for his cruel, calculating nature. His cynicism and ironic humor did little to endear him to people, and in stark contrast to his parents' piety, he enjoyed nothing better than shocking high-principled churchmen. In appearance, he was the most like his father, being of stocky, muscular build, and like him he excelled in the military arena. He also inherited the elder William's "harsh," booming voice. The nickname "Rufus" was probably intended as an insult, because red hair (which the elder William also had) was seen as a sign of wickedness.

The fact that Robert and William Rufus shared negative character traits did not create any degree of affinity between them. Indeed, the evidence suggests that they harbored an intense dislike toward each other. This animosity would become ever more obvious as the years passed. The bias shown by their parents might have fanned the flames of discord. While William favored his namesake, Matilda made no secret of her adoration of her firstborn son. What began as sibling rivalry would one day tear the ducal family apart.

Duchess of Normandy

The late 1050s and early 1060s were one of the most stable periods of William and Matilda's marriage. Their domestic harmony and burgeoning dynasty made them a formidable partnership. This was bolstered by the duke's military successes, which helped to establish Normandy's preeminence in western Europe. The growing self-confidence of the duchy was reflected in a marked cultural and economic development during the 1050s. The towns of Rouen, Caen, and Bayeux throve on the profits of merchants and artisans, while to the south, a prosperous wine trade brought wealth to the duchy from neighboring principalities and overseas.

Normandy's prosperity was reflected by the style in which its duke and duchess lived. Although little survives of their palaces at Falaise, Bayeux, Bonneville-sur-Touques, Rouen, and Fécamp, the locations still evoke a powerful sense of the past. It is easy to see why Bonneville-sur-Touques was said to be William and Matilda's favorite residence, as it commanded breathtaking views of the sea to the north and the Touques valley to the south.

There is more tangible evidence of the buildings in which they lived at Caen, where excavations carried out in the 1960s provided an impression of what the ducal palace would have looked like. It was built on a huge scale and would have dominated the entire city as well as the surrounding countryside. Designed for defense as much as for comfort, it was encircled by a thick stone wall that would have had a continuous walkway for William's guards to patrol. The entrance to the palace was through an imposing tower gateway, no doubt designed to impress visitors with the power of the residents within.

Once they had passed through the gateway, visitors would have been confronted by a bewildering array of buildings. In addition to the structure holding the duke and duchess's suite of rooms, there were also numerous private houses for their officials and attendants. At the center of the complex was the Great Hall. Measuring eighteen meters by six, this was modest compared to the halls in the palaces that William would later build in England, and was less than half the size of the Great Hall that Henry VIII would build at Hampton Court some five centuries afterward. Traces of a chapel were also found, which would have been for William and Matilda's private use.

Comfortable they may have been, but such residences were by no means as luxurious as those enjoyed by later rulers. Space was at a premium within each palace and castle, so it was common for the larger rooms to serve several purposes. The Great Hall, for example, was intended for large assemblies, but it was used as a dining hall in between times. Trestle tables were erected for meals and then removed at night so that the hall could be transformed into a dormitory for hundreds of courtiers. The lucky ones might secure a bench on which to sleep, but most would have to make do with the rushes that covered the floor.

The ducal couple enjoyed rather more creature comforts. Their private apartments were situated in the warmest—and safest—part of the castle, above the Great Hall. This area, known as the solar, included a bedchamber each for the duke and duchess. Their beds were surrounded by curtains made from heavy, richly embroidered fabric to keep out the drafts in winter, as well as to provide some privacy.

Throughout the duchy, castles were more common than palaces. Some of these, such as Falaise, William's birthplace, as well as Arques and Brionne, were made of stone, but most were the so-called motte-and-bailey construction that would later dominate England. The motte, or mound, was a raised earthwork on top of which was built the bailey, an enclosed courtyard typically surrounded by a high wooden fence. In the center would be the keep, also most often made from wood, which is why so few examples of this once prevalent type of castle survive today. All of these castles were essential to the duke's exercise of power within Normandy, and to withstand threats from outside.

William and Matilda's residences formed an important backdrop to the ducal courts, which became more frequent and imposing as their authority and prestige increased. The venue was to a large extent dictated by the duke's campaigns, although the Easter court would usually be held in the castle at Fécamp. Set within a coastal town that is as picturesque today as it was then, it is easy to see why it was so favored by William and Matilda. State business was not always conducted in the splendor of the ducal palaces, however. For example, one charter was witnessed by William as he sat on a carpet between a forester's house and the church at Bénouville, near Caen.[1]

The ducal courts were essential to the administration of the duchy. The overall function of the court was in theory to provide support and advice to the duke, although in practice it became increasingly a means by which William could assert his power. The business that was most often transacted, judging from the surviving evidence, was the confirmation by the duke of land or privileges to religious houses. The courts also fulfilled an important judicial function by settling long-running claims or disputes. The resulting charters are one of the most valuable historical sources for the period, for the clues that they provide both to Matilda's itinerary and, more important, to her role in government, which steadily grew more prominent throughout the 1050s and early 1060s.

William and Matilda's courts were attended by the most powerful nobles and churchmen in the land. Chief among the ecclesiastics were bishops Odo of Bayeux, Hugh of Lisieux, William of Évreux, and John d'Avranches, later archbishop of Rouen. Meanwhile, the counts of Eu, Mortain, and Évreux—who belonged to some of the oldest and most distinguished families in Normandy—were particularly prominent secular advisers, along with William fitzOsbern, Roger de Beaumont, and Roger de Montgomery. The latter three men all shared kinship with the duke. William fitzOsbern was one of his most trusted counsellors. His father, Osbern the Steward, had been killed while defending William from an assassination attempt during his minority. Osbern's son had probably been raised as part of the young duke's court, and the two men had struck up a close friendship. FitzOsbern's fellow adviser Roger de Beaumont was nicknamed "La Barbe" because of his mustache and beard, which made him stand out among the clean-shaven Norman crowd. His family had long enjoyed influence in the duchy. The other principal adviser, Roger de Montgomery, had one of the sharpest minds of any of the duke's courtiers. When the court was in full session, it was usually also attended by members of William's family, most notably Matilda and their eldest son, Robert.

This group of Norman aristocrats—or *comtes*—in whom William vested power was extraordinarily tight-knit. Together with the *vicomtes,* the second tier of nobles, they served as agents of ducal justice, finance, and military administration. They occupied castles on William's behalf, which gave them a pivotal role in the defense of the duchy and the maintenance of order within it. It was thus through these men that the duke implemented his authority at a local level, and the fact that national and local power was concentrated in so few hands lent William's system of government a cohesion that was unrivaled elsewhere in contemporary Europe.

As well as being the nexus of political power, the ducal court was also a center of culture and refinement, largely thanks to Matilda's influence. Her husband was a military man at heart, and this was reflected by the company that he kept. He preferred rough, bawdy entertainments to the refinements favored by more learned rulers, and he often used violence in jest. On one occasion, he beat a forester with an animal bone for querying a grant to a monastery.[2] That he took such pleasure in terrifying and humiliating the victims of his cruel jests proved him more a bully than a man of genuine humor.

Although the duke did welcome poets to court, the surviving works that were presented to him were often crude rhymes rather than the eloquent and romantic verses that Matilda inspired.[3] As one recent commentator has observed, "this was a rough existence, the life of a crude, unlettered soldier, always surrounded by men of similar accomplishments and interests."[4] This is perhaps not surprising, given that William was far more used to living off the countryside while on campaign than enjoying the niceties of court ceremonials.

But it was Matilda, rather than William, who increasingly set the tone for court life. Having been raised in one of the most cosmopolitan courts in medieval Europe, she soon brought her influence to bear on the etiquette and ceremonial of the Norman court. Given her interest in intellectual pursuits, it was no doubt thanks to her that literature flourished there. She and William became active literary patrons, and the chronicler Jumièges noted approvingly that "illustrious men excellently versed and learned in letters" surrounded the duke and his family.[5] As well as encouraging Latin poets, the Norman ruling house commissioned histories of its dynasty from the likes of Dudo of Saint-Quentin and William of Poitiers.

Matilda's role at court included overseeing the preparation of the banquets held in honor of important visitors or to mark significant days in the religious calendar. The fare served was among the finest of any court in Europe, influenced by French and Scandinavian cuisine. An array of meats and poultry was presented, including venison, pork, beef, swan, heron, and duck, all flavored with spices and dressed with rich sauces. The entertainments that followed were provided by musicians, jesters, dancers, and poets, and would last long into the night. Such occasions were devised for more than mere frivolity, however. They were a highly effective way of emphasizing the potency and prestige of the Norman dynasty.

In between the magnificent occasions of court, William and Matilda's daily life there would have followed a more routine pattern. The duchess's household, like her husband's, was strict in its observances, and she heard Mass every day. For the duke, this was followed by several hours of rigorous exercise. His great passion was hunting. A satirical poem written shortly after his death claimed: "He loved the stags so very much, as if he were their father."[6] If anyone killed a stag or a wild boar unlawfully, his eyes were "put out" as a punishment.[7] William would typically go hunting in the morning, return for lunch, and continue the chase or embark upon martial training in the afternoon.

Matilda lived a more sedentary life, but she was by no means idle. Her time would be taken up with hearing petitions, overseeing her accounts, and receiving important visitors. Her leisure hours would have been spent with her ladies, either embroidering, reading, or conversing. They may also have played or listened to music. Contemporary manuscript drawings show a variety of instruments, such as early forms of harps, viols, and horns. The resident court minstrels would sometimes be joined by singers, who performed the popular ballads of the day. Other pastimes at court included games such as chess and "tables," a form of backgammon.

✛ ✛ ✛

For all the stability and status of William and Matilda's regime that their court life suggests, the specter of the papal ban was forever in the background. But in 1059, everything changed. In January of that year, Nicholas II deposed Benedict X and was formally elected pope. The ousted Benedict soon began drumming up a powerful opposition force, and Duke William saw an opportunity. He quickly offered the new pope military assistance against Benedict in the hope that it would persuade him to revoke the ban on his marriage to Matilda. As an insurance measure, he sent representatives to Rome to reinforce his case. The duke's two-pronged strategy worked. At a Lateran Council convened that Easter, Pope Nicholas granted a retrospective papal sanction for their union. Perhaps repeating the arguments used by William's negotiators, he "wisely pointed out that if he were to order a divorce this might cause a serious war between Flanders and Normandy."[8] William and Matilda's triumph was complete.

Perhaps to appease his ecclesiastical colleagues, the Pope ordered the duke and duchess to make a penance by founding a monastery "where monks and nuns should zealously pray for their salvation."[9] This was a small price to pay for legitimacy, and William and Matilda undertook it with alacrity. Indeed, they exceeded Nicholas's instructions, founding hospitals at Cherbourg, Rouen, Bayeux, and Caen "to feed and clothe a hundred poor people, the maimed, the powerless, the infirm, the blind" in reparation.[10] But their greatest benefactions by far were the lavish new abbeys that they built. Matilda's—named La Trinité—was a convent for nuns, while her husband's, St.-Étienne, was a monastery. The couple chose the same location for their twin projects. Two centuries later, the chronicler Wace reflected:

In Caen at last their work to crown
Two abbeys rose within the town:
Two monasteries side by side,
That should for monks and nuns provide.[11]

William and Matilda wasted no time in setting their architects and craftsmen to work, and both buildings sprang up with astonishing speed—thanks in part to the preponderance of the famous white stone of Caen.[12] Before the year 1059 was out, La Trinité was operating under the supervision of the appropriately named Abbess Matilda, who was a cousin of William, and a choir of resident nuns "daily praised the Lord in their hymns." The abbey must have been built in phases, because in its final incarnation, it was a vast, elaborate edifice that could not possibly have been constructed in the space of a few months. It would be another seven years before it was consecrated, and even then it was unfinished.[13] But it is a testament to Matilda's relief and gratitude at finally having her marriage sanctified that she threw herself into the project with such abandon. She was unquestionably the driving force behind the building of her abbey—and its later success as one of the most influential and prosperous religious houses in the duchy. Her enthusiasm may also have stemmed from a possible interest in architecture inherited from her father, who commissioned a series of splendid new buildings in Flanders during his ascendancy. Her mother, Adela, would surely have proved another inspiration during the project, having herself founded several abbeys and collegiate churches in Flanders.

The attention to detail that Matilda lavished on La Trinité extended to ensuring that the abbey had a sufficiently impressive collection of relics. Once more her interest no doubt derived from her natal family. Her aunt Judith was a renowned collector of relics, and Count Baldwin had once given her a vial of the Holy Blood. Among Matilda's array were splinters of wood from Christ's manger and cross, a piece of bread that he had touched, and a strand of his mother Mary's hair. Meanwhile there was a veritable Aladdin's cave of minor saints' body parts: the finger of St. Cecile, a hair of St. Denis, the blood of St. George, and even several entire corpses. This may seem macabre to modern observers, but enormous importance was placed upon such items in the Middle Ages. Bones, body parts, or other items closely associated with saints were believed to be imbued with that saint's power, and many miracles were attributed to such relics in popular tales and legends. The better a religious house's collection, the more blessed it was considered to be.[14]

That Matilda should amass such an impressive collection for La Trinité reveals not just the meticulous care she showed in the creation of her new abbey, but her own belief in the "magical" powers of the relics. For all her political shrewdness and guile, Matilda was known to be superstitious, and during critical periods of her life she occasionally sought the advice of mystics or magicians—she is recorded to have once consulted the bones of a sheep's shoulder in the hope of foretelling the future, a practice that was common in her native Flanders.

Matilda's superstition was by no means unusual among the ruling elite. Interest in magic extended across the entire society of medieval Europe, from kings, princes, and dukes to members of the clergy and even the papacy. It also cut across social boundaries, uniting peasants and noblemen, the uneducated and intellectuals. Most communities had a "wise woman" or "soothsayer" who used the mystical arts to heal the sick or protect against evil. Reading palms, rolling dice, and using randomly selected passages from the Bible to predict the future were widely practiced by such individuals, as well as by members of the clergy. There was also a more sophisticated profession dedicated to the exploration of astrology and alchemy. Training for such a profession took place at universities and other educational establishments, but its expert practitioners were often found at court, which provided an invaluable source of patronage for their endeavors. It was common for rulers to seek the advice of these practitioners, particularly at times of crisis in their reign.

Although many ecclesiasts were involved in the practice of magic, during the tenth and eleventh centuries it was increasingly condemned by the church, which saw it as a threat to its own authority. There was thus an interesting dichotomy between Matilda's celebrated Christianity and her belief in the mystical arts. In the years to come, it was the latter that she would draw upon more at times of crisis, casting doubt on the apparently intense piety that she was always so keen to display in gestures such as the creation of La Trinité.

Like his wife, William took enormous pride in the building and fitting out of his abbey. Work on St.-Étienne apparently progressed more slowly than on La Trinité, because it was not consecrated until 1077, but like its sister abbey, it was functional from a much earlier date. Lanfranc, by now the duke's closest ecclesiastical adviser, was appointed abbot in 1063. The Italian's influence had been increasing steadily during the 1050s and 1060s, and this appointment signified the preeminence that he now enjoyed. It was said that "William venerated him as a father, respected him as a teacher, and loved him like a brother or son."[15]

Although they were built for the same purpose, William's and Matilda's churches were as different architecturally as their founders were in character. In contrast to the functional starkness of William's St.-Étienne, with its vast, unadorned west front and imposing towers, La Trinité was complex, intricate, and elaborate. As one later commentator observed: "The one is the expression in stone of the imperial will of the conquering Duke; the other breathes the true spirit of his loving and faithful Duchess."[16] Comparatively little survives of Matilda's original building today, but the fragments that do —such as the bases of the towers and the arcading of the nave—give an impression of how spectacular it must have been in its heyday.

Both St.-Étienne and La Trinité were of huge personal significance to William and Matilda. Just how much they meant to the duke and duchess is demonstrated by the fact that they would later choose to be buried in them. There could have been no more fitting a resting place. They may have been built as a penance, but there was nothing apologetic about William's and Matilda's abbeys. They were symbols of the power and magnificence of the ducal family, and of just how far William had come since the turbulent days of his minority. According to one authority, they represented a "golden age" in Normandy's history.[17]

Orderic Vitalis claims that the commissioning of St.-Étienne and La Trinité sparked a new religious fervor in the principality, providing a role model for the nobility to follow: "The barons of Normandy were inspired by the piety of their princes to do likewise, and encouraged each other to undertake similar enterprises for the salvation of their souls."[18] Suddenly, powerful magnates were vying with each other to create the most lavish ecclesiastical buildings. These would prove a lasting legacy of William and Matilda's regime.

✢ ✢ ✢

By the beginning of the 1060s, when Matilda was in her thirtieth year, she had grown in influence and prestige, not just as the wife of the duke and the mother of his children, but as a political power to be reckoned with in her own right. Her active involvement in the building of La Trinité was one indication of her influence, and it gave her the confidence to undertake other pious commissions elsewhere. In 1063, for example, she began work on the magnificent cathedral of Nôtre Dame du Pré at Emendreville, a suburb of Rouen.[19] She also founded two other abbeys, St.-George at Boscherville and St.-Florent at Saumur.

Matilda's growing importance was also beginning to manifest itself in other ways. Whereas before their marriage William had relied upon older relatives for support in government, notably his uncles Mauger, the archbishop of Rouen, and William of Arques, now he began to place his trust in his wife and children. As a result, Matilda began to play an increasingly important role in the political life of the duchy.

Nothing demonstrates this more clearly than the charters. One of the earliest documents that she witnessed as William's consort dates from 1053 and relates to Holy Trinity in Rouen. This marked the beginning of a dazzlingly successful career on the political stage. Although the lists of witnesses indicate only who was present, not who participated in any accompanying debates, the sheer frequency with which Matilda attested these documents is proof that she played an active role. During her tenure as duchess, she put her signature to a total of one hundred charters, covering a wide range of business.[20] This far outweighs the number attested by even the most powerful members of the aristocracy, second only to William himself. Often it was specified that she was acting alongside William, or that the grants were made with her consent as well as her husband's. This was particularly true of the charters relating to her abbey at Caen, but there are various other examples.[21] Her consent for such grants is sometimes placed on the same level as William's—an honor that was not even accorded to his sons.[22] Only very occasionally was Matilda able to grant charters in her own right: she did not have the financial resources to do so. She had brought a relatively meager dowry and no titles to her marriage, and the lands with which William had endowed her were confined to some modest estates in the Pays-de-Caux region of Normandy.[23] This was rather less than her predecessors had received, or than she might have expected as duchess of Normandy. The fact that she was able to lavish independent bequests upon La Trinité must therefore have required her to levy funds from elsewhere.

As well as granting land and titles, Matilda also became increasingly involved in the legal affairs of the duchy. The cases that she dealt with varied enormously in nature and complexity. One of the more unusual concerned some property at Bayeux that had been granted to the abbey of St. Peter in Jumièges. This property had formerly belonged to Stephen, the nephew of a ducal chaplain, who had married a widow named Oringa by whom he had a son. This son had died without Stephen's knowing, and Oringa had bought a replacement child from a woman named Ulburga. Stephen had made this boy his heir, but after the couple's death, Ulburga tried to reclaim her child. Oringa's relatives, realizing that they would then have to forfeit the land, prevented her from doing so, which prompted her to bring the case before William and Matilda at Bonneville-sur-Touques. It was decided that the woman ought to undergo an ordeal by carrying a red-hot iron rod, and that if she emerged unscathed, she might have her son back. Ulburga passed the test, which meant that the property was forfeit to the duke. William subsequently gave it to Matilda, who in turn passed it to Rainald, a ducal chaplain.[24]

Up until this point, women had rarely played even a supporting role in the history of the reigning dukes. They had been obscure mistresses or illegitimate offspring, easily dispensed with and rarely named in the sources. Now Matilda was enjoying a position of such prominence that she would have been the envy of consorts across western Europe. The fact that she had carved out such a position for herself was all the more impressive given that her husband was a ferocious and indomitable ruler—far from the likes of Edward II or Henry VI, whose weakness enabled their wives to gain the ascendancy. It seemed that William had met his match—and he appeared to revel in the fact.

Although Matilda's power was remarkable in the context of other ruling dynasties at the time, she was not the only woman to play an active role in political and legal affairs. Indeed, in this respect, Normandy seems to have been more enlightened than many other countries. In the collection of charters relating to the Caen abbeys, twenty-three out of thirty mention women as signatories, grantors, attestees, or involved in the transaction in some other way.[25] Wives, mothers, and even daughters became involved in the granting of property or land, not just alongside the male members of the family but sometimes, like Matilda, in their own right. For example, a contemporary of Matilda, Mabel, heiress of Bellême in the heart of Normandy, was one of the most formidable noblewomen of the eleventh century. She was as remarkably fecund as the duchess, mothering nine children, but this did not distract her from her primary objective, which was the defense of her inheritance. She had considerable resources at her disposal—it was said she traveled with a retinue of one hundred armed men—and possessed a dangerous combination of cunning and ruthlessness, poisoning her own brother-in-law and disposing of any other rival who crossed her path. Having lived by the sword, she died by it, too. According to Orderic, she was murdered in her bath by a man whose land she had taken. Her epitaph describes her as "A shield of her inheritance, a tower guarding the frontier; to some neighbours dear, to others terrible."[26]

✣   ✣   ✣

Perhaps it was the growing equality of their relationship that meant that after a decade of marriage, William and Matilda seemed to have settled into a pattern of mutual respect and harmony. The tempestuous beginning of their courtship had apparently been forgotten. William's respect and admiration for Matilda grew with every child she bore him. He was immensely proud of his large family, and even more so of his wife, "whose fruitfulness in children excited in his mind the tenderest regard for her."[27]

As far as aristocratic marriages were concerned, affection was a rare and unlooked-for quality—politics, not passion, was the driving force. But on the surface at least, that very quality was what the ducal couple seemed to enjoy. The nineteenth-century historian Agnes Strickland paints a picture of increasing intimacy and accord, claiming that the duke and duchess were "reckoned the handsomest and most tenderly united couple in Europe." She continues: "The fine natural talents of both had been improved by a degree of mental cultivation very unusual in that age; there was a similarity in their tastes and pursuits which rendered their companionship delightful to each other in private hours, and gave to all their public acts that graceful unanimity which could not fail of producing the happiest effects on the minds of their subjects."[28] A similarly rosy picture was painted by a poet of the same era who dedicated a verse to Matilda, describing her as "The fond, the faithful cherished wife/Who shared each counsel, cheered each strife."[29]

The records contain no instances of Matilda's defying William in this period, and there is indeed evidence to suggest that she had come to feel a certain degree of affection for him. Sometime between 1063 and 1066, William fell seriously ill at Cherbourg. So grave was his condition that "his life was wholly despaired of and he was laid on the ground, as at the point of death, and gave the canons of that church the relics of the saints which he carried [about] in his own chapel." As if striking a bargain with God, the duke vowed that he would establish canons in the cathedral church of St. Mary in Coutances "if God and St. Mary would raise him from this sickness." Meanwhile, Matilda went to the same cathedral and made a gift of one hundred shillings at the main altar, praying "that God and St. Mary might give her back her dearest husband." The monks were surprised by her informal attire, for she wore her hair loose—a detail they recorded for posterity. Her disheveled appearance may have been due to the fact that she had stayed by her husband's side all night, frantic with worry. After making her plea, Matilda hastened back to William. It seemed that her prayers had been answered when he made a full recovery. As a token of thanks, "she helped him in her joy to re-establish the church [of St. Mary]" and to build a new one outside the castle walls in Coutances. The couple also made various other generous bequests, and their two eldest sons, Robert and Richard, were there to witness the resulting charters.[30]

That Matilda had been so panic-stricken by her husband's illness suggests that she cared for him deeply—and this is certainly how it was interpreted by the chronicler who recorded the episode. Malmesbury approvingly noted Matilda's "willingness to please her husband," and all the sources concur that she was a useful and devoted spouse.[31] But there is another explanation for her behavior, and it is perhaps more in keeping with what we know of her character. By the time William fell dangerously ill at Cherbourg, Matilda had come to enjoy a degree of influence and prestige as duchess of Normandy that was matched by few of her predecessors or contemporaries. The active role that she played in the political sphere fulfilled the ambitions she had cherished since her youth, and she was by no means ready to relinquish them. Yet if William had died, this was precisely what she would have had to do. No matter how able she had already shown herself in the governance of Normandy, as dowager duchess the most that she could have hoped for would have been to act as regent for her eldest son until he came of age. After that, she would have been expected to retire gracefully from public life. This was not a prospect that would have appealed to Matilda's sense of ambition. At least for now, the influential position she had been building for herself depended very much upon her husband's survival.

By contrast, William's attitude to his wife seems less complex. Both his words and his actions suggest that he adored her. Malmesbury claims that Matilda's obedience and fecundity "kindled a passionate attachment in the spirit of that great man."[32] In 1079, after some twenty-eight years of marriage, the duke himself would openly declare that he had been "a companion so faithful and devoted in his affection," and referred to Matilda as "the wife of my bosom, whom I love as my own soul."[33] Even in a letter of business that he wrote to her, he prefaced the formal details with a tender address to "his dear wife," wishing her "perpetual weal."[34] These sentiments form a sharp contrast to the image of a brutish warrior. It seems that Matilda brought out a softer side to him.

The duke appeared genuinely attracted to his wife, and the sheer number of children that they had together suggests a degree of sexual compatibility. The sources certainly suggest that Matilda was an attractive wife. She regularly won praise for her beauty from the likes of Jumièges and Fulcoius of Beauvais, as well as later writers. A nineteenth-century poet extolled her elegance and poise:

Her forehead's calm and pure expanse,
Ne'er ruffled by an angry glance,
Those eyes, so steadfast and serene,
That peaceful, still and gracious mien.[35]

Meanwhile, a French account of the following century described her as "beautiful and blonde," and like "a freshly bloomed rose." It also praised the elegance of her dress, with her "fur-lined cloak and close fitting gown, her two plaits falling near to the white veil that surrounded her neck."[36] However, it is not clear upon what this account can have been based, because it matches none of the later engravings of Matilda—all of which were admittedly completed many years after her death. The description of her clothes does, however, tally with the typical apparel of a well-born lady in the eleventh century. As duchess, Matilda would have worn gowns of comparatively simple design, albeit made from rich fabrics. The fashion was for long dresses, reaching to the ground and tied around the waist with a girdle, which was often the most elaborate part of the ensemble. The gown would have been complemented by a matching cloak fastened by shoulder clasps, and a hood. Not until the twelfth century did the fashion change to more decorative and elaborate attire. Although the later engravings of Matilda show her with long, flowing tresses, in general women's hair was concealed by a wimple, which was wound about the head and thrown over the shoulder. The fact that the monks at Coutances had been so shocked to see Matilda with her hair loose suggests that she usually conformed to this fashion.

A wall painting of the duchess, executed at her command, once adorned the outside wall of an ancient chapel in the abbey of St.-Étienne in Caen, which had been built before the abbey was founded. It was destroyed when the chapel was pulled down in 1700, but an eighteenth-century engraving of it survives.[37] Though it does not help us understand Matilda's physical appearance, it does give us clues as to how she might have dressed. It shows her wearing a simple robe gathered at the waist by a belt of precious metal, possibly gold, with a cloak around her shoulders. A transparent veil covers her long, dark hair and is held in place by a crown bedecked with fleur-de-lys and precious stones. In her right hand she holds a scepter of the same design, and in her left a book—perhaps an indication of her intellect. Her graceful pose, with head slightly inclined as if to signify compliance or assent, and the simplicity of her apparel give the impression of modesty and serenity.

However, this is a heavily stylized portrait that bears more resemblance to Queen Victoria than to a woman of Norman times, so its accuracy is dubious. There is also a sketch of the fresco, which seems to date from an earlier period. This shows Matilda wearing a similar crown and carrying the same scepter, both adorned with fleur-de-lys, but her features are much plainer and her hair is shorter and fair. However, the provenance of this sketch is no more certain than that of the later engraving.

Some sources claim that Matilda's image, flanked by two lions, can be found on a capital of one of the columns in La Trinité.[38] A statue of her was also erected in the eleventh century on the west front of Croyland Abbey in Lincolnshire, toward which she had proved a generous benefactress, but it was destroyed by fire in 1091. A number of statues of Matilda can be found in French cities today, notably in the Place Reine Mathilde in Caen and the Luxembourg Garden in Paris. But these are stereotypical representations of a medieval queen, and there is no consistency in facial features.

Despite the lack of visual evidence, the written accounts of Matilda's appearance, which are overwhelmingly complimentary, suggest that she was a striking woman—and, moreover, that she retained her physical charms through much of her life. This might have helped keep her husband in thrall. Almost all of the contemporary accounts attest that William was utterly faithful to his wife. Poitiers was careful to stress that "he had learnt that marriage vows were holy and respected their sanctity." Malmesbury concurs that from the day of their wedding, "his conduct was such as to keep him free for many years of any suggestion of misbehaviour."[39] While this might be expected of one so devoted, it was highly unusual for a male ruler of the time. Aristocratic marriages being political unions rather than romantic ones, husbands tended to find sexual gratification outside the marital bed, although spousal copulation was required to beget heirs. An extreme example was King Aethelred of England, who devoted himself entirely to his mistresses at the expense of his wife, Emma. Malmesbury observed with some distaste: "He was so offensive even to his own wife that he would hardly deign to let her sleep with him, but brought the royal majesty into disrepute by tumbling with concubines."[40] Two contemporaries of William, Henry IV and Philip I (later Holy Roman Emperor and king of France respectively), would both become embroiled in similar marital scandals.

Historically, the dukes of Normandy had chosen a different but no less problematic path, not marrying at all but instead keeping a string of mistresses. Perhaps this, as well as the shame of his own birth, made William determined to break the mold, giving him a further incentive to lead a private life beyond reproach. His intense piety was perhaps also a reaction against this shady heritage. He lent his full weight to the church's campaign to prevent priests from keeping illicit wives and mistresses, and he believed in the strict teachings on marriage propagated by Lanfranc.

Whatever the cause, his sexual restraint still made his contemporaries uncomfortable. William's temperance must have seemed something of an oddity amid the red-blooded warrior types with whom he was surrounded, and they no doubt sought a more scandalous explanation than that he simply loved his wife. While the rumor that he was impotent had been thoroughly discounted, they bandied about other possibilities—was he carrying on an illicit affair and, unlike so many of his contemporaries, succeeding in keeping it a secret?

Cracks do appear in the idealized vision of William and Matilda's relationship. For example, the sources contain hints of the duke's violent behavior toward his wife. One even has him kicking her in the breast with his spur.[41] Although most of these accounts were written by hostile English chroniclers, William certainly had a strong streak of cruelty, as evidenced by the treatment that he meted out to the beleaguered citizens of Alençon. Moreover, wife beating was common in the Middle Ages, and it was not just excused but expected of a man to physically chastise his wife. It is therefore possible—even probable—that a man of William's naturally violent temperament occasionally resorted to physical force in order to quell any disobedience on Matilda's part.

But to the outside world, the duke and duchess were careful to present themselves as the head of a tight-knit family unit. The birth of two more daughters boosted this image—Matilda in around 1061 and Constance the following year, the latter named after Matilda's grandmother. The younger Matilda is the most shadowy of all the daughters. She is not mentioned by any of the Norman chroniclers, but there is reliable evidence for her existence in Domesday Book, which refers to a man named Geoffrey who was employed as her chamberlain.[42]

The apparent strength and unity of the Norman dynasty was further reinforced by William's decision in 1063 to formally designate his eldest son Robert as the heir to Normandy. William made the great nobles swear fealty to him—just as his own father had done with him almost thirty years before. He and Matilda witnessed a charter for "Robert, their son, whom they had chosen to govern the regnum after their deaths."[43] It must have been a proud occasion for Matilda, given the strong affection that she felt toward her eldest son.

In the same year, the final piece of the jigsaw was fitted into place when the duke conquered the troublesome province of Maine, which lay to the south of his principality. William had long coveted this territory, and had initially tried diplomacy to obtain it. He had arranged a betrothal between his son Robert and Margaret, a sister of the count of Maine, Herbert II. So determined was the duke to ensure the match went ahead that he had the young girl "guarded with great honour in safe places" until his son was of an age to marry her.[44] But all of his efforts proved to be in vain, for Margaret died before the marriage could take place. Malmesbury claims that the count himself subsequently asked William for the hand in marriage of one of his daughters. William agreed, but in March 1062, before the girl was of marriageable age, Herbert fell sick and died.[45] It was said that on his deathbed, Herbert promised Maine to William, "adjuring his subjects to accept no one else," and the latter wasted no time in claiming his inheritance.[46]

Acquiring Maine established William as the undisputed duke of Normandy. It also ensured that he need fear no interference from northern France in any overseas enterprise that he might undertake—a fact that would prove enormously significant during the following three years. The traditional hostility toward France had in any case been substantially reduced, thanks to Matilda's family connections. Count Baldwin of Flanders had played an increasingly active part in international politics during the years following his daughter's marriage to William. He had been assiduous in cultivating the goodwill of Henry I of France toward his son-in-law, drawing upon the strong blood ties that existed between the two dynasties. So successful were his efforts that the French king had even named Baldwin regent of France on behalf of his infant son, Philip. When Henry died in 1060, Baldwin took charge and "ruled the French kingdom with distinction for some years."[47]

The ducal couple, who together had established a spectacularly successful regime on their home turf, were on the brink of international glory. And Matilda, who had rapidly established her independence and authority as duchess of Normandy, would be central to their success.

6

Earl Harold

With their duchy secure and the papal marriage ban a distant memory, William and Matilda's prestige was greater than it had been at any time during their reign. As a result, the duke had leisure to turn his energies to an enterprise that had long been occupying his thoughts.

Whether or not Edward the Confessor had really promised William the crown of England in 1051 is a matter for debate, but in the early 1060s, bolstered by his military and dynastic success, the duke now chose to press his claim. The situation in England had changed significantly since that time, and there were other contenders for the throne. The person with the best hereditary claim was Edward's nephew, Edward the Exile, whom he ordered to be brought back to England from Hungary in 1057 so that—as Malmesbury put it—"his own lack of offspring might be made good by the support of his kinsfolk."[1] However, this nephew died shortly afterward in rather mysterious circumstances, and his son, Edgar, who was only around six years of age, inherited the claim. He was given the designation of "Aetheling"—that is, throneworthy—which might indicate that the king considered him as a potential successor. If this was the case, then his promise to William was probably little more than a diplomatic maneuver, aimed at securing a useful ally across the Channel.

Edward's flimsy promise and William's faint hereditary claim were by no means a guarantee of success. True, they both constituted qualifications for kingship in England, but there were two other such qualifications—namely, being accepted by the English nobles and being consecrated by the church. Almost all of the other claimants met at least one of these four criteria.

Within England, the most powerful contender by far was Harold Godwinson, the earl of Wessex, eldest son of the late Earl Godwine, who had died in 1053. His hereditary right to the throne was tenuous. He was Edward the Confessor's brother-in-law, and he was distantly allied with the Danish royal house through his mother, Gytha. Nevertheless, together with his brother Tostig, he had a considerable body of support among the English people, who saw him as one of their own. His immense wealth further strengthened his campaign.

Prior to the Viking invasion in the ninth century, what we now know as England was a series of independent kingdoms. They included Wessex, the kingdom named after the West Saxons, which embraced regions south of the Thames from Kent to Cornwall; Mercia, which covered much of the Midlands, stretching from the Thames to the Humber; East Anglia; and Northumbria, which began to the north of the river Humber and extended well into what is now the Scottish lowlands. The Vikings had gradually drawn each of these kingdoms into their domain. The only one to remain was Wessex, which was ruled by Alfred the Great. His descendants were able to turn the tables by steadily taking control of the Viking territories, until the last Viking king, Eric Bloodaxe of York, was driven out in 954.[2]

But England remained vulnerable to the great warrior kings of Scandinavia, who saw the kingdom as their right because of the extensive Scandinavian settlements that remained—particularly in the north of the country. One of the most dominant cultures was that of the Danes. This race was "noble of blood and fighters by nature."[3] Now that Edward the Confessor looked set to die without an heir, their king, Sweyn Estrithson, a nephew of King Cnut, began to circle his prey, as did King Harald III Hardrada of Norway. Both had the military might to pose a serious threat. In view of all of this, the chances of William's inheriting the English throne must have seemed distant indeed.

But the kingdom was worth fighting for. England was one of the most prosperous realms in western Europe, and its kings had amassed a rich treasury. It had a population of between one and a half and two million—although it could have been considerably more. Although the majority of the inhabitants lived in small villages or hamlets, there were a number of impressive urban centers, notably London, York, and Winchester—the capital of the ancient kingdom of Wessex—many of which were burgeoning centers of trade. The country was well placed to partake in both the Scandinavian and North Sea trade and the cross-Channel trade with northern France, Flanders, and the Rhineland. Archaeological finds have revealed that the landscape was also effectively exploited, from arable fields and woodland to rivers, quarries, and mines.

By the standards of the day, the system of governmental administration was extraordinarily sophisticated—certainly more so than in Normandy. Particularly impressive was the single national silver coinage and the ability of kings to levy taxes across the country, as first occurred with the Danegeld tax, which was introduced in the late tenth century in order to pay off invading Danish armies. The king could also raise a national army and navy, and he had a central secretariat to issue documents in his name. A similarly efficient organizational structure existed at a local level, with defined communities and courts within shires and their subdivisions, known as hundreds. The religious life of the kingdom was also increasingly ordered, and the English church was an effective unitary body. Comprising the two archbishoprics of Canterbury and York, numerous bishoprics and monasteries, and a huge number of village churches, it was also far more extensive than the Norman one.

Now that William had seen off his most troublesome rivals on his home turf, the idea of conquering England evolved from an appealing but distant prospect into an immediate priority. Even the most brilliant military strategist needs the occasional stroke of luck, and early in 1064, fate played into William's hands. Word reached him that Earl Harold of Wessex, one of his fiercest rivals for the English throne, had been shipwrecked at Ponthieu, on the coast of Normandy, and taken prisoner by the local lord, Count Guy. According to Malmesbury, the English earl suffered all the indignities of a common prisoner, having his hands bound and feet shackled and being kept in chains until the count decided what should be done with him.[4]

Just why Harold had been journeying to France in the first place is not known. Malmesbury's theory that he had strayed too far from the English coast while on a fishing expedition is hardly credible.[5] Meanwhile, William of Poitiers claims that it was to confirm King Edward's promise of the crown to Duke William, but this is not corroborated by any other source; moreover, it is highly unlikely that Harold—a major rival for the crown—would have been chosen to relay such a message.[6] Bishop Eadmer of Canterbury asserted that Harold had been dispatched to retrieve his brother Wulfnoth and nephew Haakon, who had been held hostage in Normandy for several years. He claimed that Edward had given Harold permission to go, but warned him: "I have a presentiment that you will only succeed in bringing misfortune upon the whole Kingdom and discredit upon yourself."[7] The Bayeux Tapestry supports this version of events, and there is a scene that appears to show the English king admonishing Harold for having proceeded with the mission.

Whatever had brought Harold to France, William was quick to seize the opportunity of having the powerful English earl on home territory. He ordered that Harold be released immediately and brought to Eu, where he received him and conducted him with all honor to his court in Rouen. Although it appeared that the duke had rescued his English visitor, for Harold it was a case of out of the frying pan, into the fire. He might have been fêted as an honored guest, but it was clear that he was just as much a captive as he had been in Ponthieu. William had no intention of releasing him without exploiting his unexpected visit to the full.

But for the time being, Harold was shown every courtesy by the duke and his family. Malmesbury records: "The duke received him with great respect, and fed and clothed him splendidly, according to the custom of his country."[8] Eager to show off his status as a powerful ruler, William ordered a series of lavish entertainments at his court. He also made sure that his wealth was ostentatiously displayed, and Harold's apartments were hung with rich jewels, fabrics, and ornaments. It is likely that some if not all of William and Matilda's children were presented to their English guest, because the duke would have been keen to demonstrate the strength of his dynasty.

Not content with these displays, William also contrived to impress Harold with his military prowess by inviting him to accompany him on campaign to Brittany.[9] The image was one of brothers in arms fighting against a common enemy, but the subtext was clear: William wanted his rival to see just how much he deserved his reputation as one of the most feared warriors in Europe. As Malmesbury neatly put it, the duke had "the deeper design of showing him [Harold] William's warlike preparations, so that he could see how much Norman swords were superior to English axes."[10]

Matilda's reaction to their English guest might have been very different. Did he spark memories of that other Saxon, Brihtric, who had so beguiled her at her father's court? Harold was said to be charming and attractive, and even Orderic Vitalis, who was highly critical of him, admitted that he was "very tall and handsome, remarkable for his physical strength, his courage and eloquence, his ready jests and acts of valour."[11] Edward the Confessor's biographer, meanwhile, described him as "distinctly handsome," graceful and brave. He also wrote admiringly of Harold's seemingly inexhaustible energy, claiming that he was "well practised in endless fatigues and doing without sleep and food, and endowed with mildness of temper and a ready understanding."[12] Whether Matilda felt nostalgic or resentful upon meeting this scion of the Anglo-Saxon race is not recorded, but she would certainly have been present for all of the elaborate ceremonials that her husband had ordered. Indeed, she played an equal part in ensuring that their English guest was "hospitably entertained," and the thirteenth-century Norwegian chronicler Snorro Sturleson describes how "Harald sat on the high seat on one side of the earl [William]; and on the other side sat the earl's wife."[13]

According to a fanciful account of their meeting written by a nineteenth-century poet, when Harold first laid eyes upon Matilda, he was struck by her beauty, which both reminded him of, and eclipsed, his mistress Edith's celebrated charms: "Ne'er hath he seen a form so fair . . . A yearning sigh escapes the guest!"[14] Matilda would then have been in her early to mid-thirties, and she was still renowned for her dignified and graceful bearing. Snorro Sturleson praised her beauty and painted an intriguing picture of a flirtation that sprang up between her and Harold. According to his account, "the earl [William] went generally to bed, but Harald and the earl's wife sat long in the evenings talking together for amusement at the drinking table."[15] Such was the apparent intimacy between them that the duke was seized by jealousy, as Matilda confided to Harold: "The earl has asked me what it is we have to talk about so much, for he is angry at it."[16]

None of the earlier sources repeat this tale, but it does have a ring of truth about it. Matilda had become acquainted with members of Harold's family during her childhood in Bruges—and perhaps even with Harold himself. She was extremely well informed about the politics of that kingdom, and could probably also speak a little of its language—an accomplishment that her husband had not achieved. She therefore had more in common with their English visitor than anyone else at the Norman court, and it is conceivable that they developed an affinity during Harold's stay.

Having thus been royally entertained at the ducal court, Harold then embarked with William for the campaign in Brittany, where they were to wage war against Count Conan II, whose rebellious barons had looked to the duke for assistance. Spying an opportunity to extend his dominions still further, William had been only too happy to oblige. His English captive distinguished himself in the fighting, even though the campaign as a whole failed to dislodge the Breton ruler.

According to the Bayeux Tapestry, it was on their return journey that William finally made his move and invited Harold to swear fealty to him as the rightful heir to the English crown. This is contradicted by Poitiers, who claims that the oath took place soon after Harold's arrival in Normandy, at Bonneville-sur-Touques.[17] Meanwhile, Orderic Vitalis writes that it was at Rouen that Harold recognized the duke as his future sovereign.[18] The fact that the sources are so contradictory casts doubt not just upon where the oath took place, but whether it took place at all. It may have been another example of later Norman propaganda to justify William's conquest of England. The only English source to corroborate it is Eadmer, and his account cannot be given full credence because it was written some thirty years after the event, by which time England was firmly under Norman rule.[19]

If Harold did agree to subjugate his own claim to William's, it was only because he had been backed into a corner. He would have known that the duke, for all his apparent geniality, had no intention of releasing him until he had wrought some advantage from his unexpected visit. Even so, it seems that he resisted as long as possible. According to both

Malmesbury and Jumièges, William was obliged to give him an added incentive by offering him his daughter Adeliza—"who was not yet of age"—in marriage, together with "the whole of her inheritance" and "half the kingdom of England."[20] Snorro Sturleson agrees, noting that the girl was "very young" (she would have been about seven years old) and that "it was resolved that the wedding should be deferred for some years."[21] Meanwhile, William asked Harold to send his sister to Normandy so that he might give her in marriage to one of his nobles.[22]

The evidence suggests that Matilda was responsible for the betrothal between Harold and her eldest daughter, and that this had been the motive behind all those intimate conversations with their English guest. When Harold learned that William was suspicious of his dealings with his wife, he immediately relayed the content of their discussions: "I have to inform you, earl, that there lies more in my visit here than I have let you know. I would ask your daughter in marriage, and have often spoken over this matter with her mother, and she has promised to support my suit with you."[23]

It is possible that the betrothal between Adeliza and Harold is depicted in the Bayeux Tapestry. One of only three women to feature in the work is a lady referred to as "Aelfgyva." She appears just after the scene in which the captive Harold is at William's palace in Rouen, and the two men are in earnest discussion. She is standing in an ornate door frame, perhaps part of the ducal palace. A priest touches her on the cheek, while a naked figure in the lower border mimics the gesture in a suggestive fashion. The action then returns to William and Harold as they depart for their campaign in Brittany. Two recent historians have claimed that the puzzling scene represents Adeliza's betrothal to Harold.[24] According to their theory, the priest is either placing a veil over the girl's head or removing it, both of which actions were involved in formal ceremonies of betrothal. She is referred to as Aelfgyva because she may have adopted this English name upon her marriage to Harold, just as Queen Emma had done when she married Aethelred the Unready in 1002.

This theory does make sense in terms of the tapestry's narrative thread. It also provides a plausible subject for William and Harold's discussion in the previous scene. However, it is by no means certain that the girl would have adopted the name "Aelfgyva" if the marriage had gone ahead. Moreover, if a daughter of William had been included in the tapestry, then she would surely have been referred to by her proper name, the tapestry being a Norman commission. The naked figure that appears beneath the scene also casts doubt upon the theory, because it hints at a sexual scandal involving the girl. Not even the most subversive of artists would have dared to cast such an aspersion upon the daughter of the king. Besides, the lady who features in the tapestry is clearly an adult, whereas Adeliza would have been a child at the time of the betrothal.

A more likely theory is that "Aelfgyva" represents the unnamed sister of Harold, whose hand in marriage William secured the right to bestow as part of the bargain with his rival. Harold had a sister called Aelfgifu, which corresponds closely with the name of the mysterious girl in the tapestry. She would also have been the right age, for she was probably in her late twenties at the time of her brother's visit to Normandy.[25]

Whatever the identity of this female figure, the tapestry does give us other clues as to the narrative of the period. For instance, in one scene it shows Harold between two altars holding sacred relics, which he touches with his hand as William, seated on a throne and holding a sword, looks on approvingly. Such a ceremony suggests that the duke was determined to make the oath as binding as possible. Even so, Jumièges attests that William retained Harold's "handsome brother" Wulfnoth as a hostage against the earl's reneging on his promise.[26]

If this oath really did take place, then it was a masterly tactic on William's part. At a stroke, he had forced one of his chief rivals for the English throne to admit that his own claim was inferior to the duke's, and he made sure that the rest of the world knew about it by arranging a great gathering of notables to witness Harold's oath. If and when the time came to invade, William could appear fully justified.

According to the contemporary sources, as soon as he had sworn fealty to William, Harold was free to return to England. As far as the duke was concerned, he had served his purpose, and the hospitality that he had been shown would no doubt have been swiftly withdrawn if Harold had outstayed his welcome. As it was, Harold was as eager to escape as William was to see him go.

Matilda no doubt triumphed in her husband's success, and she was also very satisfied at the prospect of a highly prestigious marriage for her daughter Adeliza. In fact, the betrothal—like so many others made for political gain—would come to nothing. Within a year of his return from Normandy, Harold allied himself with Edwin and Morcar, sons of Earl Aelfgar of Mercia, and sealed the pact by marrying their sister Edith. He later defended the breaking of his oath by claiming: "I have no right to set any foreign woman upon the throne of England without having first consulted the princes. Indeed I could not do so without committing a great wrong."[27] According to Eadmer, William was so determined to make Harold marry his daughter that he sent a message demanding that even if he disregarded all of the other promises he had made, he should keep this one.[28]

Orderic Vitalis claims that young Adeliza was genuinely aggrieved to lose her Saxon lord, for she spurned all future talk of marriage. That she had fallen deeply in love with him upon her betrothal is a theme continued by a nineteenth-century poet, who has Adeliza (or "Aelgiva") proclaiming:

I'd rather be than France's Queen,
The Saxon chieftain's destined bride;
I'd rather rest upon the breast
Of that stern warrior proved and tried![29]

However, given the disparity in their ages, it is perhaps unlikely that she had formed such a strong attachment to him: Harold was at least forty years Adeliza's senior at the time of their betrothal, and she was probably only about seven years old. When the betrothal came to nothing, she would presumably have continued her normal life alongside her sisters in Matilda's household in Normandy until a new fate was decided for her.

Malmesbury gives a slightly different account, claiming that the girl died before the marriage with Harold could take place, which made him feel justified in relinquishing the oath that he had made to her father.[30] However, he may have been confusing this with the death of Harold's sister, whose hand in marriage William had asked to bestow as part of the bargain. According to Eadmer, when William upbraided Harold for

failing to honor this part of the promise, he received the following pe-
remptory (and rather tasteless) reply: "My sister, whom according to our
pact you ask for, is dead. If the Duke wishes to have her body, such as it
now is, I will send it, that I may not be held to have violated my oath."[31]

Whether or not the breaking off of the betrothal really was the decid-
ing factor in prompting Harold to abandon the pact that he had made
with his great rival, events in England soon superseded it.

7

Conquest

The most famous date in English history, 1066, was a year that began with a death and ended with a coronation. On January 5, Edward the Confessor died. On his deathbed, he bequeathed his throne to Harold, knowing that of all the rival claimants, he had by far the most support among the people. Orderic Vitalis claims that Harold had persuaded Edward to name him successor by telling him of his betrothal to Adeliza, whereby William had "granted him as his son-in-law all his rights in the English kingdom."[1] But this is highly unlikely, given that Harold had already abandoned the betrothal and married another. In fact, Edward had been persuaded by the witan council, an assembly of elite secular and ecclesiastical men whose primary function was advisory, which had met in the autumn of the previous year when it became obvious that the king was dying, in order to consider the relative merits of the various claimants.

Harold's accession was recorded in the *Anglo-Saxon Chronicle*, but clearly not until some time later, because the annalists wrote retrospectively that he "succeeded to the kingdom and held it 40 weeks and one day . . . and he experienced little quietness . . . while he ruled the kingdom."[2] The Saxon had all the qualities needed to make a great ruler. Even though he dismisses him as a dishonorable usurper, Orderic Vitalis admits that Harold was also "a brave and valiant man, very handsome, pleasant in speech, and a good friend to all."[3]

Harold may have been popular in England, but powerful forces across the seas were preparing to attack. Among them was Duke William. Incensed by his rival's flagrant disregard for the oath that he had made while in Normandy, he wasted no time in making preparations for a large-scale invasion. He traveled throughout his duchy holding court with his chief magnates to drum up support, and within a few short months he had amassed a considerable army. As Malmesbury describes: "Duke William . . . spent the whole of that year in warlike preparations, using lavish expenditure to keep his own knights in readiness and to attract those of others."[4] The prospect of sharing in the riches of one of the most prosperous countries in Europe drew supporters from far and wide. "As rumours of the enterprise spread to the neighbouring regions men with a lust for war flocked to the duke and made ready their weapons for the fray . . . panting for the spoils of England they gladly threw themselves into the perils that awaited them by land and sea."[5]

In order to quell any doubts about his right to the crown of England, William wrote to Pope Alexander "to urge the justice of his campaign with all the eloquence at his command."[6] Harold failed to take the same precaution, and as a result, the Pope threw his weight behind the duke's venture. As a symbol of this support, he sent William a square white banner lined with blue and displaying a golden cross; this was to be hoisted above the invasion fleet.

In making his preparations to invade, William had the full support of his ambitious wife, who was eager to add the crown of England to their dominions. It was said that the duke asked her if he and his men "might have the benefit of her prayers and those of her ladies."[7] Matilda no doubt acceded to this request, and did a great deal more besides. La Trinité, the abbey that she had commissioned in Caen to make recompense for her marriage to William, was probably still not completed at this time, but she decided that this would be the perfect moment to dedicate it. An elaborate ceremony was planned, to which all the high-ranking members of Norman society were invited. The date assigned for it was June 18, 1066, at the height of William's propaganda campaign for his planned conquest of England. It was an important occasion for Matilda and her husband. A contemporary charter shows that as well as nobles from across the principality, all the most senior churchmen were in attendance, including Archbishop Maurilius of Rouen and four of his six subordinate bishops, eight abbots, and the heads of almost every monastery that had Duke William as its patron.

All of this may seem like a rather cynical attempt by Matilda to lend her husband's campaign religious legitimacy, but the occasion did involve a genuine sacrifice on her part. On the day of the ceremony, she and William offered up their daughter Cecilia as a novice at the abbey.[8] Giving one's child to a religious house was considered the greatest gift that one could bestow upon God. It echoed biblical tales of people offering their children, animals, or precious possessions as a sacrifice. That William and Matilda should choose to do so at such a time was profoundly significant. They were effectively striking a bargain with God: they had given Him their daughter, now He should give them England.

During the ceremony, William led the girl to the altar and, taking her up into his arms, vowed before the assembly that she would be dedicated to God, by whose grace he and Matilda had been blessed with so many offspring and other gifts. As a compliment to the ducal couple, many of the noblemen present offered their daughters, sisters, and even mothers to the abbey, along with generous bequests of land.[9]

Although the religious life was a common destiny for those daughters from aristocratic families who were not used to forge advantageous marriages, Cecilia was extraordinarily young to become a novice. She would probably have been little more than seven years old.[10] As the daughter of the duke and duchess, she would have enjoyed a less straitened existence than many of her fellow residents at La Trinité. Women of high birth who entered the monastic life were permitted their own household and chaplain. Far from being recluses who lived out their days in an obscure corner of the world in sorrow and contemplation, they gained the freedom and authority that were denied them by the male-dominated secular life.

Nevertheless, to relinquish her daughter in this way was still a sacrifice for Matilda. The meticulous attention that she had given to her daughters' education and upbringing suggests a caring and tender mother, so it cannot have been without pain that she bade farewell to the young girl. The sources do not reveal whether they had any contact after that time, but the rules of the abbey did allow Cecilia to receive visitors in her private apartments. Given how active Matilda was as a patron of La Trinité, it is likely that she saw her daughter regularly.

Cecilia's entry into La Trinité was significant enough to warrant a mention by Orderic Vitalis, who noted: "her [Matilda's] daughter, the virgin Cecilia, was consecrated to God and remained in his service for a long time."[11] He added that Cecilia was "brought up and carefully educated" by her mother's namesake, the "vigorous" abbess Matilda, who was renowned for strict discipline.[12] Jumièges also refers to Cecilia as "a virgin dedicated to God in the monastery of Sainte-Trinité in the town of Caen."[13]

As well as being intended as a sacrifice to God, Cecilia's fate may also have had a more practical benefit from Matilda's perspective. It is possible that she intended the girl to rule the abbey in future and thus secure the continuation of her family's influence there. If this was her purpose, then later events would prove that she had remarkable foresight.

Matilda did not allow herself long to mourn the loss of her daughter to the religious life. The prospect of becoming queen of England was evidently an appealing one, for she threw herself into William's invasion effort with even more directness. Her contribution was both spectacular and unique: she commissioned a magnificent new ship in which her husband might cross the Channel and lay siege to his prospective kingdom. Considering its scale, the vessel was constructed with remarkable speed, and the result was formidable. Clearly, it was built for show as much as for service. The Bayeux Tapestry depicts it as a vast ship (*magno navigo*), larger than the rest of the fleet and carrying more men.[14] It is highly decorated and modeled on the Viking style, with billowing four-cornered sails painted in stripes of red (or brown) and yellow.[15]

Matilda had planned every detail with meticulous care, and each of the embellishments was loaded with symbolism. A contemporary document known as the Ship List of William the Conqueror tells how the duchess ordered her craftsmen to make a figurehead of a golden child with his right forefinger pointing toward England and his left hand pressing an ivory horn against his lips. Although Wace believed that this represented one of William and Matilda's sons, it may have symbolized a future son rather than a present one. There is evidence to suggest that the duchess had become pregnant shortly before her husband embarked upon his invasion of England. If this was the case, then the figurehead would have been intended as a secret gesture, the true significance of which was understood only by the ducal couple themselves—or even, perhaps, by Matilda alone.[16]

It was exceptionally rare for a figurehead to be in the form of a child; they usually depicted animals or fantastical creatures such as dragons or monsters. The fact that the one commissioned by Matilda was crafted out of gold may also have been significant, for William of Poitiers described England as a land of silver and gold. Matilda's message could therefore have been that the child she was carrying symbolized the birth of a new Norman dynasty in England.[17]

This patriotic symbolism continued throughout the rest of the ship. The prow was ornamented with a lion's head, a sign of bravery and strength. In order to demonstrate that God was on her husband's side, Matilda also employed the consecrated banner that had been sent to William from Rome, hoisting it at the masthead.

The end result inspired awe in all who saw it. The ship was named the *Mora,* the literal translation of which was "mansion" or "habitation." Certain romantic historians claim that it was a knowing anagram of *amor.* Perhaps more likely is that it was a subtle allusion to Matilda's distinguished past—the Flemish counts from whom she was descended were known as the Morini. Such a gesture would have been typical of the duchess's pride in her pedigree.[18]

In commissioning such a highly decorated and sumptuous vessel for her husband to sail in, Matilda appeared to be showing him great veneration and respect. Wace observed that she had built the ship "in honour of the said Duke."[19] To achieve maximum impact, she had kept the whole project a secret from William, and it was only as he was assembling his fleet at the mouth of the River Dives in Normandy during the summer of 1066 that she unveiled the *Mora* to him. He was so delighted with the magnificent vessel that he immediately made it his flagship. His admiration for his wife was greater than ever before. To show his gratitude, he confidently promised her the county of Kent when he became king of England. This would make Matilda a rich woman, for the county was one of the most prosperous in England, and its revenues would keep her in an extremely comfortable style even if she received no other income.

According to Wace, Matilda's family contributed rather less toward William's enterprise than she did herself. He claims that the duke wrote to his father-in-law asking for his assistance. But the shrewd count refused to commit either men or money until William had told him "how much of England he would have and what part of it he would get." William promised to discuss this with his nobles, and a short while later he sent Baldwin a letter, sealed with wax. Upon opening it, the count was bemused to find that the parchment was blank, and asked the messenger what it meant. The latter replied: "You will have nothing and should expect nothing . . . He will conquer it [England] and not have any help from you."[20] Entertaining though it is, this tale is not repeated in any other source, and given that it was written more than a century after the event, its authenticity is dubious.

Nevertheless, Baldwin did indeed prove reluctant to help his son-in-law, and it was only after William had promised him an annual sum of 300 marks of silver if he became king of England that the count agreed to provide troops for the invasion. Admittedly, Baldwin was in an awkward position, for although William was his son-in-law, he was also related by marriage to another contender for the throne—Harold Godwinson's brother Tostig, who was married to his half-sister Judith. Baldwin also had to take account of the interests of his overlord, the French king. In the end, he chose to hedge his bets. As well as providing limited support to Duke William, he also supplied Tostig with ships and men to attack England.

Meanwhile, in the kingdom upon which the duke had set his sights, there was a growing sense of unease at the gathering storm. The chroniclers tell of a portentous event that occurred in April 1066, just three months after Harold's accession: "Throughout all England, a sign such as men never saw before was seen in the heavens. Some men declared that it was the star comet, which some men called the 'haired' star."[21] The phenomenon was also seen in Normandy, and Jumièges marveled: "its three-forked tail stretched far into the southern sky remaining visible for fifteen days."[22] To a God-fearing people who were ever watchful for heavenly portents, this was a sign of unprecedented significance. Great change—good or bad—must be afoot. With the wisdom of hindsight, Orderic Vitalis was more specific about what this change might be: "this portended the transfer of a kingdom."[23]

By July of that year, Duke William's preparations for the invasion were complete. He had amassed a formidable force of men. Historians disagree about its size, but William of Poitiers' claims of fifty thousand men are almost certainly an exaggeration, especially in the light of what we know of other cross-Channel invasion forces.[24] In fact William's army may have numbered as few as seven thousand. Even so, Orderic Vitalis describes how the duke "gathered an immense army of Normans, Flemish, French and Bretons" and claims that his fleet comprised as many as three thousand ships, although the actual figure was probably between seven hundred and a thousand.[25] When these were all ready to sail, "he loaded the vessels with vigorous horses and very strong men armed with hauberks and helmets."[26] Although contemporary chroniclers exaggerated the size of William's force, it would undoubtedly have presented a formidable sight. The sense of expectation, among both the troops and their leader, must have been high.

✦ ✦ ✦

Although William had achieved remarkable success in stabilizing the duchy during the previous three decades, he knew better than to trust the protestations of loyalty by his powerful noble subjects, who were no doubt already scheming to seize control as soon as he had set sail for England. He therefore had to ensure that his domain was left in the hands of someone whom he could trust absolutely to govern in his name and prove immune to corruption or rebellion. It is a testament to how much he esteemed and valued his wife that he decided that she was the only person capable of fulfilling this role.

William and Matilda's eldest son, Robert, might have expected to rule in his father's absence. At fourteen years of age, he would have already been considered a man, and he had been nominated William's heir some three years earlier. He had on one occasion been allowed to confirm a charter on his father's behalf, which he no doubt took as a sign of trust. Moreover, the fact that he had been trained in military and political affairs from his infancy meant that he had the capability—and no doubt

A nineteenth-century sketch of Matilda, which hints at her diminutive size.

An engraving of a fresco showing William and Matilda that used to adorn the walls of a chapel at St.-Étienne in Caen. The fresco, now lost, is the only known contemporary likeness of Matilda.

A nineteenth-century version of the engraving that formed the frontispiece to Agnes Strickland's Queens of England series. Here, Matilda bears a striking resemblance to Queen Victoria, which was no doubt intended to flatter the reigning monarch.

Matilda's abbey of La Trinité (Abbaye aux Dames), Caen. The abbey was dedicated in 1066, prior to William's invasion of England. Matilda was later buried there, and her tomb can still be seen today.

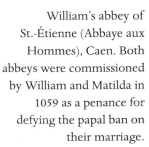

William's abbey of St.-Étienne (Abbaye aux Hommes), Caen. Both abbeys were commissioned by William and Matilda in 1059 as a penance for defying the papal ban on their marriage.

The castle at Falaise, the town of William's birth. Legend has it that it was from here that William's father, Duke Robert, spied Herleva washing clothes in a stream.

The remains of Bonneville-sur-Touques castle, said to be one of William and Matilda's favorite residences in Normandy.

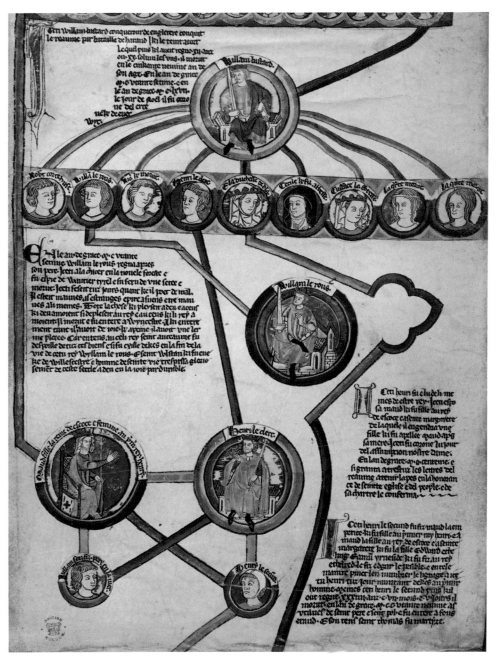

A thirteenth-century illustration showing the descendants of William and Matilda. At the top is William, and directly beneath him are the children that Matilda bore him: (left to right) Robert "Curthose," William Rufus, Richard, Henry, Adela, Cecilia, Constance, and two unnamed daughters (probably Adeliza and Matilda).

Harold Godwinson swears an oath recognizing William's claim to the English throne.

The Mora, the magnificent flagship commissioned by Matilda for her husband's invasion of England.

An imaginary portrait showing Matilda and her ladies working on the Bayeux Tapestry. The widespread belief that Matilda was responsible for the tapestry has been convincingly disproved in recent years.

A romantic depiction of Matilda watching her husband set sail for England in 1066.

The White Tower, built by William to subdue the "evil inhabitants" of London.

A modern illustration showing William and Matilda granting a charter to the city of London.

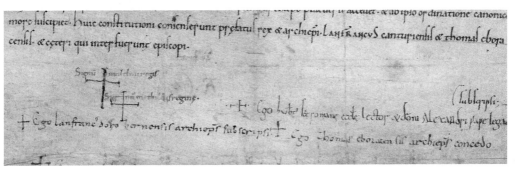

A charter bearing Matilda's signum, a distinctive Jerusalem-style cross.

Statue of Matilda, Jardin du
Luxembourg, Paris.

Matilda's tomb in the choir of La Trinité, Caen.

the desire—to rise to the challenge. After all, his father had been six years younger than he when he had assumed control of the duchy. The *Anglo-Saxon Chronicle* notes: "the best who were in the land had sworn with oaths and taken him [William] as lord."[27] But Robert was given only nominal responsibility; Matilda was to act as regent on his behalf, and it was clear that she, not the boy, would hold all the authority.

That William should bypass his eldest son in this way was no great surprise, given the disdain that he had always felt toward him. In his opinion, Robert was a feckless, pampered young man, overly indulged by his mother and with no real credibility among the aristocracy of Normandy. It would be the first of many occasions on which the duke disregarded his son's wishes, and relations between them rapidly began to sour. However, Robert's being passed over did not mark the beginning of an estrangement between Matilda and her eldest son: far from it. As the acknowledged heir to the duchy, Robert's safety was paramount, and he was therefore kept at his mother's side throughout her regency. Later events suggest that this period strengthened the bond between them, allowing Matilda to indulge the affection that she had always felt toward her firstborn.

The significance of Matilda's new role cannot be overstated. Although women were beginning to play a powerful role in the emerging dominance of the Christian church, they were still largely sidelined in political affairs. The teachings of St. Paul were held fast by most European rulers: wives should be meek, passive, and silent. Thus, no female consort before Matilda had exercised such power. Even the formidable Queen Emma, who had confidently expected that her husband, King Cnut, would name her regent in the event of his death, had seen her ambitions dashed in 1035 when his illegitimate son, Harold Harefoot, had been appointed instead.

Still, Matilda was not the first woman in western Europe to have the honor of the regency bestowed on her. In France, King Henry's widow, Anne of Kiev, was appointed coregent for their young son Philip in 1060, along with Matilda's father, Baldwin.[28] The first consort to be explicitly charged with the powers of regency was Matilda's contemporary, Agnes of Poitou, who took charge of the Holy Roman Empire on behalf of her young son, Henry IV, after her husband's death in 1056. More common was for a royal wife to be spoken of as "nourishing the young king" or "keeping the kingdom."[29] However, Agnes was not a role model to which others might wish to aspire. Her chief adviser, Henry II, Bishop of Augsburg, was despised for his arrogance and for the level of influence he enjoyed over Agnes, which led to rumors of an illicit affair. She was eventually ousted when a group of hostile noblemen abducted her son, thus depriving her of authority.

However, both Anne of Kiev and Agnes of Poitou were able to exercise sole power only after the death of their husbands. A more direct comparison with Matilda is Gunnor, the long-term mistress and later wife of William's great-grandfather, Duke Richard I. She wielded considerable authority during Richard's lifetime and remained influential long after his death, when their son Richard II was in power. Gunnor's skill in the political arena has led one recent commentator to highlight the similarities between her and Matilda, describing her as "one of those women who could make her influence felt in a predominantly masculine world."[30]

There are also examples of women who defied their conventional role in society to the extent of taking part in military campaigns. They include another of Matilda's contemporaries, Matilda of Tuscany, daughter of the powerful Italian prince Boniface III. The death of her brother in 1055 left her as sole heiress to the family's vast estates at the age of just eight. From that time onward, she was trained in military as well as diplomatic affairs, and it was said that she rode into battle on behalf of the papacy when she was in her teens. Malmesbury describes her as "a woman who, forgetful of her sex, and compared to the ancient Amazons, used to lead forth her hardy troops to battle."[31]

As regent during William's absence, Matilda would now have the power to make laws throughout the duchy, dispense justice, levy taxes, and mint money. She also had a military force at her disposal, should she choose to use it. That the duke, a staunch traditionalist, should elevate his wife to such a position ahead of the potential male candidates—who, as well as Robert, included William's half-brother Odo, and his right-hand man William fitzOsbern—would have sent shock waves throughout the duchy. Moreover, the planned invasion of England must have seemed an enormously risky enterprise, and it was very possible that William, like his father more than thirty years before, would never return. Whatever his fate, though, he seemed confident that the duchy would stay safe under Matilda's guidance. Indeed, as he stated to King Philip of France, who—perhaps disingenuously—expressed concern over his rival's departure and the future of the duchy: "That is a care that shall not need to trouble our neighbours; by the grace of God we are blessed with a prudent wife and loving subjects, who will keep our border securely during our absence."[32]

To ensure that Matilda's appointment would be honored by his subjects, William summoned a great council at the ducal castle in Bonneville-sur-Touques and forced his chief magnates to swear an oath of fidelity to his son as heir and to his wife as regent.[33] Three of his most trusted counsellors—Roger de Beaumont, Roger de Montgomery, and Hugh d'Avranches—were appointed as advisers to Matilda.[34] Of these, Montgomery was William's closest companion. Described as "a wise and prudent man," he was renowned for his learning. These qualities would have endeared him to Matilda, and she was no doubt glad to have such a man among her advisers.[35] Like her, he was also an active religious patron, and made several generous grants to monastic houses. He was married to the formidable Mabel of Bellême, and they showed their loyalty toward Matilda by naming one of their daughters after her.[36] Among the advisers, Roger de Beaumont was described as being "first in dignity," and his "mature age" lent him wisdom and experience that would be useful to the duchess.[37] Whether the duke genuinely believed that his wife would need the guidance of Beaumont and his fellow counsellors, or whether this was a sop to their wounded pride, cannot be known for certain. Either way, everyone present knew that in practice Matilda would have the power to disregard their advice if she chose and to act according to her own volition.

The challenge that Matilda faced as regent of Normandy was considerable. As her husband once observed: "The Normans are a turbulent people, always ready to cause disturbances."[38] Even though William had achieved much in establishing his authority as duke, the Norman aristocracy was still dominant in both secular and ecclesiastical affairs, and power had become concentrated in the hands of a few great families.

The fact that William had strategically appointed representatives of some of these families to assist his wife in her regency was no guarantee of their loyalty.

Not only was Matilda confronted by potential threats from within the duchy, but the French king always had an eye to exploit any sign of weakness on the part of his rival. The same was true of Geoffrey III, the count of Anjou, whose territory bordered Normandy to the southwest. Both had been temporarily subdued by William's campaigns prior to 1066, but his preeminence was unlikely to last for long. His wife was therefore a good deal more than just a caretaker; she must seize the initiative and rule as fully and effectively as her husband would have done.

✤   ✤   ✤

While William waited for favorable winds to convey him and his fleet to England, his opponent was amassing substantial forces to defend his throne. The *Anglo-Saxon Chronicle* records: "King Harold . . . gathered a greater raiding ship-army and also raiding land-army than any king here in the land had ever done before, because he was informed that William the Bastard wanted to come here and win this land."[39] But it was at this moment that his attention was diverted by a serious threat in the north of his kingdom, led partly by his own brother. Tostig had been made earl of Northumbria in 1055, but he was unpopular with the people of that region, and after suffering a decade of his ascendancy, they finally rebelled against him. He sought refuge in Flanders, the native land of his wife, Judith (Matilda's aunt), and became deeply embittered against his brother, Harold, for failing to support him. Orderic Vitalis claims that Tostig gave his wife into the care of her half-brother, Baldwin, the count of Flanders, while he went to Normandy to seek William's support.[40] Having "boldly rebuked" the duke for allowing Harold to rule in England, Tostig swore that he would secure the crown for him if William agreed to invade England with a Norman army.[41]

At the head of a fleet of some sixty ships, Tostig proceeded to launch a series of "piratical" raids along the English coast, only to be driven off by Edwin of Mercia, and Morcar, his replacement as earl of Northumbria. After taking temporary refuge in Scotland, Tostig then joined forces with Harald Hardrada of Norway, who had declared himself the rightful heir to King Cnut and assembled a fleet of three hundred ships with which to press his claim.[42] In late summer 1066, he and Tostig invaded northern England. On September 20, in the first of the three great battles of 1066, they defeated Edwin and Morcar at Fulford and captured York, the most important city in the north.

Hardrada's invasion was bad news for Harold, for, as the *Anglo-Saxon Chronicle* relates, a shortage of supplies had forced him to stand down both his army and his fleet. Undeterred, he regrouped his forces and marched north, and on September 25 he surprised Hardrada and Tostig's forces at Stamford Bridge, a few miles northeast of York. The ensuing conflict was ferocious and bloody. Malmesbury described it as "an immense battle . . . in which both nations did their utmost."[43] But with the benefit of surprise, Harold was able to gain the upper hand, and both his brother and Hardrada were killed. The king did not have long to enjoy his victory, for word reached him, probably on October 1, that William had landed at Pevensey a few days earlier. He therefore turned his troops around, headed south, and, in a remarkable forced march, reached London in just five days. He then spent about six days there gathering troops (and presumably resting) before setting off on October 11 to confront William.

✢ ✢ ✢

At St.-Valéry, where Duke William had moved his fleet because it was closer to England, he and his troops had to wait for a favorable wind to carry them to England. As the days dragged on, his men had begun to lose faith in the enterprise, and "grumbled in their tents" that their leader was "mad . . . to take over land rightfully belonging to others; God is against us, for He denies us a wind."[44] Hearing of this, William ordered that the remains of a local saint be brought among them in order to invigorate their prayers for a "favouring breeze." According to Malmesbury, this worked an immediate effect, and on September 27, the ships' sails were bolstered by the wind.[45] Not wanting to waste a moment, the duke ordered his fleet to embark immediately, even though darkness was fast drawing in. A horn was blown from the *Mora* and a lantern was lit at her masthead to give the signal. "The fleet thus ready, with a following wind and sails billowing aloft he crossed the sea."[46]

William and his army sailed through the night, and the speed of his flagship was such that at dawn, he and his crew found themselves alone in the middle of the Channel. According to Poitiers, the duke, undaunted, calmly called for breakfast, which he washed down with wine "as if in his chamber at home."[47] This episode may have been employed by William's apologist for dramatic effect, but the *Mora* did outstrip the other ships of the fleet, which is perhaps not surprising given its marked superiority. Having waited for his fleet to reconvene, he landed in Pevensey Bay in what is today East Sussex. Pevensey was an ideal landing place; the bay itself offered shelter for William's fleet, while the extensive walls of the old Roman fort of Anderida (now part of Pevensey Castle) offered a useful base from which to marshal his forces. Having overcome the bad omen symbolized by the lack of favorable winds, however, William faced another as soon as he reached England's shores. Eager to disembark from his ship, he stumbled upon the ground. While his troops looked on aghast at an incident that seemed to presage grave ill fortune, a quick-thinking knight turned the situation to William's advantage by crying: "You have England in your hand, duke, and you shall be king!"[48]

By the following day William had established himself at Hastings, where, according to the chronicler Wace, eager though he was for battle, he did not forget to pay homage to the divine presence that he claimed was at his side. Turning to his nobles, he declared: "Here I vow, that if it shall please God to give me the victory, that, on whatever spot it shall befall, I will there build a church to be consecrated to the blessed Trinity, and to St. Martin, where perpetual prayers shall be offered for the sins of Edward the Confessor, for my own sins, the sins of Matilda my spouse, and the sins of such as have attended me in this expedition, but more particularly for the sins of such as may fall in the battle."[49]

What followed has become one of the most familiar stories in English history. By October 13, Harold and his army had arrived at Senlac, close to the present-day town of Battle in East Sussex, and some ten miles from where William had first landed at Pevensey. The duke's forces were quartered about five miles away, around Hastings. It was in William's interest to bring Harold to battle as quickly as possible, for he realized that the longer he waited, the more time Harold would have to raise troops. He therefore goaded Harold by ravaging what was part of the

Saxon's old earldom. Although it might have been to Harold's advantage to delay fighting, it seems that the English king was equally keen to confront William.

Hardrada had been surprised by Harold at Stamford Bridge, but William was not to suffer the same fate: his scouts had spotted Harold's arrival. His men stood at arms all night, and on the morning of October 14 they moved up from Hastings. In fact, it was Harold who was caught by surprise, and abandoning his plans for an attack, he took up a defensive position on Senlac Ridge and awaited the Norman onslaught.

The two armies that faced each other were very different. Although many of Harold's men seem to have traveled on horseback, the English traditionally fought on foot, and they did so at Hastings. Harold's soldiers formed up in tightly packed ranks behind a wall of shields, the dragon banner of Wessex and the king's personal standard of a fighting man fluttering above them. The bulk of Harold's army was probably made up of the *fyrd,* the local militia of the time, armed with spears, swords, javelins, and throwing axes. The Saxon nobles present at the battle would have brought their household troops, or "housecarls," with them; some of these well-armed warriors carried the deadly Danish two-handed axes shown being used to such devastating effect in the Bayeux Tapestry.

William's army was more varied: it deployed with archers and crossbowmen to the front, armored infantry behind them and mounted knights in mail with lances and kite-shaped shields bringing up the rear. This diversity was to work in favor of the Normans, for while all the English could do was to stand there and take whatever their enemies threw at them, William had a range of tactical options. He could use his archers to unleash a barrage of arrows on the static English lines, then attack with his infantry while his knights probed for a weakness in the English shield wall. As a result, although the English had the advantage of occupying a strong defensive position on the top of a hill, and drove back attack after attack, they were gradually eroded by the relentless Norman pressure.

Even so, the contest was very finely balanced. Each side fought with extraordinary tenacity, and the battle lasted for most of the day, resulting in "great slaughter on either side."[50] According to William of Poitiers, who was admittedly writing to extol William's virtues, the Norman leader played a crucial role throughout—not just directing his troops from a distance, but leading by example and fighting with great ferocity in the thick of the action. When a rumor that he had been killed spread panic in his army, he was said to have taken his helmet off and ridden among his men crying: "Look at me. I am alive, and with God's help I will conquer."[51] Malmesbury records how the duke "encouraged his men by his shouts and by his presence, leading the charge in person and plunging into the thick of the enemy; so that while he carried rage and fury everywhere, three splendid horses were cut down under him."[52]

William's cunning matched his courage. When the battle seemed to be going against him, he gave the order to retreat. In fact, this was a clever ploy to break up the Saxon ranks, some of whom charged in pursuit of what they thought was a beaten and retreating enemy. Without warning, the Normans turned on them and a bloodbath ensued.[53] Although they had been "undone by a trick," the English fought on: "repeatedly they made a stand, and piled the bodies of their pursuers in great heaps of slaughter."[54] The decisive moment came late in the day, when the English king was slain. Legend has it he was killed by an arrow in the eye, but other sources suggest he was cut down by a group of knights, possibly after having been wounded by the arrow.[55]

Realizing that the battle was lost, scores of Harold's beleaguered men turned on their heels and tried to escape, running into the woods so that their enemy might lose sight of them. Some turned and faced their pursuers at a ravine that is sometimes called the Malfosse, or "evil ditch." But it was to no avail. "The Normans, though strangers to the district, pursued them relentlessly, slashing their guilty backs and putting the last touches to the victory."[56] Their leader, William, Duke of Normandy, would henceforth be known as William the Conqueror.

8

"A Fatal Disaster"

Hastings, as decisive as it was, marked the start, not the end, of William's campaign to conquer England. It would be nearly five years before he was finally able to establish full control over the country. Even so, it was at this battle that the English lost not only their most effective leader, but also their best chance of turning back the Norman invader.

This was something that Englishmen of the time were all too well aware of, and the half-English William of Malmesbury later described the "day of destiny" as "a fatal disaster for our dear country as she exchanged old masters for new."[1] The chroniclers estimate that as many as fifteen thousand men perished in the battle. While this figure was again almost certainly an exaggeration, it had clearly been one of the bloodiest and hardest-fought conflicts that England had ever seen.[2] "The fields were covered with corpses, and all around the only colour to meet the gaze was blood-red. It looked from afar as if rivulets of blood, flowing down from all sides, had filled the valleys, just like a river."[3] The battle had wiped out much of the English ruling elite: "The mangled bodies that had been the flower of the English nobility and youth covered the ground as far as the eye could see."[4] As well as Harold, his brothers Leofwine and Gyrth had been killed, and "many good men."[5] The victorious duke of Normandy ordered the burial of all his fallen men, but he left the English dead unburied, "to be eaten by worms and wolves, by birds and dogs."[6] He defended this apparently callous action on the grounds that they had supported a tyrant and did not therefore deserve a Christian burial. Neither did he accede to a request by Harold's grieving mother that she might be given her son's body so that she could arrange a fitting burial. According to Orderic, even when she offered him "Harold's weight in gold for his body," William angrily refused.[7]

A rash of Norman accounts appeared soon after the battle, praising William as a magnificent warrior and justifying the cruelty of his actions. The size of the English army grew with each telling, so that the feat of the Normans appeared all the more remarkable. Tales of cowardice and disorganization among Harold's men were contrasted with Norman bravery and tactical brilliance. Writing almost sixty years later, Malmesbury decried the bias with which the story of the battle had been told: "Those men seem to me wrong who exaggerate the number of the English and diminish their courage, thus bringing discredit on the Normans whom they mean to praise. A mighty commendation indeed! That a most warlike nation should conquer a set of people who were disorganised because of their numbers, and fearful through cowardice! On the contrary, they were few in number and brave in the extreme, who disregarded the love of their own bodies and laid down their lives for their country."[8]

The reports that were sent back to Normandy in the immediate aftermath of the battle were no less biased than those of which Malmesbury complained. Among the first to hear the news was Matilda. She was in the Benedictine priory of Nôtre Dame du Pré, a small chapel that she had founded in 1060 on the banks of the river Seine near Rouen, praying for William's safety, when a messenger arrived with the news. Upon hearing it, she joyfully proclaimed that the priory should henceforth be known as Nôtre Dame de Bonnes Nouvelles (Our Lady of Good News).[9] She had good reason to rejoice, for she was now queen of England—an honor that she could not possibly have hoped for when she had agreed to become the wife of "William the Bastard" some fifteen years earlier.

Determined to celebrate her husband's success and revel in her exalted new status, Matilda embarked upon a series of well-planned public gestures. She made a number of high-profile—and extremely generous—religious bequests, giving thanks to God for her husband's victory. Orderic Vitalis wrote admiringly: "The alms which this princess daily distributed with such zeal brought more succour than I can express to her husband, struggling on the field of battle."[10] It might have been at Matilda's command that in 1068 her chaplain,[11] Guy, bishop of Amiens, composed an epic poem—*Carmen de Hastingae Praelio*—"praising and exalting William" and "abusing and condemning Harold."[12] The theme that ran throughout this piece of blatant Norman propaganda was that the duke had only taken what was rightfully his. The prologue declares: "For manfully he recovered a kingdom of which he had been deprived, and by his victory extended the boundaries of his ancestral lands across the sea—a deed worthy to be remembered forever."[13] Throughout the poem, William is hailed as a triumphant leader, comparable to Caesar, whose nobility and virtue excelled those of all his contemporaries.[14] It is a straightforward tale of hero versus villain, usurper versus rightful king.

According to popular legend, Matilda's most powerful and iconic commemoration of the Battle of Hastings was the Bayeux Tapestry, which told the story of the battle from a Norman perspective and reinforced the justice of William's claim to the English throne. For many years, it was assumed that it was the work of the duchess and her ladies, an idea recorded by the Benedictine historian Bernard de Montfaucon, who discovered the Bayeux Tapestry in the late 1720s. He subsequently published a reproduction of it in his *Monuments de la monarchie française*, in which he reported: "The common opinion in Bayeux is that Queen Matilda, wife of William the Conqueror, had the tapestry made. This opinion passes for a tradition in the region. It seems highly probable."[15] His theory was soon widely accepted, and gained greater currency when it was reiterated—and embellished—by the prolific nineteenth-century historian Agnes Strickland in her Queens of England series.[16] It has since proved remarkably enduring, to the extent that most French people today know the work not as "La Tapisserie de Bayeux" but "La Tapisserie de la Reine Mathilde." Indeed, a modern-day visitor to Bayeux will encounter numerous references to Matilda as being the orchestrator of the work—from the Hotel Reine Mathilde to a plaque outside the museum that houses the tapestry bearing her name.

That Matilda was responsible for the Bayeux Tapestry is in many respects a natural assumption to make. It was customary for queens and noble ladies to embroider hangings for churches or monasteries depicting the glorious successes of their families. Bertha, wife of Matilda's grandfather, Robert the Pious of France, commissioned just such a hanging for the abbey of St.-Denis. Meanwhile, Duchess Gunnor, wife of Duke Richard I of Normandy, presented an exquisite embroidery in silk and linen to the church of Nôtre-Dame in Rouen.

It would therefore have been entirely commensurate with Matilda's role as a dutiful wife to the Conqueror, eager to promote his successes, that she should have commissioned the Bayeux Tapestry. The image of the new queen of England and her ladies assiduously working on the tapestry during their idle hours while their husbands completed the obliteration of the Saxon kingdom fits neatly with the conventional view of women's role in society. Moreover, Matilda certainly was an accomplished seamstress, having been taught the art of embroidery as a young woman in her parents' household, and she bequeathed some fine needlework in her will.

Beguiling though the image conjured up by Montfaucon and Strickland is, however, it is fundamentally flawed. There is no doubt that Matilda had been a dutiful wife up until this point, and she was shrewd enough to realize the importance of justifying William's tenuous claim to the English throne. But in the aftermath of his victory, she was fully preoccupied with the regency of Normandy, so the notion that she was able to idle away countless hours sewing with her ladies is questionable in the extreme. At best, she might have commissioned the tapestry and set her female attendants to work on it, providing only occasional supervision.

However, as early as the nineteenth century, historians were questioning whether Matilda was involved in the making of the Bayeux Tapestry at all. One of them claimed that the tapestry was produced after her death, attributing it instead to her granddaughter and namesake, the empress Matilda.[17] Other historians of the period began to voice doubts that any royal woman could have been responsible. Their reasoning says much about the age in which they were writing. The tapestry contains some overtly sexual images in its borders, and it was felt that neither queen could possibly have been involved in such a shockingly crude piece of work.

More important in understanding the provenance of the tapestry are recent painstaking investigations providing compelling evidence that it was in fact made not in Normandy, but in the conquered land, England. The style of decoration mirrors that found in English manuscripts, and some of the Latin names are spelled the English rather than the Norman way. Moreover, Anglo-Saxon women were renowned for their skill at embroidery, and many of them were employed in this profession. William of Poitiers, who was hostile toward the English, admitted that "the women are very skilled at needlework and weaving gold thread."[18] The late King Harold's sister, Edith, was among them, and it is possible that if any royal lady had a hand in the work, it was she rather than Matilda.

The case for the tapestry's having been made in England rather than Normandy is also supported by a fresh interpretation of the story it tells. One recent historian has argued convincingly that it was not the great statement of Norman triumphalism that it appears, but a subversive work loaded with hidden meaning. For example, the images depicted in the tapestry imply that Edward the Confessor did not support William's claim to the English throne, as the Norman chroniclers would have us believe. Furthermore, the scenes in which the Battle of Hastings is played out suggest that it was the French, not the Norman troops, who assumed the starring role. These troops were under the command of Count Eustace II of Boulogne (which was then part of Flanders), who although nominally on William's side in the battle was otherwise one of the duke's most troublesome northern French rivals. In fact, Eustace is one of only three Normans who are singled out in the tapestry as being present at Hastings (the others being Bishop Odo and William himself), which again suggests that this was hardly a work celebrating that duchy's triumph.[19]

That the artist was a supporter of Eustace adds weight to the notion that the Bayeux Tapestry was a subversive work, and it may also be possible that Eustace himself had commissioned it.[20] But the more commonly accepted view is that its patron was Matilda's brother-in-law, Bishop Odo. In 1824, a French antiquarian, Honoré François Delauney, one of those nineteenth-century historians who did not believe that Matilda was responsible for the tapestry, put forward the theory that it could have been given to Bayeux Cathedral by an immoral cleric.[21]

Bishop Odo perfectly fitted the bill. His lax morality was notorious, and he made little secret of the fact that he had a mistress and a son. The fact that Odo was bishop of the cathedral in which the tapestry was discovered might seem to strengthen the case for his being its originator, but it was his connections in Kent that have proved more significant. Soon after the Battle of Hastings, William made him earl of that region. Canterbury was its principal town, a thriving artistic center. Any patron intending to commission an embroidery on such a grand scale would naturally have turned to the artisans of this city.

It is with this in mind that most historians are now agreed that the tapestry was made in Canterbury at Odo's orders with a view to decorating the magnificent new cathedral that he was building at Bayeux. He may have unveiled it at the elaborate consecration ceremony in 1077, which Matilda herself attended. The idea that Matilda was in any way connected to it has thus been cast into grave doubt. She could claim the credit for a number of similarly high-impact gestures to mark her husband's victory in England, but it is unlikely that the Bayeux Tapestry was one of them.

✢ ✢ ✢

When William triumphed at Hastings, Matilda had only been regent of Normandy for a little over two weeks, but there was no prospect of her tenure's coming to an end in the near future—her husband still had much to do in his newly conquered land. He might have won the English crown, but his campaign to subdue the rest of this hostile, rebellious country was only just beginning. His apologist's bold claim that he "subjugated all the cities of the English in a single day" was wildly exaggerated.[22]

William's first task was to take the city of London, which was so far from accepting the Norman duke as its ruler that it had elected Edgar the Aetheling, great-nephew of Edward the Confessor, as king instead. William rapidly reassembled his forces and advanced toward the city. They brought terror wherever they went, for William's tactic was to force his recalcitrant new subjects into submission with brutality and bloodshed. Entire villages and towns were razed to the ground, and their citizens raped or murdered. The major strategic strongholds of Dover and Southwark were laid waste by the Norman troops as they advanced toward London—"a most spacious city, full of evil inhabitants, and richer than anywhere else in the kingdom."[23] Meanwhile, the duke ordered a detachment of his army to Winchester in order to secure its surrender and that of Queen Edith, Edward the Confessor's widow and Harold's sister, who had become a figurehead for the beleaguered English. Within a few short weeks, both cities had capitulated. Then, in early December, William marched to Berkhamsted, some thirty miles northwest of London, where Edgar the Aetheling had taken refuge. Upon the Conqueror's arrival, Edgar immediately relinquished the crown, and William was declared king of England.

Eager to formalize his new status, William set about organizing his coronation. He had originally wanted to defer the ceremony so that Matilda might join him, "since if God granted him this honour, he wished for his wife to be crowned with him." This was more than just devotion: he knew full well that Matilda's presence—given her ancestral ties with previous English kings—would lend the occasion much-needed legitimacy. However, he had been dissuaded from doing so by his advisers, who had urged him that it was crucial to consolidate his position as soon as possible.[24]

Plans for the coronation duly proceeded, and the ceremony took place on Christmas Day 1066 in Westminster Abbey, where Harold had been crowned and Edward the Confessor buried. To further legitimize his position and emphasize the continuity of his accession, William ordered that the service should follow that used for previous English kings. He also commissioned a magnificent new crown in the style of Solomon (the ancient king of Israel renowned for his wisdom), "fashioned out of gold and precious stones," including a sapphire, an emerald, and a large ruby at its center.[25] But there was no fooling his new subjects, who still viewed him as a foreigner, a bastard, and a usurper.

Indeed, far from being a cause for celebration, William's coronation was a tense, somber affair. The crowds that had gathered outside the abbey to witness the arrival of their detested new king were silent and subdued. The only cheering came from the Conqueror's own men, who were there as much to suppress any trouble as to support their leader. During the ceremony, one of William's Norman bishops, Geoffrey of

Coutances, sought the assent of those present for their new king, as tradition dictated. Their affirmations were so loud that they alarmed the guards keeping watch outside the abbey, who, fearing an uprising, went on the rampage and torched a series of houses in order to terrify the inhabitants into submission. Meanwhile, the congregation took flight, and the ceremony had to be hastily concluded by the handful of "terrified" clergymen who had stayed behind. The episode tested the nerve of England's newly crowned king, who, according to one chronicler, was "trembling from head to foot."[26]

Still, the English were now forced to acknowledge William as their sovereign, however reluctantly. In doing so, they were also accepting Matilda as their queen. But William was not content with her sharing in his newly won status by association only; he resolved that she, too, would be crowned with full pomp and ceremony as soon as she could join him in England. This met with some opposition from the English barons, because it had not hitherto been the practice of the Saxon kings to gratify their wives with the title of queen. But William was determined. In his eyes, no woman was fitter than she for such a position. Matilda herself was eager to be crowned, and even before she joined her husband in England, she began styling herself queen of that kingdom.[27] She was no doubt highly satisfied when she received news of her husband's plans for her separate coronation. The prospect of playing as active a role in England as she did in Normandy would have appealed to her keen sense of ambition.

It would in fact be two years before Matilda joined her husband in his new kingdom. The reason for this delay is a matter for debate. It is possible that William considered the situation there too volatile, but as we have seen, Matilda's unquestionable pedigree and heritage would have made her presence advantageous in the duke's attempts to quickly establish his authority. Moreover, Matilda herself was keen to see her new kingdom—and take possession of her landed wealth. Upon becoming king, William had granted her extensive lands—perhaps as much as a quarter of the total at his disposal. These included rich estates in Buckinghamshire, Surrey, Hampshire, Wiltshire, Gloucestershire, Dorset, Devon, and Cornwall.[28]

These lands made Matilda a wealthy woman in her own right, for she could levy taxes, or "geld," from them. According to Domesday Book, this earned her in the region of £1,070 per year, a staggering sum for the time—equivalent to around £500,000 today. This income alone made her the richest woman in England. But as queen, she was also entitled to claim "Queen Gold," which was one-tenth of every fine paid to the crown. There were numerous other financial privileges associated with her new position. The city of Warwick, for example, was obliged to provide her with one hundred shillings for the use of her property. Not all of Matilda's revenue was paid in cash. For example, as well as sending her tolls on all goods landed at Queenhithe, the city of London provided oil for her lamps and wood for her hearth.[29] The city of Norwich, meanwhile, had to deliver a palfrey to her each year.

Considering the riches that lay in wait for her in England, it must have been a compelling reason that kept Matilda in Normandy for so long, especially as she had so successfully quelled the threats both within and outside its borders during her regency. One of the stronger explanations is that she had been pregnant when William had set sail for England in September 1066. If she had conceived another child before her husband's departure, then she would have given birth no later than June 1067.[30] As the birth dates of Matilda's sons do not fall within this period, the child must have been a girl, and it is most likely to have been the one whose name appears in the sources more than any of the other daughters, thanks to her later career: Adela.

The choice of name was significant. Adela was the name of Matilda's mother, daughter of the king of France, and as such it would have reminded William's rebellious new subjects of the legitimacy of his dynasty. A poem written in around 1079 by Godfrey of Rheims, chancellor to the French king, provides further evidence. He alludes to Adela's birth as occurring just after the Norman Conquest:

> The duke's child would rise to become an excellent woman,
> The goddess did not think it sufficient for her to be of ducal status.
> The royal virgin obtained by fate that her father would be a king.
> In order for Adela to be the daughter of a king,

The Fates allowed the father to establish himself as a king.
Because the virgin was not allowed to leave the womb
Her father owed the kingdom of England to her.[31]

If, as the evidence suggests, Matilda was pregnant during the weeks leading up to her husband's invasion of England—arguably the most crucial
moment of their reign—then, given her belief in the mystical arts, she
might well have consulted soothsayers at court on the significance of the
pregnancy and how she might use it to ensure a favorable outcome. As
Godfrey implies in his poem, the safe delivery of the child thus became
inextricably linked with the successful conquest of England.[32]

✢   ✢   ✢

Whatever her reason for remaining so long in Normandy, it did mean
that Matilda was not present to witness the brutal early months of William's reign. After being crowned, he was formally referred to as "the
great and peacegiving King," something that his new subjects would
have found deeply ironic.[33] The *Anglo-Saxon Chronicle* describes the mer-
cilessness of William's regime, which butchered thousands of Englishmen, laid vast swaths of land to waste, and imposed "stiff" taxes and
other strictures upon the beleaguered natives. Any who dared to defy
him were either mutilated or put to death. The twelfth-century chronicler John of Worcester describes how William punished his recalcitrant
subjects "by gouging out their eyes or cutting off their hands."[34] The
English commentators clearly believed that the Norman invasion was a
punishment from God for their manifold sins. "They built castles widely
throughout this nation, and oppressed the wretched people; and afterwards it always grew very much worse. When God wills, may the end be
good."[35]

The prospect of assimilation between the conquerors and conquered
looked bleak indeed. The Norman Conquest was the second successful
invasion of England in the eleventh century, the first being led by the
Danes in 1013–16. The latter had been overthrown by the native English
less than thirty years later, and it remained a strong possibility that the
Normans would be ousted in similar fashion.[36]

The invading Normans presented a stark contrast to the people of

England. They certainly looked very different, with their clean-shaven faces giving them the appearance more of priests than of fighting men. They were also "well-dressed to a fault." It was with a mixture of curiosity and scorn that they regarded the "long-haired denizens of England" with their mustaches and "skin tattooed with coloured patterns." William of Poitiers derided "the long-haired sons of the northern lands," who appeared rough and ill-kempt next to the neatly cropped style of the Normans. According to Malmesbury, their appearance was mirrored by their uncivilized ways, which included "eating till they were sick and drinking till they spewed"—although he admitted that the conquering army inherited these bad habits.[37]

In religion, at least, the Normans were in accord with their new subjects. The Saxon were Christians who now found themselves in the hands of one of the most devout Christian peoples in Europe. Malmesbury claims that the Conquest greatly enhanced the religious life of the English: "you may see everywhere churches in villages, in towns and cities monasteries rising in a new style of architecture; and with new devotion our country flourishes."[38] Great Romanesque churches were erected across the country, becoming as much a sign of Norman preeminence as the imposing castles with which William and his men would later stamp their authority. As in the political sphere, the higher ecclesiastical offices were now held by Normans, and the English clerics were gradually (or in some cases, summarily) ousted from their positions.

The new king personified his race's emerging piety, but he also symbolized its strident self-confidence, which was viewed as arrogance by resentful Saxon subjects. He trusted none of the English nobles who had survived Hastings and the campaigns that followed. To be fair, they had done little to earn his trust, proving all too ready to rebel against him—"behaviour which so exasperated his ferocity that he deprived the more powerful among them first of their revenues, then of their lands, and some even of their lives."[39] William's privileged inner sanctum, then, was dominated by Normans. Odo of Bayeux, Roger of Montgomery, Roger de Beaumont, Robert of Mortain, Alan of Brittany, Geoffrey of Coutances, Earl Hugh of Chester, Richard fitzGilbert, and William of Warenne seem to have been the most active in his government, judging from the frequency of their witness marks on the charters. Almost all of these "wise and eloquent men," as Orderic described them, had served the royal couple ever since their marriage, and some even before that time.[40] Their loyalty was richly rewarded with large estates, honors, and titles. As well as the relentlessly acquisitive Odo, William's other half-brother, Robert of Mortain, and his close associate Roger of Montgomery also profited from a share of the spoils after 1066.

William was not alone in his disdain for the English people. Lanfranc, still one of his closest advisers, felt such an aversion toward them that he begged to be excused from the post of archbishop of Canterbury when it was offered to him by William and a convention of powerful ecclesiastics. "I pleaded failing strength and personal unworthiness, but to no purpose; the excuse that the language was unknown and the native races barbarous weighed nothing with them either." Neither did his opinion of the English improve after he was obliged to take up the office. He complained to Pope Alexander II: "Now I endure daily so many troubles and vexations and such spiritual starvation of nearly anything that is good; I am continually hearing, seeing and experiencing so much unrest among different people, such distress and injuries, such hardness of heart, greed and dishonesty, such a decline in holy Church, that I am weary of my life."[41]

For all of his determination to sweep away every remnant of the Saxon regime, England's new king found himself conforming to at least some of it. For example, William himself recognized that the English system of government was more sophisticated than that of his dukedom. Within this system, the king was assisted by the witan council. This William adapted, albeit under a different name (the *curia regis*), and he would surely have retained many of the existing personnel if they had not proved so rebellious. His kingship was much as Edward the Confessor's had been, superior only in the formidable military power that supported it.

At a local level, the system of government more closely mirrored that of Normandy. Instead of *comtes* and *vicomtes* there were earls and sheriffs, but the function they performed was essentially the same. They were responsible for the collection of royal revenues, acted as executants of royal justice, held castles on behalf of the king, and played an important financial role. The key difference was the degree of autonomy these men had. In Edward the Confessor's time, the kingdom had been divided into earldoms, and each earl had enjoyed immense power. They thus constituted a threat to royal authority, and the king was often subject to their will. All of this changed with the accession of William the Conqueror. He replaced any surviving Saxon incumbents with Norman men whose loyalty was proven and who were firmly under his control.

One of William's first acts after the Battle of Hastings was to reassure Londoners that they would have the same rights of inheritance that they had enjoyed in Edward's day. Upon the death of a father, his child would inherit his estate, with no interference from the crown. As a rare gesture of conciliation on the part of the arrogant and all-powerful new king, this offered some reassurance. However, in practice, the heavy casualties suffered by vast swaths of the native landowning classes at Hastings and the battles that followed made this privilege of dubious value. It certainly did little to stop the major social revolution that took place between 1066 and 1100, during which the great majority of Saxon estates fell into Norman hands.

The contemporary chronicler Abbot Ingulphus, of Croyland Abbey in Lincolnshire, abhorred this situation. "So inveterately did the Normans at this period detest the English, that whatever the amount of their merits might be, they were excluded from all dignities; and foreigners, who were far less fitted, be they of any other nation whatever under heaven, would have been gladly chosen instead of them."[42] A powerful inner ring of high-ranking Normans, related by ties of blood and loyalty to the royal court, came to control nearly a quarter of the landed wealth of England. William himself controlled a fifth, and the church and remaining barons almost half between them. Even Orderic Vitalis was forced to admit that "foreigners grew wealthy with the spoils of England, whilst her own sons were either shamefully slain or driven as exiles to wander hopelessly through foreign kingdoms."[43]

Rather than curtailing her husband's excesses, Matilda initially joined in. She ordered the abbey of Abingdon, the loyalty of which was questionable, as it had been closely affiliated to the Godwine family, to send her a selection of precious ornaments. The monks duly obliged, but upon receiving their treasure, she declared it inadequate and demanded richer items.[44]

With wealth came corruption, and many of the Normans who had profited from their lord's generosity "arrogantly abused their authority and mercilessly slaughtered the native people."[45] As scores of English abbots were ousted from their posts and replaced by greedy, tyrannical men, the same corruption spread to the country's religious life. Orderic Vitalis observes: "Between such shepherds and the flocks committed to their keeping existed such harmony as you would find between wolves and helpless sheep."[46]

There seemed to be no end to the Norman oppression. New laws were introduced that were heavily weighted against the native population, while even the humblest followers of the Conqueror were protected. If any of them was attacked by a Saxon, the perpetrator faced a considerable fine. By contrast, the attempted murder of a native Englishman would go unpunished if the attacker was a Norman.

The revolution did not end there. In almost every sphere of life, the customs and traditions of old England were gradually swept away by the new ruling class. Referring to the disdain with which the conquerors viewed the traditional English ceremony for conferring knighthoods, Ingulphus lamented: "And not only in this custom, but in many others as well, did the Normans effect a change."[47] Even the native language was systematically eroded. The conquering Normans may have learned sufficient English to administer their newly acquired estates, but otherwise they spoke Latin and French, and these now became the dominant languages of the ruling and upper clerical classes. "The very language even they abhorred with such intensity, that the laws of the land and the statutes of the English kings were treated of in the Latin tongue," observed Ingulphus, "and even in the very schools, the rudiments of grammar were imparted to the children in French and not in English. The English mode of writing was also abandoned, and the French manner adopted in charters and in all books."[48] Before long, all government business was transacted in Latin rather than English. William himself had made a rather halfhearted attempt to learn English so that he could understand his new subjects without the aid of an interpreter, but he soon gave up. Orderic Vitalis excuses this failing on the grounds of William's "advancing age" and "the distractions of his many duties," but it is difficult to imagine that he tried very hard.[49]

The gradual erosion of their language was one of the most tangible losses suffered by the native English people. If the Normans had been a civilized and diplomatic race, this might have been easier to bear. As it was, their leader epitomized the often shockingly rude, even barbarous manners of the conquering regime, which made a mockery of the ancient chivalric values cherished by the Saxons. In the early years at least, William's English court lacked the refinements of the former royal and noble households. Nor was the flowering of intellectual life that had begun before the Conquest sustained. Instead, the brutish, boorish people of the new regime seemed to derive all their pleasure from the cruelty of their military exploits. Even the great Norman castles that later sprang up across the country were, in their earliest incarnation, little more than ugly barracks thrown up as a temporary means of defense against the intransigent natives.

Women had even more cause for complaint in this dramatically changed culture and society. Rape became commonplace, as Orderic Vitalis describes: "Noble maidens were exposed to the insults of low-born soldiers, and lamented their dishonouring by the scum of the earth." Those women who escaped such violence on account of their age were no less wretched. "Matrons, highly born and handsome, mourned the loss of their loving husbands and almost all their friends, and preferred death to life."[50] Moreover, women found themselves oppressed by the law. For example, new marriage customs put them at a disadvantage, as they were now expected to bring with them considerable dowries, whereas in Anglo-Saxon times the onus had been on the man to arrange a more equitable settlement. As one authority on the subject neatly put it: "Favour lay with the spear not with the spindle in Norman days."[51]

With precious few exceptions, then, the changes wrought by the Norman Conquest proved both dramatic and unwelcome for the native population. Even sixty years later, Malmesbury had cause to lament, "England has become a dwelling-place of foreigners and a playground for lords of alien blood. No Englishman today is an earl, a bishop, or an abbot; new faces everywhere enjoy England's riches and gnaw her vitals, nor is there any hope of ending this miserable state of affairs."[52]

Orderic Vitalis's account, however, provides a stark contrast. He paints a picture of harmonious integration in which the Saxons gladly accepted the civilizing influence of their Norman conquerors: "English and Normans were living peacefully together in boroughs, towns, and cities, and were inter-marrying with each other. You could see many villages or town markets filled with displays of French wares and merchandise, and observe the English, who had previously seemed contemptible to the French in their native dress, completely transformed by foreign fashions. No one dared to pillage, but everyone cultivated his own fields in safety and lived contentedly with his neighbour."[53]

On this latter point, at least, the *Anglo-Saxon Chronicle* is in agreement: "Among other things, the good order he [William] made in this land is not to be forgotten, so that a man who was of any account could travel over his kingdom with his bosom full of gold, unmolested." It also attests that after the initial wave of violence against the native population, England's new king gradually imposed a set of strict laws against crimes such as murder and rape: "No man dare kill another man, however great a wrong he might have done the other. And if any common man had sex with a woman against her will, he immediately lost the limbs with which he played."[54]

But this account was written at the end of William's life, which indicates that the change had been gradual. Orderic Vitalis's claim that the Conqueror's civilizing influence had taken full effect within the space of just four years was an idealized and inaccurate view, as would be proved by the continuing unrest and resentment among the English population. William's struggle with his rebellious subjects was to be a long and bitter one, and he would never enjoy the luxury of feeling secure on his throne.

9

Queen of England

I f the situation looked bleak in England, it was a good deal brighter
in Normandy, thanks to the efforts of its duchess. Ever since taking the reins of power on the eve of her husband's invasion,
Matilda had ruled the duchy with great shrewdness and political acumen. Throughout her initial two-year tenure, there was no erosion of
ducal power or loss of territories to foreign magnates. In fact, the duchy
enjoyed a more stable period than it had for many years. This achievement must not be underestimated. Normandy was, as one leading authority of the period has termed it, "a province notoriously susceptible
to anarchy," and the absence of its powerful duke and most of his army
had made it dangerously vulnerable to antagonistic forces.[1] Orderic Vitalis describes the political infighting with which Matilda had to deal:
"One would try through jealousy to oust another from his position, and
various disturbances broke out which caused wretchedness to the poor;
troubles such as these delighted the cruel and distressed all who loved
justice and seemliness."[2] Such rebelliousness was, he claimed, endemic
among the Norman people as a whole: "They tear each other to pieces
and destroy themselves, for they hanker after rebellion, cherish sedition,
and are ready for any treachery."[3]

Yet Matilda, a mere woman, had established her authority from the
start and had brought this turbulent duchy firmly under her control. As
a result, her husband had been able to concentrate upon the urgent need

to consolidate his victory in England, which could have been seriously threatened if his attention had been continually diverted by affairs back in Normandy.

Acting as regent would have absorbed all of Matilda's time and energy. Contemporary ideals required rulers to be always accessible to their subjects, and this was particularly important when there were potential threats to their power. For Matilda, this meant traveling from city to city and holding court in as magnificent a style as possible. There was very little room for privacy in her life. Among the places she visited most often would have been her and William's chief residences at Fécamp, Rouen, Caen, Bayeux, Bonneville-sur-Touques, and Lillebonne. In order to reinforce the strength of the Norman dynasty, she might have taken some or all of her children with her on the most important occasions, but otherwise her duties must have involved long periods of separation from them.

By making such sacrifices and working hard to maintain the stability of the realm, Matilda had won the respect of ministers and subjects alike. There could have been no clearer demonstration of her political skill or of her loyalty to William. Even William of Poitiers praised the "wisdom" of "our dearest mistress" and admitted: "Its [Normandy's] government had been carried on smoothly by our lady Matilda." However, the fact that he did not use her royal title may have been intended as a slight, and he could not resist musing that the absence of rebellion or invasion during her regency "must, we think, be attributed primarily to the king himself, whose return they feared."[4]

As a female regent, Matilda was arguably at a disadvantage when it came to bringing her subjects to heel. But she overcame the perceived weakness of her sex, and in the eyes of her grateful husband, her worth soared to even greater heights than before the conquest. To a woman of Matilda's ambition, this reward was greater than any riches. As an indication that he trusted her above all others, William made it known that in future she was to act with the fullness of his authority in whichever of his domains he needed her. Matilda, Duchess of Normandy, now faced the appealing prospect of being queen of England in more than just name.

Having "united the two shores of the channel," William returned in triumph to Normandy in the spring of 1067.[5] Though he was delighted to find that his wife had kept the duchy in such good order, there were rumors that she had been less than faithful to him in other ways. One of the duke's knights, Grimoult du Plessis, who had stayed behind in Normandy during the conquest of England, repeated a tale that Matilda had been sleeping with another man during William's absence. Enraged, the duke was said to have dragged his wife from her bed and fastened her hair to a horse's tail before parading her naked through the streets of Caen. The more detailed accounts attest that she was dragged from the end of the Rue de Vaucelles to her husband's abbey, thus crossing the entire town. On the way, she passed by a road that she subsequently baptised Rue Froide (Cold Road)—not, as one might assume, because of her lack of attire, but because of the indifference of the inhabitants who lived there. Tradition has it that she also had a monument built on the site where the humiliating parade began, and named it the Croix Pleureuse (Cross of Tears).[6]

On their return to the chateau, William had his wife locked up in a dungeon. Only after Matilda continued to plead her innocence did he eventually agree to restore her. Finally convinced of his wife's fidelity, he wrought a horrific revenge upon the knight who had told him such a scandalous falsehood, ordering his men to hunt him down and skin him alive with a wooden knife. Grimoult's corpse was then quartered by four horses. According to the legend, William kept fragments of the knight's skin under his saddle as a trophy.[7]

This extraordinary tale is typical of the salacious rumors that were put about by chroniclers sympathetic to the English cause, and there is no reference to it in any other source. In fact, Grimoult du Plessis had been one of the rebels who had fought against William at the Battle of Val-ès-Dunes in 1047. He had subsequently been captured and held prisoner at Rouen, where he later died. As William's captive, he would hardly have been in a position either to witness Matilda's infidelity (if such it was) or to relate the tale to William, let alone suffer such a gruesome fate. More to the point, it is highly unlikely that Matilda would have risked her position by playing the whore during her husband's absence. Even if she had been so inclined, she would hardly have had the time. The regency of Normandy was very much a full-time occupation.

While this rumor can be given little credence, there is another that has a rather firmer grounding in the contemporary records. Although she was on the surface a calm and pragmatic ruler, there is evidence to suggest that Matilda did not flinch from using her power for an altogether more sinister purpose than the just government of her realm. It had been almost twenty years since her humiliation at the hands of Brihtric, the Saxon lord who had spurned her proposal in Flanders, but time had apparently not lessened the implacable hatred that she felt toward him. For Matilda, revenge was a dish best served cold. During the first year of her husband's reign, she demanded possession of the manor of Tewkesbury, which had been held by Brihtric since before the Conquest.[8] The *Chronicle of Tewkesbury* claims that she also deprived his town of Gloucester of its charter. The vengeful queen then "stirred up the king's wrath against the Saxon nobleman." William ordered that Brihtric should be seized at his house at Hanley in Worcestershire on a day that should have been one of glory for his captive, witnessing as it did the consecration of a chapel that he had had built by Wulfstan, the bishop of Worcester. The Saxon was taken with all haste to Winchester, where he was thrown into prison, apparently without cause. He languished there for two years before dying in mysterious circumstances. It was widely rumored that Matilda had ordered his murder.[9]

The truth of what happened to Brihtric will probably never be known. The evidence against Matilda is far from conclusive. If she had deprived Brihtric of his estates and his life, then she must have done so through an agent, because she did not arrive in England until the following year. Moreover, there is evidence—overlooked until now—to suggest that Brihtric might have been present at Matilda's coronation. Among the charters is a grant by William to Giso, the bishop of Wells, restoring some land in Banwell, Somerset, which the late King Harold had appropriated.[10] This diploma has been dated to Whitsun 1068, and the considerable body of witnesses who attested it suggests that it was among the charters that were approved at Matilda's coronation. The last name on the list is that of Brihtric. This makes it unlikely that Matilda had ordered the seizure of his lands the previous year, and impossible that she had ordered his imprisonment at the same time. It is deliciously tempting to imagine England's new queen confronted by the sight of her former

lover amid the pomp and ceremonial of her coronation. Forced to re-
strain her emotions for fear of causing a scandal that would ruin the
most important day of her life, she may have resolved to exact her revenge at the earliest opportunity. If this is a flight of fancy, then it is certainly feasible that something had prompted Matilda to seek redress for
the slight that she had suffered all those years ago. Seeing Brihtric at her
coronation would have been the perfect provocation.

We know from Domesday Book that Matilda did inherit a considerable portion of Brihtric's estates. These dominated the west of England,
encompassing Cornwall, Devon, Dorset, Wiltshire, Worcestershire, and
Gloucestershire.[11] His lands in the latter—his home county—besides
Tewkesbury, included Avening, Fairford, Thornbury, and Old Sodbury.[12]
Matilda retained these during her lifetime, but she gave many of Brihtric's
other estates away. She donated some of his most prized lands in Dorset
and Devon to the abbeys of St. Mary's Le Bec, La Trinité, and St.-Étienne.[13]
Was this a penance for ordering Brihtric's imprisonment—or, worse, his
death? A nineteenth-century source supports such a notion. According
to this account, a year before her death, Matilda transferred the owner-
ship of her manor of Nailsworth in Gloucestershire, together with all its
rents and dues, to her abbey in Caen. This manor had apparently been
part of the spoils that she had wrested from Brihtric, so the fact that she
gave it to the church during her final illness can be interpreted as an attempt at atonement for past sins.[14]

However, there are question marks surrounding the theory of Matilda's revenge. For example, the charter for Gloucester was removed before her arrival in England. What is more, Domesday Book tells us that
Brihtric had inherited the manor of Tewkesbury in 1020, which suggests
that he would have been in his sixties when he died—a comparatively
advanced age for the time. It is therefore at least as likely that he died
from natural causes as at the orders of the woman whose proposal he
had so callously rejected all those years ago. Indeed, it might have been
his death that caused his manor to become available and subsequently
granted to the queen.

Another explanation for Brihtric's reputed fall from grace could be
that he took part in the Exeter rebellion of 1068. He was one of the few
Saxon magnates who had not been immediately dispossessed after the

Battle of Hastings, and as such it is possible that he became a figurehead for opposition to the Norman regime. His loyalty to the Norman king was unlikely to have been strong, and he might well have decided to throw all of the wealth and power at his disposal behind the rebels' cause. The fact that his principal manor of Tewkesbury subsequently suffered "destruction and dismembering" at the hands of one of the king's most trusted companions, William fitzOsbern, adds weight to this theory.[15]

But still the rumors persisted, and the prospect that Matilda had a hand in his death remains a tantalizing one. It was in keeping with her pride and strength of will that she would have harbored a simmering resentment against the man who had so humiliated her in Flanders—and a determination to wreak revenge if ever she had the opportunity. And if this revenge was as terrible as the rumors suggest, then she rivaled even her husband in ruthlessness and brutality.

✢   ✢   ✢

In early 1067, the same year that Matilda allegedly took revenge upon Brihtric, her daughter Adeliza was again the focus of marriage negotiations. The potentate upon whom her father had fixed his sights was Alfonso VI, King of León, part of modern-day Spain. Alfonso had inherited León upon his father's death in 1065, while his elder and younger brothers had acquired other parts of the vast Spanish empire over which King Ferdinand had ruled.[16] Even though Alfonso was only the middle son, his overweening ambition drove him to make war with his brothers and lay claim to their territories. He was a fierce warrior, who earned himself the nickname El Bravo (the Brave), and contemporary sources variously depict him as a valiant hero and a ruthless oppressor. Determined to gain the upper hand over his brothers, he set his sights on a daughter of the new king of England, and the evidence suggests that Adeliza was once more chosen as the intended bride.[17]

The fact that such a powerful ruler was again singled out for Adeliza suggests that she was considered an appealing match—Orderic describes her as "a most fair maiden,"[18] and she was perhaps the most beautiful of Matilda's daughters. It also lends weight to the notion that she was the eldest, because as such she would have been the most highly prized in the international marriage market. William of Poitiers claims that two Spanish kings fought for the honor of marrying her. "A bitter quarrel arose between them on her account: for, far from being unworthy, she was in every way worthy of such a parent, and shone with such virtues and such zeal."[19] According to another account, the two combatants were Alfonso of León and Robert Guiscard, the duke of Apulia and Calabria. However, the latter can surely be discounted, because he was already married at the time.

Adeliza had inherited some of her mother's strong will, and upon hearing that she was to marry Alfonso of León, she reacted with as much distaste as Matilda had shown for William of Normandy. According to Orderic Vitalis, "she who had not enjoyed union with her first betrothed [Harold Godwinson] shrank with loathing from a second marriage."[20] The chroniclers add that Adeliza had also grown into an extremely pious young woman and fervently desired to eschew such worldly concerns by entering a convent. One account claims that she was already a nun when her father decided that she would be more useful to him as a bride to barter with.

Despite her aversion to the idea of marriage, there was little that Adeliza could do to resist her father's wishes. It is hard to imagine that William had much patience or sympathy with the girl, for he was a staunch traditionalist where his children were concerned, believing that the only useful function daughters could fulfill was to further his political ambitions. There is no record of Matilda's part in the matter. If she felt any empathy with her daughter, then she either failed to persuade William to abandon the scheme or realized that it was futile even to attempt to change his mind.

Negotiations duly proceeded. Anxious not to let this desirable bride slip away, Alfonso sent proxies to take part in the wedding ceremony on his behalf, as was the custom in diplomatic marriages when the bride and groom lived many miles apart. He must have been impatient to seal the agreement, for it would have taken his prospective bride only a matter of weeks to travel to Spain. Adeliza remained miserable at the prospect of marrying the Spanish king, whom she knew only by his reputation as a grasping and ruthless leader. Orderic even goes so far as to claim that she still felt too strong an attachment to the late King Harold to marry another: "She had seen and loved the Englishman, but she was terrified of the Spanish husband she had never seen."[21]

The poor girl prayed fervently that she might be released from her fate and never set foot on Spanish soil. According to Orderic, her prayers would be answered, but not without great cost, for she died on her way to her prospective new land. Her body was brought back to Normandy by the same entourage that had accompanied her on the journey to Spain. Orderic concludes his tale by claiming that Adeliza was then given a fitting resting place at the church of St. Mary the Virgin in Bayeux.

However, there is good reason to doubt the tragic end to Orderic's tale. Although other sources suggest that Adeliza died young, they do not relate the deadly divine intervention that saved her from marrying the Spanish king. Such a tragedy would have been much talked of at the Norman court, and yet William of Poitiers, whose account was written at the time that Orderic claims her death occurred, does not mention it at all. In fact, there is evidence to suggest that Adeliza was released from her betrothal to Alfonso by some other means—perhaps the collapse of diplomatic negotiations. Furthermore, Orderic himself claims that a daughter of William and Matilda was betrothed to Earl Edwin of Mercia, a powerful English magnate, when the duke returned in triumph to Normandy in the spring of 1067, and the most likely contender is Adeliza.

Edwin was one of several high-ranking Englishmen whom William brought with him to Normandy that spring. The others included Edwin's brother, Earl Morcar, and Edgar the Aetheling, the young man whom William's recalcitrant subjects had proclaimed king. William clearly wished to abide by the old adage of keeping one's enemies close. These men served as hostages for peace in England during the new king's absence, depriving the kingdom of any possible figureheads for a rebellion. In order to neutralize the threat of at least one of them still further, the evidence suggests that William betrothed his eldest daughter, Adeliza, to Edwin during this visit.[22]

Determined to celebrate his triumph in England to the full, William kept a magnificent court that Easter at the old ducal monastery of Fécamp.[23] He was joined by Matilda, together with "a brilliant galaxy of bishops and magnates" from across the duchy who flocked to the palace.[24] Members of the French aristocracy were also there, in recognition of the fact that William was no longer the vassal of the king of France, but an equal. Men and women of more humble status also thronged the route of their duke's triumphant return. "Old men, boys, matrons and all the citizens came out to see him; they shouted out to welcome his return, so that you could have thought the whole city was cheering."[25] Even the weather appeared to hail the duke's victory. William of Poitiers claims that "the sun seemed to shine with the clear brightness of summer, far more strongly than usual at this season."[26]

The feasting and entertainments that William and Matilda ordered were so lavish that Normandy had never seen the like. All marveled at "the splendid garments, interwoven and encrusted with gold, worn by the king and his court," which made their own clothes appear poor by comparison. Indeed, now that they were king and queen of England, William and Matilda's clothes were more lavish than before. Brightly colored and highly decorated, they would have been made out of priceless materials such as shot silk taffeta and gold thread.

The foreign visitors sent home enthusiastic reports of the couple's attire, as well as of the rich tapestries and "vessels of silver and gold, of whose number and beauty incredible things could truthfully be told."[27] Poitiers describes "a great banquet" at which William and Matilda "drank only from such goblets or from horns of wild oxen decorated with the same metal at both ends," proudly adding that the visitors would have "noted many such things, fitting the magnificence of a king, which they praised on their return home because of their novelty."[28] It is likely that Matilda was responsible for this spectacle, for it was the role of the consort to manage and exhibit the family treasure and adornments, and displays of ostentation such as those at the Easter court would have fallen within her remit. It was also the consort's job to ensure that royals stood out from the crowd, and with the adornments she now employed, the message was clear: William and Matilda were no longer merely duke and duchess of Normandy, but king and queen of England, with all of the associated majesty and splendor.

The celebrations to mark William's triumph continued long after the assembly at Fécamp. At the beginning of May 1067, he ordered the consecration of the abbey of St. Mary in St.-Pierre-sur-Dives, which attracted a considerable audience.[29] Two months later, on July 1, he and his wife attended the dedication of the magnificent new abbey church of St. Mary in Jumièges. The church, which was situated on the river Seine in Rouen, was one of the most important in Normandy—it had strong ties with the ducal family, and its abbots had played a leading role in both government and church reform. The works had been started by Robert of Jumièges, Edward the Confessor's archbishop of Canterbury, who had undertaken an ambitious program of building more than twenty years before. The result was an imposing new Romanesque church, which rivaled even William and Matilda's great abbeys in Caen.

‡ ‡ ‡

While the new king and queen of England were parading their magnificence throughout the duchy, an event occurred that cast a shadow over their celebrations—for Matilda at least. On September 1, 1067, her father, Count Baldwin V, died. There is no evidence that Matilda had seen her father since her marriage to William. This was by no means unusual: distance and domestic duties meant that when daughters of ruling families were married to foreign potentates, they often bade farewell to their family forever. Nevertheless, she seems to have maintained good relations with both of her parents, perhaps through regular correspondence, and she remained proud of her family connections, as well as of Baldwin's burgeoning prestige. Little wonder, therefore, that she was said to be "overwhelmed with grief" at her father's death, as well as by pity for her widowed mother.[30] Ever the dutiful daughter, she was no doubt glad that she and William had already provided for Adela some years before, when they had arranged for Abbess Elisabeth of Montvilliers to pay her an annual pension in return for her gift of land in the Pays-de-Caux.

As Baldwin had acted as regent of France, his death signaled the resumption of the traditional hostility between Normandy and France. For now, though, the duke had other concerns. Toward the end of 1067, he began making preparations to return to England. In his absence, Odo and fitzOsbern had been unable to quell the rising antagonism to the new regime among the Saxon people, and rebellions had broken out in Kent and Herefordshire. Trouble was also brewing in the west, signaled by the dangerous uprising in Exeter. As well as being a principal city, this was also the home of Harold's mother, Gytha, who provided a figure-head for dissenters to the Norman regime. Anxious to hold on to his crown, William decided that he must return to his new kingdom with all haste. He had no hesitation in continuing to leave the government of Normandy in the hands of his wife, confident that she would again prove how fit she was to rule.

This time, Matilda was invested with even more independent author-ity to act in her husband's name. Roger de Montgomery, who had been appointed to advise her on previous occasions, accompanied William to England. Matilda now possessed a level of power enjoyed by few of her female contemporaries. Even Orderic Vitalis, who tends to underplay her influence, admits, "Queen Matilda was now a powerful ruler with vast resources at her command."[31]

Having taken his leave of her, William set sail from Dieppe on De-cember 6. He resolved that their separation would not be of long dura-tion, however, for he was impatient to see her crowned in England. In early 1068, by which time he had quashed the rebellions that had flared up during his absence, he sent ambassadors to his wife in Normandy with instructions that she was to join him across the Channel.[32] Their son Robert was to take charge of the government of the duchy in her absence. Jumièges and Orderic imply that this would henceforth be a permanent arrangement, but there is no evidence for this. Indeed, the charters attest that Matilda continued to be as active a regent during her husband's subsequent absences as she had been since his conquest of England.

Much as she might have enjoyed the power of acting alone in Nor-mandy, Matilda was no doubt eager to see her new kingdom, and Ord-eric Vitalis records that "she gladly obeyed her husband's commands."[33] By now in her mid-thirties, she had never before left the shores of conti-nental Europe, so the prospect of a sea voyage must have appealed to her sense of adventure. There is no record of her journey, but we know that she was accompanied by an impressive retinue that included scores of servants and noblewomen. The chronicler Langtoft describes a "rich company of ladies and maidens" in her train.[34] As befitted her rank, a number of prominent clergymen were among her attendants, including her chaplain, Guy of Amiens, her physician, Baldwin, abbot of St. Edmundsbury, and the bishop of Lisieux. She may also have been accompanied by some of her children on this or subsequent visits to her new kingdom. Her son Richard was certainly present at her coronation, for he was among the witnesses to a charter that was drawn up at the time, and we know from the evidence of Domesday Book that her daughter Matilda resided in England for some time, because she had her own household there.[35]

England's new queen arrived shortly after Easter 1068, which fell on March 23 and had been celebrated by her husband in Winchester. Her appearance in England was noted by the *Anglo-Saxon Chronicle:* "At this Easter the king came to Winchester . . . And soon after that the Lady Matilda came here to the land."[36] She was viewed with some suspicion upon her arrival in England, and her new subjects referred to her as "the strange woman." Their suspicion was rooted in the fact that she was spoken of as "la Royne" by the Normans, which implied that she was a female sovereign in her own right, rather than being merely the wife of the king.[37] It soon became clear how shocking a concept this was to her new subjects.

The lukewarm reception that his wife received in England did nothing to disrupt William's plans for her. Until now, he had attempted to subdue the English by force alone. However, with Matilda at his side, he now intended to emphasize the magnificence—and legitimacy—of his dynasty. This was greatly helped by the fact that Matilda was almost certainly pregnant at the time of her arrival.[38] She had probably conceived toward the end of William's visit to Normandy and would therefore have been in the early months of her pregnancy. It would be her ninth known child—and her last. The fact that she endured an arduous journey by land and sea at such a time is again a testament to how much she desired to claim her new crown. Furthermore, it was crucial to the establishment of the Norman dynasty that the child she had carried in her womb across the Channel should be born on English soil. Attuned as she was to popular feeling, Matilda fully appreciated this, and she therefore resolved to stay in her new country for the remainder of her term.

✢ ✢ ✢

The attention that was paid to the aesthetics of the new English royal court soon after her arrival suggests that Matilda was quick to bring her influence to bear. Even the pro-English chroniclers could not help but be impressed by the opulent spectacle that the couple presented, clad from head to toe in gold-encrusted robes and eating their sumptuous meals from gold and silver platters. They proceeded to hold another great court at Westminster for Whitsuntide, which was attended by a host of English notables.

As soon as these celebrations were out of the way, plans began in earnest for the main purpose of Matilda's visit: her coronation. The event was loaded with significance. Besides being vital to William's efforts to reinforce his legitimacy in the eyes of his new subjects, Matilda would be the first queen of England to be formally styled "Regina." Before that, a female consort was simply referred to as the wife or companion of the king, a practice that was viewed with some disdain by the ninth-century commentator Asser, who observed: "The West Saxon people do not allow the queen to sit next to the king and do not even permit the king's wife to be entitled queen."[39]

There were, however, exceptions. Matilda's ancestor Judith, daughter of Charles the Bold, married Aethelwulf, king of the West Saxons, in 856 and became the first consort to be formally consecrated as queen. This concession was probably made on account of Judith's distinguished pedigree, as well as the influence of her husband, who "commanded that she should sit beside him on the royal throne, against the perverse custom of that people."[40]

But even though Judith had set the precedent of consecration for a queen in the mid-ninth century, the initial wariness that Matilda's new subjects had shown toward her proved that the notion of a queen as distinct from a king's wife was still not fully accepted by the end of the following century. Indeed, the coronation ordo (a collection of prayers, ceremonies, and hymns) used for Aelfthryth, wife of King Edgar, in 973 emphatically limited the role of the female consort to the production of heirs. Although her successors had achieved some recognition of the broader potential of their role, the fertility of a queen was still viewed as her primary function. Only with the consecration of Cnut's second wife, Emma, did the situation begin to change. The rites used for her consecration as Cnut's queen in 1017 stressed that she was to share in his power and rule, not just be a passive, silent partner according to the traditional model for consorts.

In order to emphasize the significance of Matilda's coronation as the first one ever staged just for a queen, the ceremony had to eclipse even that of the king in splendor and magnificence.[41] Every detail was planned with meticulous care. The date that was chosen was heavily symbolic. The coronation was to take place on Whit Sunday (May 11), one of the most important dates in the Christian calendar, which is celebrated fifty days after Easter (hence its Latinate name, Pentecost) and commemorates the descent of the Holy Spirit upon the disciples of Christ.[42] The message was clear: conjoined with her husband, Matilda had been chosen by God as the savior of the people of England.

The ceremony was to take place at Westminster Abbey and be presided over by Archbishop Ealdred of York.[43] He had been one of Edward the Confessor's foremost prelates, and some sources claim that he had crowned Harold Godwinson as king of England. Even though his loyalties clearly lay with the native English people, it was a shrewd move on the part of the royal couple to choose him for the task, helping to retain an element of continuity in their accession to the throne.

Matilda's coronation was probably the last to follow the ordo used for her predecessors. At the beginning of the ceremony, she was led into the church and prostrated herself in prayer before the altar. This symbolized the end of her previous personality and the birth of her new one as queen. Next she was anointed with holy oil, just as her husband had been at his coronation. This part of the ceremony was intended to emphasize the monarch's divine status. The new queen was then given a ring to symbolize her "marriage" to the kingdom, as well as to the king in his public duties. Finally she was crowned. The overall effect—a combination of splendor, ritual, and pious stagecraft—inspired awe in everyone who attended, and as such achieved its purpose.

Special laudes—ritual chants—were written for Matilda, probably by Archbishop Ealdred himself. It is likely that this was the first time laudes were used at the crowning of an English monarch, and they were no doubt designed to impress the audience with a Continental practice.[44] The words emphasized both the legitimacy and the power of Matilda's position as queen. Three crucial phrases were introduced: *constituit reginam in popolo*—the queen is placed by God among the people; *regalis imperii . . . esse participem*—the queen shares royal power; and *laetatur gens Anglica domini imperio regenda et reginae virtutis providential gubernanda*— the English people are blessed to be ruled by the power and virtue of the queen.[45] This conveyed a strong message: Matilda's authority was constitutional, not customary. Never before had a queen's power been so formalized—or so equal to that of the king. The "manly" nature of her authority was stressed by the omission of the female saints traditionally referred to in a queen's laudes; instead, her intercessors were all male apostles. Matilda had apparently transcended even her sex in becoming England's new queen, and the coronation marked the dawning of a new era for royal consorts. No longer confined to the narrow domestic sphere, she and her successors were expected to play an unprecedentedly active part in the political, judicial, financial, and spiritual life of their kingdom. Matilda would fulfill this role so effectively that she would become a model of ideal queenship for centuries to come.

The "very rich festival" was followed by a magnificent banquet, the ceremonial of which was so admired that it established a series of precedents that endured for many subsequent coronations.[46] They included the entrance of a "champion" to challenge any man who dared to question the queen's authority. This was a Norman tradition, unknown to the Saxons, and this first champion, a man named Marmion, was from the conquering land. When the company was all seated for the banquet, he rode into the middle of the hall, fully armed, and declared: "If any person denies that our most gracious sovereign, lord William, and his spouse Matilda, are not king and queen of England, he is a false-hearted traitor and a liar; and here I, as champion, do challenge him to single combat."[47] There is no record that any man rose to the challenge on this occasion.

Meanwhile, William granted his cook, a man named Tezelin, the manor of Addington "for composing a dish of white soup called dillegrout, which especially pleased the royal palate."[48] The office of "grand pannetier" was also instituted at Matilda's coronation banquet. His role was to carry the salt and carving knives from the pantry to the royal table and to serve bread to the king and queen. In return for his service, he received the salt cellars, spoons, and knives laid on the royal table, as well as a fee for the bread. It became something of a custom for the officials who served the royal couple at banquets to be rewarded with the precious cups, bowls, or other utensils used during the meal. There are many contemporary accounts of unseemly squabbles breaking out as men jostled with each other for the right to perform such tasks (and thus share in the spoils), and on occasion they even came to blows, but there is no record of any such fracas at Matilda's coronation. In fact, the occasion seemed to pass remarkably smoothly, particularly compared to that of her husband eighteen months before. This may be an early indication of the influence that Matilda would bring to bear over formal occasions of state.

Two charters that were granted at the time give a sense of the scale and demographic of the assembly that gathered for the ceremonials. In contrast to her husband's coronation, it was very much an Anglo-Norman congregation. Archbishop Ealdred aside, the other leading English prelate, Stigand, the Archbishop of Canterbury, was in attendance, as well as scores of English bishops and abbots. Three of the foremost English earls, Edwin, Morcar, and Waltheof, came to pay homage to their new queen, as did retainers such as Tofi, the sheriff of Somerset. The high-ranking Normans were also there in force, including the king's half-brothers, Bishop Odo and Count Robert of Mortain, and his most trusted advisers, Roger de Montgomery, Count Robert of Eu, and Bishop Geoffrey of Coutances.[49]

The fact that Matilda's coronation was attended by both English and Norman dignitaries was no accident. With her English lineage, she was key to a carefully planned strategy to integrate the two cultures. Her subjects' acceptance of their new queen was perhaps eased by the departure of the most high-profile Anglo-Saxon women, principal among them Gytha, the mother of King Harold. Ironically, when these women, "the wives of many good men," set sail from England, most of them were bound to Matilda's homeland of Flanders.[50] The departure of Agatha, widow of Edward the Aetheling, and her daughters Margaret and Christina for Scotland shortly after Matilda's coronation meant that

England's new queen was now the principal female focus for her sub-jects.

The replacement of the mother figures of the Anglo-Saxon dynasty by a Norman queen was mirrored farther down the social scale. The chronicles paint a picture of sorrowing Saxon womenfolk making way for a new generation of Norman wives and mothers. But the higher ech-elons of Saxon women were essential to the new king. By arranging marriages between the remaining Saxon heiresses and his Norman no-bles and knights, William perhaps seemed to be further implementing his policy of positive Anglo-Norman integration. At the same time, though, he was able to gain control of even more land and wealth than his military conquests brought him. Although Domesday Book records 350 female landowners in Edward the Confessor's time, the majority of female-owned estates were concentrated in the hands of just thirty-six Saxon noblewomen.[51]

The holders of this land did not all give in to their fate meekly. Some followed Gytha's example by going into exile, whereas others escaped marriage to an invader by entering a convent. Edward the Aetheling's granddaughter, Matilda, the future queen of Scotland, spent most of her childhood in convents for this very reason. Indeed, so many others chose this path that even William's leading churchman, Lanfranc, who might arguably have approved of their choice, became concerned that it would impede the integration that his master was so keen to achieve. Neverthe-less, by the end of the twelfth century, the process of uniting the blood of the Saxons with their Norman conquerors was well advanced. Evi-dence can be found in the predominance of Norman names among the English population. Most of the major chroniclers of the period were born of mixed marriages, including William of Malmesbury, Orderic Vi-talis, and Henry of Huntingdon.

But such integration would have seemed a distant prospect in the wake of Matilda's coronation. The new queen now faced the seemingly insurmountable task of winning over her resentful subjects.

"The English Tumults"

While Matilda was preparing for her lying-in, her husband's attention had been diverted by events in the north. Of all the regions in his newly conquered kingdom, Northumbria and Yorkshire were the least under his control. The proximity of the former to the Scottish border did not help matters, for the Scottish king, Malcolm III, was all too ready to assist any rebels against William. The brother earls, Edwin and Morcar, had been dispatched to their estates in the north after Matilda's coronation, and although they had sworn fealty to William, they soon began whipping up opposition to the Norman regime. At about the same time, to make matters worse, Edgar the Aetheling had left court and taken refuge with the king of the Scots.

Fearing a rebellion, in the summer of 1068 England's new king hastened to York, the principal city of the north, from where he could prepare his own forces to quell any uprisings. According to the *Anglo-Saxon Chronicle,* he fortified other key strategic towns on the way. "Then when the king was informed that the people in the north had gathered together and would stand against him if he came, he went to Nottingham and built a castle there, and so went to York, and there built two castles, and in Lincoln, and everywhere in that region."[1] Within a matter of months, large swaths of the Midlands and north were littered with these new defenses, which, being built from wood and according to tried and tested Norman designs, could be constructed with staggering speed. Jumièges also described this tactic, in typically admiring prose: "The king surveyed the less fortified places of his realm, and to meet the danger he had powerful strongholds built at strategic sites, which he entrusted to excellent military garrisons and large numbers of mercenaries."[2] The distinctive motte-and-bailey-style castles that were so prevalent in Normandy symbolized William's predominance, and by the end of the eleventh century at least eighty-four had been erected across England.[3] The building of these castles necessitated the destruction of thousands of dwellings in order to make way for them, as Domesday Book testifies. They proved one of the most effective means by which the king could advance and consolidate his conquest of the country, effectively placing the English in a stranglehold.

As William's reign progressed, he gradually replaced the more strategically important castles with stone structures. As well as being easier to defend, they were also more comfortable for the inhabitants, because they kept out the elements. The risk of fire was not as great as in wooden buildings, so large hearths could be installed, and there were few if any leaks during wet weather. Among the first of the king's fortresses to be rebuilt was what became known as the Tower of London. Given that the inhabitants of London were among the most hostile in the country, William wanted to ensure that this new fortress would be stronger and more imposing than any the city had ever seen. The mighty stone tower (the White Tower) took several years to complete, so thick and high were its walls. It would dominate the capital for centuries to come.

At Winchester, the other major city of the south, the royal palace was already a fitting residence for England's new king and queen, but since Edward the Confessor had bequeathed it to his wife Edith, it would have been a public relations disaster to wrest it from her. William therefore set about building another, buying up land from the monks of the New Minster "upon which in the fourth year of his reign he built a new hall and palace in handsome fashion."[4]

But William and Matilda were able to make use of some of the residences that they had inherited from their predecessors. These included King Edward's former palace in Westminster, which is featured in the Bayeux Tapestry, and although heavily stylized, it still gives an impression of grandeur. William's court soon outgrew the palace, however, and in around 1069, the king ordered a substantial extension, effectively doubling the size of the old palace and adding a new hall.

Meanwhile, at Gloucester, the old royal palace used by William's predecessor served for the royal court's Christmas gatherings each year. This was probably the old palace of Kingsholm to the north of the city, which is referred to as "the king's hall" in twelfth- and thirteenth-century documents. There are no descriptions of what the palace might have looked like, and it subsequently disappears from the records, but it must have been of sufficient size and grandeur to accommodate the vast court that assembled for the Christmas celebrations.

✢ ✢ ✢

Although the Conqueror's strong-arm tactics intimidated the hostile inhabitants of the north of England, they did little to gain their loyalty and respect. Perhaps sensing an opportunity to win over their recalcitrant subjects another way, in late summer 1068, Matilda decided to join her husband in Yorkshire. She must have been motivated by more than the desire "to enjoy her husband's company," as one chronicler asserted. Assuming she was then at the court in London, this involved a journey of some two hundred miles—a considerable enough feat in itself, let alone for a woman who was by then heavily pregnant. It is a testament to the bravery and physical fortitude of this diminutive woman that she should embark upon such a venture. At around thirty-seven years old, she would have been considered of an advanced age to be giving birth. It was rare for a woman to experience a successful pregnancy beyond the age of thirty—most women by then would have endured many years of childbearing, as was the case with Matilda—and many did not survive long beyond their twenties. To take such a long and arduous journey in her condition suggests a definite determination on Matilda's part: it seems she was intent on giving birth to her child in Yorkshire and thus inspiring greater loyalty among her subjects there.

Indeed, Matilda was always prepared to set aside her own comfort in the interests of the Norman kingdom. Her royal life was an exhaustingly peripatetic one. All travel in the eleventh century was slow, uncomfortable, and dangerous. Roads were rudimentary and took the form of dusty or muddy tracks, according to the season. Men tended to travel on horseback, whereas noblewomen enjoyed the relative luxury of riding in wagons covered with richly decorated cloth to denote their rank. Although this shielded them from the worst of the elements, they would have been uncomfortable—particularly on long journeys—as they bumped and jolted over the uneven roads. This was also the slowest mode of transport, particularly in wet weather, when the carts laden with goods and passengers frequently became stuck along the muddy tracks. The considerable entourage by which Matilda was accompanied would have made progress even more cumbersome and difficult.

Moreover, Matilda's new kingdom required her to make an exceptional number of journeys by sea. Between her first visit to England in 1068 and her last in 1080, she crossed the Channel at least eight times. These are just the occasions that are recorded in the contemporary sources—the number may have been higher, her ceaseless energy and visibility being so vital to the success of the Norman dynasty. Despite involving greater exposure to the elements, often in cramped and unsavory conditions, Matilda's cross-Channel voyages would still have been preferable to her travel within Normandy and England. A calm crossing would be infinitely more comfortable than arriving sore and bruised after an arduous journey by road. If travel within her domains required a great deal of time and organization, Matilda's frequent crossings to and from England would have constituted a major operation. The evidence suggests that both she and her husband retained a household that comprised many of the same officials in both England and Normandy. They would serve and follow the king and queen wherever they went.

The rigors of travel were—for the royal couple at least—partially off-set by the comforts of the residences that were waiting for them on their arrival. One of the most detailed descriptions of the royal living quarters is provided by Baudri, the abbot of Bourgueil and archbishop of Dol in Normandy, who was also something of a poet. In a long verse that he later addressed to William and Matilda's daughter, Adela, he describes her bedchamber:

The walls are covered with tapestries, woven according to her [Adela's] design, and all seem alive: on one wall, creation, the fall and fratricide, the flood with fish on mountain tops and lions in the sea;

sacred history from Noah to Abraham, Jacob, Joseph, the glory of Moses, and David to Solomon on a second wall; the Greek gods and myths, Phaethon, Ganymede, Cadmus, Pyramis and Thisbe, Hermaphroditus, Orpheus, Troy, and Roman kings on a third . . . On the ceiling, the sky with its constellations, the signs of the zodiac, the stars and planets described in detail. On the floor, a map of the world with its seas, rivers, and mountains, named along with their creatures, and the cities on the land masses of Asia, Europe, and Africa. The bed is decorated with three groups of statues, of Philosophy and the liberal arts, the quadrivium (music, arithmetic, astronomy, geometry) at the head of the bed, the trivium (rhetoric, dialectic, and grammar) at the foot. The third group represents medicine, with Galen and Hippocrates, the humors and physical characteristics, herbs and unguents.

Baudri goes on to describe "a wonderful tapestry" that surrounded Adela's bed. This sounds remarkably similar to the Bayeux Tapestry, for it included scenes depicting the comet, the Norman council and preparations, the fleet, the Battle of Hastings with the feigned flight of the Normans and the real one of the English, and the death of Harold. However, from Baudri's description it seems that the work was on a much smaller scale than the Bayeux Tapestry and was fashioned from richer materials than the original. Nevertheless, it still provides an interesting insight into the pride that Adela felt in her father's achievements.[5]

Baudri would at best have caught only a glimpse of the chamber of which he paints such a vivid picture, so much of the detail must be imaginary. He himself admitted: "I described what would be most appropriate more than what existed." But his account still provides a valuable insight into contemporary tastes and fashions, and hints at the lavish and luxurious style in which Matilda and her family might have lived.

Without accounts such as these, it can be difficult to imagine the color and spectacle of the palaces and churches that Matilda knew, both as queen of England and duchess of Normandy. Those buildings that do survive have plain, imposing stone walls that show little sign of the vibrantly painted murals and rich decorations that would have adorned them originally. Such decorations had long been in fashion. The Anglo-

Saxon poem *Beowulf* describes a hall bedecked with drapes "embroidered with gold" and "many a sight of wonder for those that delight to gaze on them."[6] But such grandeur was not just hollow opulence; it served a vital purpose: to reinforce William and Matilda's right to the English throne.

There were no such lavish palaces in the place where Matilda was obliged to halt her progress northward in 1068. Despite her determination to give birth to her latest child in York, in the end she made it only as far as Selby, some fourteen miles south of the city. It is possible that William had sent word that it was not safe for her to venture farther, given the fragile state of affairs in the region. Or perhaps the onset of labor had forced her to rest there. Whatever the reason, the fact that Matilda sought refuge smacks of a hasty rather than a preplanned decision. Even though Selby was a sizable town, it was by no means as fitting a venue for the birth of a royal prince as York, the "capital" of the north.

Matilda's confinement would be her last. It resulted in a fourth son, who was named Henry after Matilda's uncle, King Henry I of France. This may seem an odd choice given the difficult, rivalrous relationship that had existed between William and the French king before the latter's death in 1060. However, the royal couple clearly wished to further legitimize the boy and the family in the eyes of their subjects by reminding them yet again of Matilda's impeccable pedigree. Moreover, she herself was always keen to emphasize her affinity with the French royals, and in many of the charters that she attested she is described as "niece of Henry, most illustrious king of the French."[7]

By giving birth to a male heir on English soil, Matilda had achieved a vital step toward Anglo-Norman integration, inspiring greater loyalty among her subjects than her husband had during the many hard-fought campaigns he had waged since the Battle of Hastings two years earlier. Indeed, many Saxons would come to regard Henry as the only legitimate heir to the throne, taking precedence over Robert, Richard, and William. According to Orderic Vitalis, Matilda encouraged this view by making him heir to all of her lands in England, probably soon after his birth.[8] It is equally possible that she did so out of a special fondness for her youngest child, and William also seemed to favor the boy. Malmesbury records that Henry enjoyed "his father's blessing and his mother's inheritance" and that he was "well supplied with money."[9] Matilda and William

founded a Benedictine abbey at Selby the year after his birth, presumably
to give thanks to God for the safe delivery of their son.[10]

Henry might have been viewed as the rightful heir to the throne by
most Englishmen, but for all the royal commemoration of his birth, it
was out of the question that he would supplant his three elder brothers.
It would set a dangerous precedent to so flagrantly disregard the natural
order of succession. Instead, William and Matilda intended for him to
follow the usual path of youngest sons and embark upon a career in the
church. To this end, he was given a more extensive schooling than his
brothers, and was tutored by their father's closest adviser, Lanfranc, who
from about 1070 had held the post of archbishop of Canterbury, despite
his initial reluctance.[11] So effective was Henry's education that he grew
up with a passion for intellectual pursuits, and is said to have remarked
that an illiterate king was little better than a crowned ass.[12]

Among Henry's most important lessons was English, and he became
more fluent in this language than any of the rest of his family—a fact
that further endeared him to the native population. He could also read
and write in Latin, which, together with his command of English, later
earned him the nickname "Beauclerc." Moreover, the young Henry apparently possessed the opposite temperament to his father, for Malmesbury claimed that he "preferred contending by counsel, rather than by
the sword." He would grow up to be much more withdrawn than his
outgoing and flamboyant elder brothers, Robert and William Rufus, but
his natural reserve masked a shrewdness and cunning that would one day
make him the most successful of all Matilda's sons.

✧ ✧ ✧

It seems the royal family overestimated the healing effects of Henry's
birth on the Saxon population. At the end of 1068, they felt their monarchy secure enough to return to Normandy to celebrate Christmas, where
they no doubt enjoyed the traditional festivities at court.

But William had misjudged the situation. The imposing fortresses he
had erected across the country had become a target for rebellion, and
within a few short weeks, fresh trouble had broken out. Edgar the Aetheling, who had been steadily building support from his base in Scotland,
headed south to Northumbria and led a huge uprising. His intention was

to seize the throne from William and thus reestablish the Anglo-Saxon monarchy. His cause attracted large numbers of men hostile to the Norman regime, and in February 1069 the rebels won a major victory by taking the city of York in William's absence.

William had no choice but to set sail for his new kingdom once more. He left Matilda behind, presumably as regent—her position being that much higher than that of her son Robert, who had guarded the kingdom in his parents' absence. By April 1069, he had succeeded in retaking York. Any conciliatory feelings toward the English that this victory, together with the birth of his fourth male heir, might have inspired were soon forgotten. Outraged, the king exacted a terrible revenge. Throughout 1069 and well into the following year, he launched a series of blistering attacks on a vast swath of territory stretching from the Humber to the Tees. During this "Harrying of the North," his forces showed no mercy as they razed villages, destroyed crops and livestock, and slaughtered thousands of men and women—innocent and guilty alike. Over a period of two years, thousands more—one account estimates as many as a hundred thousand—died of starvation after their food stores had been laid to waste.[13] As Malmesbury observed: "the citizens perished by famine or sword."[14] According to Orderic, the severity of the attack was such that William himself later repented of it: "In mad fury I descended on the English of the north like a raging lion, and ordered that their homes and crops with all their equipment and furnishings should be burnt at once and their great flocks and herds of sheep and cattle slaughtered everywhere. So I chastised a great multitude of men and women with the lash of starvation and, alas! was the cruel murderer of many thousands, both young and old, of this fair people."[15]

Even by William's standards, this was ruthlessness on an unprecedented scale. It appalled contemporaries and alienated many who had previously been sympathetic to the Norman cause. The horror of it was still raw when Orderic Vitalis wrote his account forty years later:

He [William] cut down many in his vengeance; destroyed the lairs of others; harried the land, and burned homes to ashes. Nowhere else had William shown such cruelty . . . My narrative has frequently had occasion to praise William, but for this act which condemned the innocent and guilty alike to die by slow starvation I cannot commend him. For when I think of helpless children, young men in the prime of life, and hoary greybeards perishing alike of hunger I am so moved to pity that I would rather lament the griefs and sufferings of the wretched people than make a vain attempt to flatter the perpetrator of such infamy.[16]

Another contemporary, Simeon of Durham, was appalled by the devastation that he witnessed firsthand:

So great a famine prevailed that men, compelled by hunger, devoured human flesh, that of horses, dogs, and cats, and whatever custom abhors; others sold themselves to perpetual slavery, so that they might in any way preserve their wretched existence; others, while about to go into exile from their country, fell down in the middle of their journey and gave up the ghost. It was horrific to behold human corpses decaying in the houses, the streets, and the roads, swarming with worms, while they were consuming in corruption with an abominable stench. For no one was left to bury them in the earth, all being cut off either by the sword or by famine.[17]

Even William's apologist, Jumièges, admitted: "by sword and fire they [the Normans] massacred almost the entire population from the very young to the old and grey."[18]

But even this dreadful campaign did not stamp out the resistance of William's most recalcitrant subjects. Thousands rose in support of Sweyn Estrithson, King of Denmark, when he invaded Yorkshire in the summer of 1069, assisted by William's now-perennial enemy, King Malcolm III of Scotland. The rebels recaptured York in September. Although Sweyn was in theory acting in support of Edgar the Aetheling, he had long coveted the English throne for himself, so his intervention added a dangerous new dimension to an already highly volatile state of affairs.[19]

Matilda had returned to England in early spring 1069.[20] Jumièges claims that during her absence from Normandy, the regency was again entrusted to Robert, who, being a minor, was no doubt still surrounded by strong advisers.[21] It may seem puzzling that she should leave Normandy at a time when her husband's attention was so diverted by his English kingdom. Although the duchy was stable by comparison, this stability could never be taken for granted, with ambitious noblemen ever watchful for an opportunity to seize power. Matilda had already proved adept at keeping all threats to ducal power at bay, so it might reasonably have been expected that William would have wished her to remain there as regent until the situation in England had improved. Yet perhaps she and her husband recognized the importance of having a figurehead for the royal family in the south of their new dominion. While William struggled in the north, a strong presence was required to guard against any sympathetic uprisings elsewhere. Matilda, already gaining favor among the English people thanks to her dignified bearing and gentle demeanor, formed a welcome contrast to her husband's brutality. She was therefore ideally suited for this task.

Having returned to England, Matilda embarked upon a series of carefully planned public relations opportunities. These included the Easter celebrations that were held at the court in Winchester. Here, in a display of family unity no doubt intended to remind the populace of the strength of the Norman dynasty, she was joined by her second son, Richard, as she presided over the ceremonials. But while she was intent upon promoting goodwill, her husband had other ideas. At a council meeting held as part of the Easter gathering, he confirmed the perpetual security of a grant of property to the abbey of Holy Trinity in Rouen "by a knife which the king playfully gave the abbot [Rayner] as if about to stab his hand." Given William's notorious cruelty, the poor abbot must have been greatly alarmed. Matilda was there to witness her husband's tasteless prank, for her signature appears on the grant that Abbot Rayner hastened away with.[22] No doubt thanks to her influence, the rest of the celebrations passed without incident.

Religious festivals such as Easter and Christmas provided an important focus for court ceremonials. William and Matilda were quick to realize the potential of such dates as a means of showing off their power and majesty. Malmesbury describes the splendor of these occasions, and was clearly not fooled by the intention that lay behind them:

The dinners in which he [William] took part on the major festivals were costly and splendid—Christmas at Gloucester, Easter at Winchester, Whitsun at Westminster in each of the years in which he was free to stay in England; all great men of whatever walk of life were summoned to them by royal edict, so that envoys from other nations might admire the large and brilliant company and the splendid luxury of the feast. Nor was he at any other season so courteous or so ready to oblige, so that foreign visitors might carry a lively report to every country of the generosity that matched his wealth.[23]

A medieval queen played a crucial role in such gatherings. She acted as housekeeper, the traditional duty of women at every stratum of society—only on a much greater scale. One of her primary concerns was the provision of hospitality. The ninth-century commentator Hincmar claimed that the queen was responsible "for good order . . . for the presentation of the king in dignified splendour, for annual gifts to the men of the household."[24] Thus the feasting, pageantry, and other social aspects of life at the royal court would have been superintended by Matilda, just as they were in Normandy. She would preside over feasts and entertainments, ensuring that every detail was in place for the comfort and enjoyment of her guests. This was regarded as a natural feminine duty, and any queen who did not fulfill it would be much criticized. In the poem *Beowulf,* the fictional queen Radegund courted disapproval by leaving the care of the royal hall to others, arriving late to meals and failing to preside at the nobles' feasts.[25]

A whole host of attendants would be on hand to serve the royal couple at these banquets. Duties included "giving the king water for his hands . . . bearing a towel before the queen . . . serving the king with his cup . . . being the king's butler . . . being the king's pantler . . . making wafers when the king wears the crown . . . being turnspit."[26] The king's table was covered with a cloth, and the servants would carry clean napkins for the use of the most important guests. They would serve the king and queen on bended knee with a selection of dishes and wine.

Even the royal couple's daily meals retained an element of grandeur and ceremony. Although William and Matilda ate breakfast in private, they were joined by the rest of the court for dinner (which was usually taken at around eleven o'clock in the morning) and supper (at five or six o'clock in the afternoon), supplemented by substantial snacks in between. No matter what the occasion, they and their courtiers were presented with a staggering array of dishes to choose from at each meal.

Fish was an important part of the eleventh-century diet. Much of it was fresh, as it was common for fishponds to be created at royal palaces and castles. Otherwise, it was salted. The royal diet was also rich in meat, except during Lent and on certain other religious days, and it tended to be roasted on spits. Beef, mutton, pork, and venison were all popular fare, along with a vast array of poultry, ranging from swans, ducks, and herons to blackbirds, pigeons, and greenfinches. The scarcity of fresh meat during the winter months meant that most of it was salted, and its pungent flavor would often be disguised by spices imported from the East. Bread was also a staple of the Norman diet. The highest ranks of society ate wheat bread, which was served in the shape of flat cakes embellished with a cross or other decoration, whereas the lower ranks had to make do with rye bread.

Other dishes would include dillegrout, a soup made from capons, almond milk, and spices, which had become popular since being served at Matilda's coronation. This would have been eaten with a spoon, but Norman diners—including the king and queen—used their fingers to eat most of the food that was put before them. "Forks were not among the royal luxuries at the board of the mighty William and his fair Matilda, who both, in feeding themselves, verified the proverb which says 'that fingers were made before forks.' "[27] It was therefore customary for diners to wash their hands before and after a meal. Anything they did not wish to eat was thrown on the floor for the dogs or beggars who frequented the feasts. All of the fare served at court was washed down with vast quantities of wine, as well as a beverage called Neustrian cider, which was famous throughout Normandy.[28]

The luxury enjoyed by the court was essential to uphold the royal dignity. But this dignity came at a price. Keeping the court supplied with food was an enormous undertaking, particularly for landowners in the south of England. Domesday Book recorded that each year the estate of Edward of Salisburys, sheriff of Wiltshire, yielded "130 porkers, 32 bacon hogs . . . 480 hens, 1,600 eggs, 100 cheeses, 52 lambs, 420 fleeces and 162 acres of unreaped corn"—and this was just in case the royal household's usual suppliers ran out of produce.[29] Even on an average day, the queen's table was furnished with viands costing forty shillings, and each of her female attendants received a daily allowance of twelve pence for her sustenance.[30]

Such luxury was also evident in the queen's apparel. Matilda, keenly aware of her status, "dressed in queenly purple, in a prosperous condition, with sceptre and crown," according to one eyewitness.[31] The contemporary accounts suggest that her attire was much more lavish as queen of England than it had been as duchess of Normandy. She commissioned dresses from English embroideresses, who were renowned as being the best in the world. Among the possessions mentioned in her will is a "tunic, worked at Winchester by Alderet's wife, and the mantle embroidered in gold . . . two golden girdles."[32] She also employed a woman from Wiltshire named Leofgeat, "who made and makes the King's and Queen's gold fringe."[33]

Both Matilda and William kept their jewels and robes in a small chamber adjoining their bedroom, which became known as the wardrobe. During the winter months, they and their attendants wore fur-lined garments to guard against the cold and drafty interiors of their palaces and castles. Surprisingly, though, the custom was to go to bed naked, swathed in rich fur-lined coverlets. Contemporary artists did not shy away from sketching images of kings and queens in bed wearing only a crown to delineate their rank.

Superintending the spectacle of court life was just part of Matilda's role as queen of England. Appreciating the need to be as visible as possible during her latest stay there, she subsequently traveled to Wells for the Whitsun Council in late May or early June 1069 and witnessed a charter to the city's cathedral. It may be a measure of the queen's success in generating support for the Norman regime that there were no reported troubles in the southern counties during this time.

Despite the relative calm that prevailed in the south, it is an indication of just how threatening the situation had become elsewhere that William sent "his beloved wife Matilda" back to Normandy soon afterward, charging her "to pray for the speedy termination of the English troubles, to encourage the arts of peace in Normandy, and to take care of the interests of their youthful heir."[34] According to Orderic, this visit was simply "so that she might give up her time to religious devotions in peace, away from the English tumults, and together with the boy Robert could keep the duchy secure."[35] It is unlikely that either William or Matilda envisaged her having much peace. Indeed, the evidence suggests that the duke was concerned to maintain his authority in Normandy and prevent his overmighty subjects from taking advantage of the troubles in England and the young regent in his homeland. Unable to make the visit himself at this critical juncture, he would have known that his wife was more than capable of flying the ducal banner on his behalf.

11

"Mutual and Lasting Hostility"

he exact date of Matilda's return to Normandy is difficult to determine, but it would have been sometime between the Whitsun Council[1] and the beginning of the northern uprising in the autumn of 1069. She assumed the regency, with Roger de Beaumont and Archbishop John of Rouen (an influential ecclesiastic who mirrored Lanfranc's role in England) as her advisers. It would prove her longest and most challenging tenure to date.

As usual, one of the most pressing demands upon Matilda's time as regent was the administration of justice. The cases over which she presided would have varied enormously in nature and complexity. For example, among the many disputes upon which she had previously passed judgment was one that involved the abbey of St.-Martin in Marmoutier, which had been granted an income from customs by William. The new *vicomte*, Robert Betran, denied all knowledge of the grant and kept the money for himself. One of the monks, Goscelin, was dispatched to England to seek justice from the king in person. Upon hearing the case, William angrily sent the monk back to Normandy so that the queen could deal with it. It was clear that if any Norman sought redress from him rather than Matilda, they would receive short shrift. And indeed Matilda wasted no time in reprimanding Betran and demanded that he restore the funds to the abbey.[2]

The legal affairs of Normandy were no less demanding during Matilda's latest regency, and her authority in such matters was stronger than ever before. However, a series of crises meant that she had a good deal less time to devote to them. Although the situation within the duchy itself was stable when she returned there in 1069, trouble was brewing beyond its borders. She had only been back in Normandy a short while when the province of Maine, which William had conquered in 1063, broke out in rebellion. It was led by the powerful nobleman Geoffrey de Mayenne, who gained a huge groundswell of support from inhabitants of the province (known as the Manceaux) who wanted to regain their independence from Normandy. Before long, the capital city, Le Mans, had been lost to the rebels, and Normandy's hold on the province began to crumble.

Matilda was now faced with a hostile and dangerous neighbor on her duchy's southwestern border. Worse was to come. Later in 1069, two of William's bitterest rivals, the king of France and the duke of Brittany, joined forces and launched an attack on Normandy. The duchess sent an urgent request to her husband for military assistance: evidently the troops that she had at her disposal in Normandy had been depleted by the constant need for reinforcements in England. Alarmed, William immediately dispatched the son of his trusted official William fitzOsbern to defend her—presumably with a retinue of men.

Matilda had barely had time to recover from this when word reached her of yet another crisis. This time it was not in Normandy, but her native land of Flanders. On July 16, 1070, Matilda's brother, Count Baldwin VI, died unexpectedly, leaving his son Arnulf as heir. Because Arnulf was then only about fifteen years old, his mother, Richildis, the countess of Mons and Hainault, was appointed regent. As was so often the case, the accession of a minor sparked unrest. This time it was the nominated heir's own uncle who rebelled.

Robert the Frisian, as he was known, was Matilda's brother, and the younger of the two recorded sons born to Baldwin V and Adela. Like his sister's, his marriage had been arranged for political gain.[3] His bride was Gertrude, the countess of Frisia, whose homeland bordered Flanders on the northern side. Residing with her in Frisia, Robert had evidently maintained a close interest in his native land, for he immediately seized the initiative upon his brother's early death and began rallying support for his own claim to the throne. He found a willing ally in the form of Henry III, the German emperor, who had long been an adversary of the Norman dynasty and was therefore happy to help cause trouble in Matilda's homeland.[4]

It is interesting to note that one of the chief chroniclers of the age blamed the unrest not upon Robert the Frisian's overweening ambition but upon the failings of the Flanders regent, Arnulf's mother, Richildis. According to Malmesbury, "she, with a woman's ambition, was forming plans beyond her sex," and had levied an onerous new tax upon her people that incited them to revolt. Robert was merely answering their calls for assistance rather than attempting to seize power for himself.[5] This account owes more to the misogyny of the author than the truth of what occurred, and it reflects the widespread prejudice against female rule that Matilda was forced to overcome. The fact that there were no disparaging remarks about her own regency suggests that she demonstrated exceptional strength and ability.

Matilda was greatly distressed when she heard of the turmoil caused by her brother's treachery and immediately wrote to her husband asking for military assistance. William seemed rather reluctant to intervene in what he viewed as a family dispute, but out of respect for his wife, this time he dispatched William fitzOsbern himself[6]—"the bravest of the Normans"—with a small force (according to one account, just ten Norman knights) to assist the young Count Arnulf.[7] Interestingly, Jumièges—not usually generous in his praise of Matilda—accords her a greater role in the crisis than any of the other sources. He claims that it was she, not William, who sent fitzOsbern to Flanders, and that he was accompanied by "a large army."[8] Such power and independence were unmatched by any other consort's across western Europe.

William's reluctance may have been due in part to the fact that the situation in England was once more volatile and he could ill afford the loss of men and munitions. The latest threat of rebellion came from Edwin of Mercia, who together with his brother Morcar had posed a constant danger to William's regime ever since his victory at Hastings. Edwin had been betrothed to William's eldest daughter in 1067, but the king refused to set a date for the wedding and four years later he reneged on the deal altogether. Orderic blamed the king's change of mind on his "listening to the dishonest counsels of his envious and greedy Norman followers," after which he "withheld the maiden from the noble youth."[9] During the rebellion, which took place in 1071, Edwin was treacherously killed by his own men. They subsequently made their way to court and presented the earl's severed head to William, thinking it would please the king. But the latter was so horrified upon seeing the grisly spectacle that he was moved to tears. Adeliza was said to be devastated upon hearing that yet another engagement had come to nothing. She eschewed all further talk of marriage and entered a nunnery. It is to be hoped that she was not driven to do so by witnessing the sight that had so shocked her battle-worn father.[10]

Meanwhile, William fitzOsbern had journeyed to Flanders "gaily as if to a tournament."[11] He apparently did not take the crisis there as seriously as Matilda did. But help came from another quarter, too. There is little record of Matilda's mother, Adela, since she attended her daughter's wedding at Eu around 1050 and spent some time in the Norman court during her grandson Robert's infancy. If the two women had met or corresponded since then, the evidence has been lost. But this does not necessarily mean that they had not been in contact: the letters of medieval women—even those of high standing—were often lost or destroyed, being considered of no importance next to the deeds of their male counterparts. Adela certainly shared her daughter's horror at the events that were unfolding in Flanders. Even though Robert the Frisian was her son, she abhorred his attempts to overturn the rightful succession and was determined to stop him. Calling upon her family connections, she urged King Philip of France to intervene.

The young French king seemed to hold his aunt in some esteem, for he consented to her request and duly sent troops to Arnulf's aid. However, this was not enough to counter a surprise attack by Robert's forces at Cassel on February 22, 1071. Among the Frisian's troops was Gerbod, the earl of Chester, the man inaccurately described as a son of Matilda by her alleged first marriage. Evidently he considered his loyalty to Robert greater than that to either Arnulf or King William. It was he who struck the killer blow in an encounter with the young Arnulf. William fitzOsbern was also slain in the battle. Matilda's brother won the day and seized control of the principality.

With his forces tied up in England, William had no choice but to accept Robert as the count of Flanders. The French king, too, now washed his hands of the affair. Matilda herself was deeply affected by these recent events, and she would have drawn scant comfort from the fact that her mother had apparently managed to gain a foothold in Robert's court. According to Orderic Vitalis, she was "overwhelmed with grief at . . . the cruelty of her brother, who had brought about the ruin of another brother, a dear nephew, and many friends."[12] Although Robert had made a concession by granting their younger nephew, Baldwin, the territory of Hainault, which had been annexed to Flanders upon the accession of Baldwin VI and Richildis, this did little to offset her bitterness at the treachery of his actions.

As we know, Matilda had always been proud of her heritage, but her brother's usurpation had put a stain on the family name. Moreover, it had destroyed the alliance between Flanders and Normandy. Orderic Vitalis describes the "mutual and lasting hostility" that "arose between the Normans and Flemings, partly because of the slaying of the queen's brother [nephew] and other kinsfolk, but chiefly because of the fate of Earl William fitzOsbern."[13] Thus when Richildis and her surviving son, Baldwin, withdrew to Hainault and attempted to drum up support for recapturing Flanders, William and Matilda both supported their quest.

For his part, Robert the Frisian was openly hostile to Normandy, and as count, he would prove a thorn in William's side for many years to come. He married his daughter Adela to King Cnut of Denmark, one of William's most powerful opponents, and would later assist him in an attempted invasion of England.[14] In the meantime, he made Flanders a refuge for English opponents of William's regime. They included Edgar the Aetheling, who arrived there in 1072. Robert had also formed a dangerous alliance with William's archenemies closer to home. Principal among these was King Philip of France, whose friendship was soon "easily won."[15] To seal their newfound alliance, Philip married Robert's stepdaughter, Bertha of Holland. Matilda's brother further strengthened his connections with Normandy's hostile neighbors by courting the goodwill of Geoffrey Martel, the count of Anjou, and Conan, the duke of Brittany.

According to Orderic Vitalis, the three men "hatched many plots" against William, "but though they hoped for great gain and laid cunning traps they never secured what they desired."[16]

Although the end result was not as she might have wished, the fact that Matilda had been so determined to use her position as regent of Normandy to try to resolve the political turmoil in her native Flanders hints at a strong sense of justice, as well as tenacity and resourcefulness. These were qualities that would increasingly come to the fore during the years that followed. Moreover, during the next few years, Matilda would consistently urge her husband to go on the offensive against her usurper brother, which is perhaps testament to another of her defining qualities: ambition. As Robert's sister—and possibly the oldest of all Baldwin V's children—she had a strong claim to the principality, and she was surely keen to govern Flanders herself. Her esteemed position as duchess of Normandy and queen of England served to strengthen this claim still further. But there was little she could do without her husband's military might. No matter how much William might have wished to satisfy his wife's wishes, his forces were fully engaged in England and Normandy, and he rightly judged that an attempt upon Flanders would overstretch his resources.

However, Matilda's ambitious side would become increasingly apparent in the future, and she would grow ever more independent from her husband as her confidence in her own abilities grew. This latter development would have devastating consequences for both her marriage and the Norman dynasty as a whole.

12

"Matilda, Wealthy and Powerful"

In another attempt to bolster her husband's public image, Matilda returned to England in the spring of 1072 and joined in the celebrations for Easter at the royal court in Winchester. An ecclesiastical council was held there in April—an indication that the royal couple were using it as a base from which to conduct government business. By Whitsun, Matilda had moved to Windsor, which suggests that she was keen to maintain a high profile. However, her tour came to an abrupt end a short while later, when the situation in England again appeared volatile due to a threatened invasion from the Scottish king. She therefore returned to Normandy and was once more appointed coregent with her son Robert—although it was again clear that she held the reins of power.

It did not take William long to neutralize the Scottish threat, using his accustomed strategy of meeting aggression with aggression in order to bring his enemy to terms. He and Malcolm agreed to a truce in the autumn of 1072. "At last, for a while, the storm of wars and rebellions dying out, he [William] now powerfully holds the reins of the entire English monarchy and even more prosperously reigns in glory."[1] Jumièges may have been overstating the case, but the situation in England did appear more settled. After 1072, the frequency of William's journeys home increased dramatically. From that time until his death, he spent around 130 of 170 months in Normandy, which effectively made him an absentee ruler in England.[2] Although there were genuine calls upon his attention in Normandy, such as the revolt of Maine, it was clear that he had a strong preference for his native land.

But though William was often absent from England during the 1070s, it remained vital that he and Matilda continue to reinforce their author- ity there. One of the most powerful expressions of this authority was the court, and Matilda in particular was keen to ensure that they made the most of their increasingly infrequent visits by living in as magnificent a style as possible. Thus her apparently domestic duties as superintendent of feasts, pageants, and the other great gatherings of court were in fact loaded with significance and vital authority.

Nowhere was the magnificence of William and Matilda's court more blatant than at the great "crown-wearings" that were held at regular in- tervals throughout their reign.[3] Although there are some references to Edward the Confessor wearing his crown at certain court festivals, the crown-wearings as a distinct court gathering seem to have been a Nor- man invention, and they soon became integral to William and Matilda's exercise of majesty. There is no record of the order of ceremony that was followed at these occasions, but they probably involved an appear- ance by the royal couple in front of their ordinary subjects as they pro- cessed from the palace to the church. They usually took place at Winchester at Easter, Windsor or Westminster at Whitsun, and Glouces- ter at Christmas.[4] Again, full of pomp and ceremony, they were designed to emphasize William and Matilda's legitimacy as king and queen of England.

The *Anglo-Saxon Chronicle* hints at a sense of the scale and grandeur of the crown-wearings. "All the great men of England were assembled about him: archbishops, bishops, abbots, earls, thanes, and knights."[5] Many of these men would bring a host of attendants of their own, thus swelling the numbers further. There would also often be foreign envoys and visitors, who would be accorded a lavish reception so that they might report back on the splendor of the English king and his court. The wit- ness lists of the charters that were granted during these occasions give a sense of both the number and quality of the attendees. For example, at

the crown-wearing held in Winchester at Easter 1069, a charter for the
abbey of St.-Denis was signed by William, Matilda, one of their sons,
William's two half-brothers, his right-hand man, William fitzOsbern, and
a plethora of archbishops, bishops, and other high-ranking churchmen.[6]

In such charters, Matilda is almost always styled "Regina," and occasionally she is given the more elaborate title of *regina Anglorum et comi-
tissa Normannorum et Cenomannorum* (queen of England and countess of
Normandy and Maine).[7] Her illustrious ancestry is also reinforced in the
numerous bequests made by the great nobles of England, which refer to
prayers and gifts for the souls of the whole royal family.[8] Matilda's inclu-
sion in such bequests, along with that of her sons, suggests that only as
head of his dynasty was William viewed as the rightful king: on his own,
without Matilda's validating presence, he was little more than a bastard
usurper. Combining the pageantry and splendor of the crown-wearings
with the practical business of granting titles and estates gave out a clear
message: the court was the center of power, patronage, and favor, a symbol of the entire kingdom.

Although great occasions such as crown-wearings swelled the ranks
of those paying attendance upon the royal couple, even on ordinary days
their court would have been filled with hundreds of noblemen, ecclesiastics, military men, and visitors. Many of these formed part of William
and Matilda's permanent staff. It was considered essential to royal dignity
that a large body of servants be maintained. "A worldly king has many
thegns and stewards," observed the tenth-century writer Aelfric. "He
cannot be glorious unless he has the dignity which befits him and many
serving men who wait on him in obedience."[9]

The personnel of the royal household reflected the military and ad-
ministrative function of the court. It was more sophisticated than the
ducal household back in Normandy, and had a long-established structure
and officials. The king and queen had their own chapel, which held services, housed the royal relics, and fulfilled some of the couple's secre-
tarial needs. Their household also contained the royal treasure, which
was largely the responsibility of the chamberlain. In theory, this traveled
with the court wherever it went, but by the eleventh century, the palace
at Winchester served as almost a permanent treasury. The contemporary

records also include references to an array of domestics—from cooks and washerwomen to grooms, carpenters, smiths, falconers, swineherds, dog handlers, clerks, and jesters.

Evidence from Domesday Book suggests that the queen had a household of her own that mirrored the structure and functions of the larger one. It could exist either as a separate entity or as part of the overall household. The officials referred to in Domesday Book are for the most part the same as those in the main royal household, with the exception of the queen's personal attendants. They include a chaplain, chamberlain, butler, cooks, goldsmiths, hunters, stewards, and geld collectors.[10] Matilda's own household included a host of male and female servants to meet her every need. Many of them were drawn from high-ranking families in each country, as was customary. It is difficult to ascertain the precise number of men and women who served Matilda, but it is likely to have been in the region of seventy to eighty. This includes both those who served her at court and those who held land for her or worked on her estates. Although little is known of her household in Normandy, this was probably considerably smaller, particularly as the bulk of her landed estates were in England.

The servants of Matilda who are listed in Domesday Book include Humphrey the chamberlain, who was evidently one of the queen's most loyal attendants, because he received a great deal of land in recognition of his royal service. There is also Albold the cook, who held lands in Mapledurham, Hampshire, which had formerly been held by his mistress. It is possible that she bequeathed these to him prior to her death. A reeve named Goscelin farmed some of Matilda's manors in Devon and held land from her in Halberton, near Tiverton. Wulfweard White is listed as another official, and Bernard, the bishop of St. Davids, was her chaplain.[11]

Matilda's presence seemed to have a civilizing influence upon court life when she was in England. As in Normandy, she welcomed men of letters to court, adding to its luster. They included the celebrated poet Godfrey of Winchester. The queen made such an impression upon him when they met that he was inspired to write about her in his epic work, *Epigrammata Historica*.[12]

There was a marked deterioration in standards during Matilda's long sojourns in Normandy. The twelfth-century chronicle of the life of Lanfranc recounts that at one of his crown-wearings, William was seated on his throne, magnificently dressed in gold and jewels, with Lanfranc seated beside him. Upon seeing the king, a jester cried out in mock adulation: "Behold, I see God! Behold, I see God!" William was on the point of laughing at this joke, but the shocked Lanfranc ordered that the man be flogged. William agreed, but if his archbishop had not intervened, he would no doubt have been happy to indulge his jester's blasphemy.[13] It is hard to imagine this incident happening if Matilda, who was widely renowned for her piety, had been present.

There is no doubt that the queen was becoming increasingly and unprecedentedly powerful. In part, this was due to the fact that court life in the eleventh century was intimate, and there was little or no differentiation between public and private spheres of life. As king, William's court—the *curia regis*—in a sense differed little from the *curia ducis* that had surrounded him as duke. The business it considered was identical to that of the ducal court in Normandy, for it was largely concerned with confirmations of land or privilege, and it played a judicial function in the settling of claim disputes. Both were dominated by members of his family—notably his wife and sons—as well as by a select group comprising the chief magnates and churchmen of his realm. And as most of the latter were drawn from Norman families, there was a strong continuity between the two courts. Crucially, the *curia regis* was always held at a royal residence.

In any palace, the Great Hall or "common room" was where the king and his court ate, slept, and governed. This meant that the queen was constantly at his side. Therefore, even though a consort's role was in theory limited to her family and domestic arrangements, in practice this gave her a great deal of influence in what we would today consider the public or political arena. As one recent commentator has observed: "The nature of personal rule ensures that she who has the king's ear may help direct the course of events."[14] Such power was never openly acknowledged, however, and a wise queen would be discreet in employing it—as Matilda herself proved to be.

However, by the early 1070s, Matilda had carved out a more dynamic and visible role for herself in the public affairs of her English kingdom than any of the queen consorts who had gone before her. The constant to-ing and fro-ing between England and Normandy, as well as the considerable travel that she undertook within each domain, might be expected to have taken its toll on the queen, who was by now in her early forties and the mother of at least nine children. But there is no record of her ever failing in her duties on account of sickness, and she seemed to endure the rigors of her position with remarkable fortitude.

The queen was particularly active in the sphere of justice. There are frequent references in Domesday Book to her hearing English legal cases during William's absences, especially those involving disputes over property. The crowds that gathered to support their kinsmen or friends in such disputes were huge, and their numbers were swelled even more by royal officials, sheriffs, underlings, churchmen, jurors, and witnesses. To wield authority over such a gathering would have tested the mettle of the most formidable king or magnate, let alone a mere woman. But Matilda proved more than equal to the task, for she presided over these assemblies time and again, often acting as sole adjudicator. This is one of the clearest testaments to her personal presence and authority, as well as to the respect that her English subjects felt toward her.

One of the most notorious cases involved the abbey of Abingdon, then part of Berkshire but now in the county of Oxfordshire. Like so many others, although it centered on a dispute over property, at its heart lay the ongoing feud between native Englishmen and their Norman oppressors. The case was brought by a royal official named Alfsi who had sought out Matilda at Windsor and complained to her of the violent treatment that he had suffered. Although what it represented was of a very serious nature, the case does have an element of farce about it. Alfsi, who was by all accounts an arrogant and overbearing official, had harassed the local population surrounding the abbey by plundering their woodland and using their oxen to transport lead for the king's use. This so enraged the abbot that he beat the man with a stick, threw the lead to the ground, and returned the oxen to their owners. When Alfsi came back a second time, the abbot once more seized the load that he was carrying and obviously made as if to beat him again, for the terrified man fled on horseback. So desperate was he to escape the furious prelate that he waded across a river, "wet up to his neck," rather than cross the nearby bridge and risk encountering him.

In seeking out Matilda, the royal official was no doubt confident of winning his case, for she had shown no scruple in plundering the abbey herself shortly after her arrival in England, demanding a selection of its finest treasures. But the wily abbot acted swiftly by offering a sum of money to atone for his violent behavior, and Matilda subsequently ordered that there should be no further exploitation of land or goods, either by Alfsi or any other royal official.[15] From a localized squabble, the case was thus transformed into one of enormous national significance. It also proved the apparent lack of Norman bias that Matilda displayed in her role as royal justiciar.

The only women with similar legal authority to Matilda's were to be found on the Continent, in the persons of Beatrice of Lorraine and Matilda of Tuscany, both of whom wielded considerable influence in the judicial sphere. But this had never been the case in England. Neither of Matilda's direct predecessors, Queen Emma or Queen Edith, had had any involvement in the administration of justice. Indeed, both women had found themselves on the receiving end of the law. Edith had been suspected of being involved in the murder of Gospatric, a Northumbrian noble and a rival claimant to the throne. Both she and Emma had also been accused of adultery and had been forced to prove their innocence—in Emma's case perhaps even by ordeal.[16] Matilda had therefore transformed the role of queen consort in England from that of victim of the law to master of it. In doing so, she provided a powerful role model for her successors and descendants—none more so than her daughter Adela, as her later career would prove.

‡ ‡ ‡

Religion was another sphere in which Matilda was actively involved. In April or May 1072, she and her husband cast judgment upon the primacy of the church of York—an issue that struck at the heart of the English church—and they were the only members of the laity present. The case had first been heard during the Easter celebrations at Winchester, and the royal couple, together with numerous other dignitaries, had convened in the royal chapel within the castle.[17] After hearing the case, William and Matilda decreed that the church of York should be subject to the archbishop of Canterbury, Lanfranc, along with the bishoprics of Worcester, Dorchester, and Lichfield—the only ones not to have submitted to the prelate's authority thus far. Lanfranc's supremacy over the entire religious community of England was therefore confirmed.[18]

Besides the vexatious issue of York, Matilda was at the center of other important religious debates of the time in England. For example, she played a part in settling a dispute between the powerful churchmen Bishop Osbern of Exeter and Bishop Giso of Wells, persuading Osbern to return a contested church to his rival.[19] She also independently directed a change in management of the important bishopric of Wells in Somerset, which had formerly been the concern of Queen Edith, informing "the sheriff and all the men of Somerset" that at her request the church of Wedmore was to be transferred to Bishop Giso of Wells.[20] Moreover, in assemblies at the cathedrals of Wells, Exeter and Bury St. Edmunds, and the London church of St.-Martin-le-Grand, she would have been the only lay person present, apart from William, and certainly the only woman.[21]

According to Eadmer, as archbishop of Canterbury Lanfranc "always took great pains both to make the King a faithful servant of God and to renew religion and right living among all classes throughout the whole Kingdom."[22] Both Matilda and her husband were of course actively supportive of this campaign in England and Normandy. The two abbeys that they had founded at Caen—La Trinité and St.-Étienne—had set a new standard for ecclesiastical life across the duchy, and between 1072 and 1076, Lanfranc organized a series of reforming councils to impose the same rules upon the English church as existed in Normandy. These included the outlawing of clerical marriage and simony (the sale of church offices), the latter practice being "detestable" to him, according to Orderic Vitalis.[23] The backing that William gave to these councils was not entirely due to a genuine religious fervor, however, for they were obviously another potentially useful means of forcing the recalcitrant English to adopt Norman ways.

During the early 1070s, Matilda continued to make increasingly generous bequests to the English church, fulfilling the pious and charitable role expected of medieval queens. She was described as "munificent and liberal of her gifts" and "indefatigable at alleviating distress in every shape." It was said that she "frequently relieved the poor with bounteous alms." Her epitaph later claimed that such generosity had "left her in need," but this is unlikely to be true, given the enormous resources at her disposal—and her natural instinct for self-preservation.[24]

Considering this celebrated munificence toward the church, it is perhaps not surprising that Matilda could count some of the most influential ecclesiastics of the day among her acquaintance. Besides Archbishop Lanfranc, they included his protégé Gundulph, a monk from St.-Étienne who came to England after the Conquest and was appointed bishop of Rochester. Gundulph claimed to enjoy a close friendship with Matilda, which had no doubt been forged during his time at her husband's abbey.[25]

Thanks to William's generosity, Matilda owned a considerable amount of land in England, the administration of which formed a constant demand upon her time. She was assisted in this by her viceregal council.[26] The wealth that she had amassed after the Norman Conquest also enabled her to play an active role in patronage. She was particularly generous toward the scores of her countrymen who had come to England in the wake of the Conquest, and she encouraged the artisans among them to teach their trades to the English people. She patronized Flemish architects, sculptors, and painters from her native land, and she promoted poets and chroniclers.[27] The influence of her countrymen was also felt in the religious and political life of England. The tyrannical abbot of Glastonbury, Thurstan of Caen, forced his monks to abandon their English chants and learn "an alien and novel chant from Flemings and Normans."[28] By the early twelfth century, the number of Flemish people in England was so high that they were considered a burden to the state, and Matilda's son Henry was forced to gather them all together "as though into some great midden" and banish them to Wales.[29]

✣ ✣ ✣

The impressive variety of English charters in which Matilda was involved—from founding a market at Tewkesbury to rewarding loyal subjects with estates—attests to her versatility in business matters.[30] As well as granting land and money, she could also appoint officials to manage her estates and local interests. Word of her preeminence soon spread beyond her kingdom. The contemporary biographer of her kinsman, Count Simon of Crépy, referred to her as "The queen of the English, Matilda, wealthy and powerful."[31] Little wonder that she attracted petitioners in her own right, not just because she was the king's consort. This gave her a position of considerable influence and authority at the English court. While she was seen as more diplomatic and benevolent than her fearsome husband, her power and influence earned her a reputation as a formidable woman. One unnamed Englishwoman offered her estate in Surrey to the queen in return for her protection.

It seems undeniable, then, that Matilda had become something of a powerful royal in her own right. Not only did she have the king's ear and the crucial role of managing all royal spectacles, but she was now firmly installed at the heart of legal and religious matters and had established her own enormous independent wealth. Her influence was such that her name became extremely popular among the royalty and aristocracy of France and England, who were keen to flatter her by naming their daughters after her. However, this emerging authority was the cause of some unease among contemporary commentators. Any royal female authority beyond that derived only from being mother of the heirs and mistress of the household was viewed with suspicion by the chroniclers, who were quick to accuse women of witchcraft, scheming, and even murder. Malmesbury's account of Queen Emma's reign is typically scornful. Although he admitted that she was a formidable queen, he was highly critical of the wealth that she accumulated and claimed that she wasted all of it on jewels.[32]

A similar undertone is evident in the accounts that would emerge of Matilda's own reign, both as duchess of Normandy and queen of England. For every account that praised her benevolence to the church or her dignity of bearing, there was another depicting her as a defiant traitor or an insatiable adulterer who was dragged through the streets

naked as a punishment for her sin. The only way that her husband's mi-
sogynistic biographer, Poitiers, could reconcile himself to the degree of
power that Matilda had attained was to describe her as a "woman of
masculine wisdom."[33]

Most chroniclers also felt uneasy about the conflict at the center of a
queen's role; that on the one hand she must be pious and chaste, but on
the other she must be a "fruitful mother."[34] The Virgin Mary was the
ultimate symbol of motherhood and purity, and the chroniclers believed
that royal wives should aspire to her example. Little matter that immacu-
late conception was difficult to come by in most royal marriages. Indeed,
if a queen showed any hint of sexuality, she was immediately condemned
as a wicked seductress. The same was not true of kings, who were expected to take mistresses and would suffer no diminution of their prestige as a result. It is an indication of the general prejudice against women
that only they, not their husbands, could be accused of adultery. Equally,
if a marriage was barren, it was the wife, not the husband, who was to
blame.[35]

Nevertheless, from the mid-eleventh century onward, there were the
beginnings of a profound change in the perception of women in society.
Ladies of high birth became more conspicuous in the contemporary records as owners of titles and estates. Female royals and noble ladies also
emerged as prominent patrons of literature. This literature itself sparked
a new tradition of courtly love that placed women at center stage as the
belles dames sans merci who could bestow or withhold favor as their will
dictated. The idealized view of womanhood and maternity was inspired
by the cult of the Virgin, as well as by developments in theology that
placed much greater emphasis upon the sacred nature of marriage.

The new respect for women that this literature implied harked back
to an earlier time. The famous eighth-century Anglo-Saxon poem Beowulf presents a very positive image of queenship—and of womankind
in general. There are more female characters in Beowulf than in any other
Old English poem. Among them are five queens, all of whom display
what the author considers to be typically feminine virtues of pacifism,
diplomacy, hospitality, and wisdom. The male characters are imprudent
and boorish by comparison, embroiled in incessant wars and military af-

fairs. Despite the various battles that are waged in the story, it is the women, more than the men, who assume heroic status.[36]

If Matilda read this famous poem, she might well have reflected upon the parallels with her own position. As duchess of Normandy, she had already proved that she had an abundance of the feminine virtues described in *Beowulf*, while her husband conformed to the warfaring stereotype of its male characters. The contrast between their characters would become even more marked as their reign in England progressed.

13

A "Wholly Wretched Mother"

In contrast to his previous visits, when William returned to Normandy on a more or less permanent basis in late 1072 or early 1073, he did not spend time with his wife parading the splendor of their court in a series of well-planned public engagements. He had more pressing business. Now that he had achieved a degree of stability in England, he could focus his resources upon reclaiming the province of Maine, which had rebelled against Norman rule three years earlier. Together with a sizable "raiding-army," which included English as well as Norman troops, he launched a blistering attack on the province, employing the same brutal tactics he had used in the north of England. According to the *Anglo-Saxon Chronicle*, it was the English soldiers who caused the most devastation: "[they] greatly despoiled it; they did for vineyards, burned down towns, and greatly despoiled the land, and bent it all into William's hands, and afterwards they turned home to England."[1] By the end of March 1073, the entire county was back under William's authority. According to Eadmer, William was now "so powerful that there was no one in all England, all Normandy, all the Province of Maine who dared lift a finger against his rule."[2]

Even though her husband had returned to Normandy, the fact that he was immediately preoccupied by campaigns to secure its borders meant that Matilda effectively continued to exercise authority as regent. She was formally appointed as such again in early 1074, when William briefly returned to England, and once more around autumn 1075, when a revolt by a dangerous alliance of English earls forced him to endure a more prolonged spell there. This lasted until the following year, during which time Matilda had sole authority to confirm grants on her husband's behalf. This is surprising, given that her son Robert was now in his twenties and was already being referred to as duke in some quarters,[3] and it might have been expected that he would assume the regency. As on previous occasions, he may have shared the title with his mother, but it was clear that she had been appointed to act on his behalf once more, and his power was very much circumscribed by hers. The fact that William had so often chosen his wife over their eldest son as regent of Normandy was due at least as much to his faith in her as to his antipathy toward Robert— an antipathy that would soon have disastrous consequences.

Matilda had done much to earn William's faith, in contrast to his half-brother, Odo, and his late right-hand man, William fitzOsbern, to whom he had entrusted the viceregency of England during most of his visits to Normandy. Odo in particular was motivated more by a desire for self-aggrandizement than by loyalty to his overlord. By the 1080s, he owned land in twenty-two English counties, which gave him an annual income of around £3,000—a staggering sum for the time.[4] Orderic Vitalis describes him as "a second king," whose authority was "greater than all earls and other magnates in the kingdom." The *Anglo-Saxon Chronicle* agrees that he was "the foremost man next to the king," and Eadmer describes his power as "absolute."[5] Although he was a high-ranking churchman, Odo's piety was questionable. "In this man . . . vices were mingled with virtues, but he was more given to worldly affairs than to spiritual contemplation." He did not scruple to plunder the English church for his own gain.[6]

There is evidence to suggest that both Odo and fitzOsbern encouraged cruelty and corruption by the Norman forces. Orderic Vitalis claims that the two men "were so swollen with pride that they would not deign to hear the reasonable plea of the English or give them impartial judgement . . . And so the English groaned aloud for their lost liberty and plotted ceaselessly to find some way of shaking off a yoke that was so intolerable and unaccustomed."[7] The *Anglo-Saxon Chronicle* concurs that Odo and fitzOsbern "distressed the wretched folk."[8] This exacerbated the already fragile relations between the English and their conquerors, and made the former even more ready to rebel. As a result, William was frequently obliged to cut short his stays in Normandy in order to deal with trouble in his new kingdom.

The damage that Odo and fitzOsbern inflicted upon the reputation of the Norman dynasty in England was to some extent repaired by Matilda's benevolent influence. The evidence suggests that she gradually succeeded in persuading her husband to adopt a more conciliatory stance toward his conquered subjects.

It had taken a great deal of patience, however. For the first five years of her queenship, many people had still looked to Edward the Confessor's widow, Edith, as the figurehead of the old regime. A charter written in 1072 reverently described Edith as "the Lady, King Edward's widow" and dismissed Matilda as William's "gebedde" (bedfellow).[9] Although a later document referred to Matilda as "the Lady," even this was rather less a title than she deserved as queen of England.[10]

It was unlikely that Matilda could ever attain the level of popularity enjoyed by an Anglo-Saxon queen such as Edith. But the native population gradually abandoned their initial suspicion toward her. Her natural dignity and apparently mild disposition formed a welcome contrast to her brutal, arrogant husband. And her presence lent a much-needed feminine, civilizing influence to William's court. Whereas William relied upon interpreters, Matilda had apparently mastered English—perhaps as a result of her cosmopolitan upbringing in the Flemish court. Making the effort to speak their language would have greatly endeared her to her subjects, and it was indicative of the respect that she showed them.

Everyone was impressed by the queenly dignity of this diminutive woman. Fulcoius of Beauvais claimed that "the common people, the rich, every gender and age, the whole clergy, every tongue, every class" admired her "just" and "prudent" character.[11] William ruled by force, Matilda by diplomacy. Through her tact and charm, she did more to win over her resentful subjects than the relentless brutality of her husband's campaigns ever could. The fifteenth-century chronicler Thomas Rudborne describes the benign influence that Matilda exerted over her husband: "King William, by the advice of Matilda, treated the English kindly as long as she lived."[12]

A prime example of this concerned the death of the dowager queen Edith in December 1075. William ordered that her remains be conveyed from Winchester to Westminster with great honor so that she might be interred in the abbey next to her husband, King Edward.[13] There, a tomb "lavishly decorated with gold and silver" was erected, and William also paid for a suitably ostentatious funeral.[14] Matilda was much more in tune with the mood of the English people than her husband, and Malmesbury asserts that it was "the same deep feeling" that he cherished for his wife that persuaded William to this uncharacteristic act of kindness.[15] By restoring Edith to a place next to her husband, the king was also seen to be honoring the institution of marriage—something that he and Matilda remained consistently keen to do, given the old doubts over the legitimacy of their own union.

To this end, they had restored good relations with the papacy, and the evidence suggests that this was largely thanks to Matilda's efforts. The previous year, Pope Gregory VII had replied to a letter he had received from her, praising her as a pious wife who had saved her husband from falling into excess. The tone of his correspondence suggests that they were on familiar and affectionate terms. He referred to Matilda as "beloved daughter," and he clearly respected her distinguished pedigree, assuring her: "You who are noble by blood may live the more nobly by virtue, after the custom of saints." He then implored her to use her influence with William to increase his piety. "Be instant with your husband; do not cease from suggesting things profitable for his soul. For it is certain that, if as the Apostle says an unbelieving husband is saved by a believing wife, even a believing husband is increased for the better by a believing wife."[16]

This letter reveals more than just the widespread reputation for piety that Matilda enjoyed. The fact that she was regarded by the Pope as a calming and restraining influence over the king is a hugely significant indication of the power that she now wielded as queen and duchess.

When Pope Gregory wrote again six years later, the content of his letter suggests that he and Matilda had become regular correspondents. As well as exchanging letters, they also used intermediaries to convey oral messages that perhaps related to more confidential or sensitive matters. Gregory's esteem for her had increased during the intervening years, no doubt because she had made many high-profile benefactions to the church. In a letter (now lost) that Matilda had written to him shortly beforehand, she had pledged whatever lands and property the pontiff might desire. "With what love, dearest daughter, we have received this and what gifts we desire from you you may understand thus. For what gold, what gems, what precious things of the world, are more to be looked for by me from you than a chaste life, the distribution of your goods to the poor, and love of God and your neighbour?" He ended by urging Matilda to constantly endeavor to make her husband as pious as she was herself.[17]

Matilda evidently heeded his words, for the sources contain numerous references to her inspiring greater piety in her husband and acting on his behalf when he overlooked his ecclesiastical duties. For example, when her husband missed the dedication ceremony by Lanfranc of his former abbey of Le Bec in 1077, and she herself was prevented from attending owing to "royal preoccupations," she made sure to send a donation so that he did not appear neglectful. According to Jumièges, she also sent a courteous note of apology for her own absence: "Queen Matilda would willingly have been present had not other royal affairs detained her; she was, however, present through the generosity of her gifts."[18]

Similarly, it seems to have been at Matilda's prompting that William relieved the cathedral of St.-Julien in Le Mans of all dues and customs. It is recorded that the king issued a charter, drawn up "with the praise and agreement of queen Matilda," so that they had sufficient funds to repair the damage that William's campaign of 1073 had caused to the cathedral—a clear demonstration of the influence that she now exercised over her husband.[19] Similarly, in 1081, William granted freedom from tolls and customs to the abbey of St. Mary and St. Aldhelm at Malmesbury, "at the request of queen Matilda."[20] In another charter of around the same time, he notified his wife that he had granted the church of Nôtre Dame in Les Pieux to the abbey of Marmoutier, specifying that both the church and the abbey's lands should be free from all customs. The charter ends with the special request that Matilda should "direct Hugolin of Cherbourg to interfere no more therein."[21]

Matilda's influence over her husband was also recognized further down the ecclesiastical hierarchy. Abbot Ingulphus of Croyland Abbey in Lincolnshire expressed his deep gratitude for the many occasions upon which she had used her influence with the king for the good of the abbey, as well as being a generous benefactress in her own right. "My most illustrious lady, queen Matilda . . . had always used her good offices for me with my lord the king, had often relieved me by her alms-deeds, and had very frequently aided me in all matters of business and cases of necessity."[22] It may have been at his orders that a statue was later erected at the abbey in her memory.

✧   ✧   ✧

The satisfaction that Matilda must have derived from her growing influence was soon overshadowed by tragedy in her personal life. The records suggest that the king had taken his second son, Richard, with him to England in the wake of the Conquest, and that the boy had resided there on a more or less permanent basis ever since. This was something that his elder brother Robert had wished for but had so far been denied, and it implies that Richard was more of a favorite with their father. Little is recorded of him in England, so it is not clear whether his stay was continuous or whether he sometimes accompanied his mother or father back to Normandy. Only when tragedy struck do we hear of him again.

Like all Matilda's sons, Richard had been raised to love hunting, and this had become one of his favorite pastimes. The New Forest, a vast area of woodland situated close to the court at Winchester, had been created by his father as a hunting ground by laying waste to scores of dwellings. It was one of the best in the country, and Richard and his younger brothers—together with their father when time permitted—would spend many hours there in the chase. As one contemporary observed: "There he would gladly pass his time, there he rejoiced to hunt for many—certainly months, for of days I say nothing."[23]

But this pleasurable pastime would cost Richard his life. On one of his excursions, he had a riding accident that was so severe that he died from his injuries. Quite how it happened is not certain. Robert of Torigni claims that Richard had been riding at full speed when he had either failed to see, or was too late to avoid, an overhanging bough. This had struck him on the head and he had fallen from his horse. Orderic Vitalis gives a slightly different version of events, describing how Richard was "galloping in pursuit of a wild beast" when he was "badly crushed between a strong hazel branch and the pommel of his saddle, and mortally injured."[24] Meanwhile, in a version of his *Gesta Regum Anglorum,* Malmesbury surmises that the cause of death was either a blow to the neck or that Richard was "hanged by the throat on the branch of a tree when his horse ran underneath it."[25] It is not clear whether he was killed instantly or, as Orderic asserts, died of his injuries a few days later.[26]

The date of this tragic accident is as uncertain as the cause. Accounts vary wildly, with the earliest date cited being 1069 and the latest 1080. Given that Richard was considered to be tragically young when he died, it is likely to have taken place by 1075. Malmesbury and Orderic agree that his death occurred before he had been dubbed a knight, which meant that he would have been less than twenty-two years old—and, given the other evidence, probably around nineteen.[27]

Richard's death was said to be "to the great grief of many"—none more than Matilda.[28] The evidence suggests that she felt the loss keenly, for she ordered that some of her extensive lands, those belonging to a widow named Eadgifu at Edmondsham, Dorset, be freed of geld (a form of taxation) in memory of her second son.[29] Her pious bequests also increased around this time. Among the many ecclesiastical houses to benefit from her generosity was the abbey of St.-Corneille in Compiègne, which received a reliquary decorated with gold and precious stones. Meanwhile, St. Florent in Saumur was given a golden chalice, and Cluny Abbey in Burgundy benefited from a chasuble "that was so rigid because of the metal that it could not be folded."[30] In 1076, Matilda's generous donation funded an extension to the church of Nôtre Dame de Buibray, which had previously been too small to house its congregation.[31]

Although it is typical for laudatory accounts to appear about a person who dies young, in Richard's case they seem to have been justified. Malmesbury describes him as an "elegant boy" with "high ambitions" and claims that his father had great hopes for him—apparently more than for his older brother.[32] He was wise, gentle, and discreet, which formed a marked contrast to the boisterousness and boorishness of his brothers—Robert in particular. He seems to have inherited more of his mother's qualities than his father's, and the affinity between them no doubt intensified her grief. It was said that Matilda had been told of a prophecy that she would lose three sons in the New Forest. Given her belief in mystics and superstitious practices, this would have seemed a dread warning indeed, and she must have been horror-struck when Richard's death appeared to confirm it. Fortunately, she would not live to see the day when the prophecy would be further fulfilled by another of her sons.

Around the time of Richard's death, Matilda's much-betrothed daughter Adeliza was again the subject of marriage negotiations. Little had been heard of her since her betrothal to Edwin of Mercia ended in tragedy in 1071, and it is not certain whether she returned to her mother's household or lived for a time in a nunnery. After three failed betrothals, she would have been forgiven for abandoning any further hope of marriage, but her father had one more candidate in store for her.

In around 1074, Duke William suggested a match between Adeliza and his former protégé, Simon of Crépy, the future count of Amiens, Valois and the Vexin, who had been raised in the ducal court and may also have spent some time with William and Matilda in England.[33] The count's anonymous biographer describes the encounter. Having requested a secret audience with Simon, William told him: "Because I have long since known your faithfulness and love and because I raised you, I wish to increase feelings in you. I have chosen you as the future husband of my daughter who has been asked for in many conversations by the messengers of King Anfurcius of Spain and Robert of Apulia." Although he professed his gratitude, Simon was clearly not keen on the idea, and claimed that the union would be banned by the church because he was related to the girl's mother, Matilda: "My lady the queen, your wife, and I, as they say, are bound by ties of blood and close kinship in such a way that we have to ask wise men their advice if this marriage is at all possible and why." William's response is interesting. Even though he himself had fallen afoul of the laws on consanguinity, he dismissed Simon's concern, telling him that he would ask his ecclesiastical advisers to "look round and search whether a gift of alms or the building of a monastery or anything of that kind deals with this problem legally."[34] For all that he was so often hailed as a pious monarch, William clearly believed that godly sanction could be bought—just as he and Matilda had done by building their abbeys at Caen.

The idea that William offered one of his daughters to Count Simon is supported by the autobiography of Guibert, abbot of Nogent-Sous-Coucy, who asserted that Simon was betrothed to "a young girl of high rank" but subsequently turned his back on the world to become a monk. Upon hearing "that her lover had renounced herself and the world, and not enduring to be considered inferior to him, [the girl] joined the virgin bands that serve God, determined to remain a virgin herself."[35] However, Guibert was reporting this as hearsay, and was writing some years later. The tale is suspiciously similar to the one that, according to Orderic, had unfolded with Alfonso of León seven years before, so it is likely that the accounts became confused—and probably elaborated.

Still, while the evidence is patchy for Adeliza's fate after her final betrothal, it seems likely that this pious young girl did end her days as a nun. Certainly, she could not have died on her way to marry Alfonso around 1067 because of the number of times that her name subsequently appears in the contemporary records. Of all Matilda's daughters, she most closely fits the identity of the girl whom Baudri of Bourgeuil refers to as having joined her for a time at La Trinité.[36] She was probably also the same girl who "made a pious end" at the nunnery of St.-Léger of Préaux.[37]

A compelling piece of evidence has recently been brought to light that supports this view. It is a letter to the young princess from St. Anselm, prior of the neighboring abbey of Le Bec. It seems that upon entering the religious life, Adeliza had written to the famed prelate for spiritual guidance. She asked for a selection of psalms upon which to base her life, and those that Anselm chose for her suggest that she had been in some distress, because they all promote contemplation and peace of mind. The letter that St. Anselm wrote to accompany them also hints at some discord between Adeliza and her parents. Referring to the collection of prayers that he included along with the psalms, he explained that two of them in particular, relating to St. Stephen and Mary Magdalene, were aimed at transforming feelings of hatred into love.[38]

After so many failed betrothals, Adeliza would have been justified in harboring some resentment against her parents, who had apparently shown scant regard for her feelings as they moved from one potential suitor to the next in their quest for political gain. She may also have blamed herself for the fact that each betrothal had come to nothing, believing that this was a punishment from God for her sinful life—hence the need to atone by entering a nunnery. Although he sought to heal the rift between Adeliza and her parents, St. Anselm could not disguise his distaste for William's violent profession, for he praised the girl's life as being nobler than that of her father. He seemed to imply that Adeliza should not blame herself for her sorry fate.[39]

The date of Adeliza's death is not recorded, but the sources imply that she was still very young—"of marriageable age," according to Orderic.[40] The letter from St. Anselm was written while he was still prior of Le Bec, which dates it to 1078 or earlier. This means that Adeliza was probably in her early twenties at most. Bayeux and La Trinité are both cited as her place of burial, even though she was probably not serving at either when she died.[41] Despite suffering so many tragedies during her short life, her faith remained unshaken to the end. Malmesbury claims that "after her death the callus found on her knees bore witness to her constancy in prayer."[42]

Whatever the date or location of her death, the loss of Adeliza must have grieved Matilda sorely, especially if she, like her brother Richard, died young. The idea that the girl had been wretched at the seemingly relentless string of failed betrothals, for which she had harbored increasing resentment against her parents, would have aggravated her mother's sorrow. But one of Matilda's other daughters assuaged her grief. Cecilia had apparently flourished in the cloistered world of her mother's abbey at Caen, and at Easter 1075 she was ordained as a nun by Archbishop John of Rouen. Both William and Matilda were present for the lavish celebrations that accompanied the ceremony, and they would no doubt have looked on with great pride as their daughter took her final vows. It had been almost nine years since Cecilia had entered La Trinité as a novice, which was an unusually long period of training. It is possible that William and Matilda arranged that she should not become a fully ordained nun until their other daughters—who were all destined for political marriages—had survived the perilous years of childhood.

The poet Fulcolus of Beauvais wrote a poem in honor of the occasion, comparing William with the biblical hero Jephthah, an illegitimate son who triumphed over his enemies and offered his daughter to God as a sacrifice before the battle. One of the lines implies that Matilda had felt the loss more keenly than her husband, and that her grief was still raw nine years later, for the girl declares: "I am the only daughter of my father and my wholly wretched mother."[43] Although Cecilia was not the only surviving daughter, this declaration would have been consistent with the closeness that seemed to exist between the duchess and her daughters, over whose upbringing she had taken such assiduous care. It is not known how often—if at all—Matilda had seen Cecilia during the intervening years, but it cannot have been as often as she would have liked, as a result of both her own and her daughter's obligations.

✢ ✢ ✢

Despite the turmoil and tragedy of her family life during the middle years of the 1070s, for Matilda it was still a case of business as usual. For example, the queen's name can be found on a charter that was signed shortly after, if not actually at, the ceremony for Cecilia's dedication.[44] It seems, then, that if Matilda felt any resentment toward William for the loss—in different ways—of her daughters, she did not let it interfere with her official duties. This suggests a certain hardness to her character, a pragmatism honed from her years at the heart of Normandy's political affairs. These qualities may not have made her the most tender of mothers, but they did equip her well to deal with the duties expected of her as William's consort. Besides, another of her daughters provided her with ample consolation. Adela, who at the time of her siblings' deaths would have been about ten or eleven years old, had grown into a remarkably intelligent and precocious young woman. Despite the pressures of Matilda's political role in Normandy and England, she had taken the same care over Adela's education as she had that of her other daughters, and the girl was probably educated for a time at the abbey of La Trinité in Caen, along with Cecilia.

Adela responded to her studies with enthusiasm. Recognizing her daughter's ability, Matilda encouraged her learning by advising her that academic prowess was one arena in which women could surpass men—a lesson that she herself had learned as a child. Adela took this to heart and would grow up to become a noted literary patron, something that few women could lay claim to in that age. Her talents would be widely praised by contemporary writers and intellectuals. Baudri de Bourgueil,

Archbishop of Dol, enthused: "She surpasses her father in her apprecia-
tion of poetry and her knowledge of books. She rewards the merits of
poets, she has critical judgment, and she has her own store of songs and
poems to dictate."[45] Others noted her accomplishments, and she would
receive letters, poems, and dedications from various celebrated intellectuals during her lifetime, including St. Anselm and Hugues de Fleury.

However, the pride that Matilda took in her youngest daughter was
soon to be overshadowed by a dramatic turn of events concerning her
eldest son. These events would shatter the unity not just of her marriage,
but of the entire ducal family.

14

"A Faithless Wife"

For the first twenty five years of her marriage, Matilda had been a model wife. Loyal, steadfast, and wise, she had proved an exceptionally capable regent and consort, enabling William to both consolidate his victory in England and maintain his hold over Normandy. United by matrimony and ambition, theirs seemed to be an invincible partnership. As one contemporary observed: "The queen adorned the king, the king the queen."[1]

But toward the end of the 1070s, free at last from the unrelenting cycle of childbirth, Matilda began to display the independence of spirit that had caused such ructions with her husband in the very earliest days of their courtship. It would transform her from model wife and consort into one of William's deadliest enemies.

Around this time, rumors began to circulate that her husband was looking elsewhere for sexual gratification. Perhaps Matilda, who was by now in her mid- to late forties, had begun to lose her famed beauty. The many pregnancies and births that she had endured must also have taken their toll on her body. Some of the rumors can be easily dismissed, however. For example, William was said to have fathered two sons outside his marriage: Thomas of Bayeux, Archbishop of York, and William Peverel. Both stories stem from local tradition, and neither has any basis in fact. Thomas of Bayeux was of the right age to have been William's son and was close enough to him to write the epitaph for his tomb, but there is nothing else to support the theory. Neither is there a case for believing that William Peverel, mentioned in Domesday Book, was a natural son of the Conqueror. The only reference to it is in an account by the seventeenth-century antiquarian William Dugdale.[2] It is possible that he consulted sources that have since been lost, but the fact that a tale of such significance is not mentioned by any of the major chroniclers of the period makes it dubious in the extreme. Neither is there any reliable evidence to support the rumor that William had a bastard daughter, who later married Hugh du Château-sur-Loire.[3]

The eighteenth-century novelist known as the Abbé Prévost was responsible for some of the other aspersions as to William's fidelity. He confidently asserted that when William's marriage began to grow stale, he *"se mit à garçailler"* (took up wenching). Although he based his account upon references in the contemporary sources, some of his tales were almost certainly of his own invention. There is, for example, one particularly winding story, which not only questions William's uxorious qualities, but also casts Matilda as a jealous, retributive spouse. The tale goes that one day, while hunting in the forest of Pont-Audemer, which lay in the heart of Normandy, William encountered two pretty young novices from the abbey of Préaux. The girls had been placed in the convent against their will and were making their escape. They were greatly alarmed when they saw the duke, but he allayed their fears and escorted them to one of his hunting lodges in the forest of Lyons. Although he assured them that they would be safe from harm, he confided to his men that he intended having his way with "one of the two or perhaps the two together." But such was William's respect for his wife that by the time he returned the following day, his conscience had gotten the better of him and he decided instead to find husbands for the girls.

In the meantime, word had reached Matilda that under the pretext of going hunting, her husband was meeting two mistresses in secret every morning in the forest. In a fit of jealous rage, she sent an armed guard to drag the girls from their secret hiding place and bring them to her. But her husband intercepted the men on his way back from seeing the young novices and, suspicious of their intentions, killed three of them and put the rest to flight. He was shocked to discover afterward that they had been sent by his wife.

When the duke returned to court, he sought out Matilda and assured her that it had all been a misunderstanding. Far from having any adulterous intent, he had merely been concerned for the girls' welfare. Meanwhile, he secretly arranged marriages for them. But the young girls would have been better advised to stay at Préaux, for both of them died within a year of their wedding. Upon hearing this, the duke immediately suspected that his wife had ordered their deaths, and as a punishment he had her dragged through the streets of Caen by the tail of a horse.[4]

This story is of course typical of the salacious novels of the eighteenth century, and it has only the barest relation to the known facts. William did have connections with the abbey of Préaux through his daughter Adeliza, but nothing else about the tale rings true. Indeed, from the point of logistics alone, it would have been impossible, because the locations that Abbé Prévost mentions are too far-flung for the protagonists to have visited on foot. Moreover, the ending is identical to that other scandalous rumor about William and Matilda's marriage—when the duke returned to Normandy after the conquest of England to discover that his wife had been unfaithful—which in itself is suspicious.

Rather more intriguing is a persistent rumor that resulted from malicious gossip by the wife of Hugh of Grantmesnil, an influential Norman nobleman whom William had appointed governor of Winchester. This lady had "conceived a particular ill-will against her sovereign" and therefore determined to cause trouble for him in Normandy.[5] She began by circulating reports among the wives of absent Norman nobles that their husbands were being unfaithful during their long sojourns in England. This caused such a furor that many of the husbands in question were obliged to return home and defend themselves, thus creating a void in the government of England.

Lady Grantmesnil then turned on William directly, claiming that the king had tried to seduce her. This story was seized upon by Gytha, mother of the late King Harold, who then sent word of it to the king of Denmark—but not before she had added an embellishment of her own. According to her version of events, William had also tried to seduce the daughter of one of the canons of Canterbury Cathedral. The young girl in question was the niece of a Kentish nobleman named Merleswen, who joined a rebellion (possibly the Kent rebellion of 1067) against the king upon hearing of it.[6]

Such rumors were prevalent, and William of Malmesbury could not resist including some of them in his twelfth-century history of the English kings. No doubt anxious to safeguard his credibility as a chronicler, he derided the "scandal-mongers" who had circulated such stories to begin with, but he repeated them with such relish that he was little better than they. He related the claims that William had "abandoned his early continence when royal power came to him." The tale that seems to have fired Malmesbury's imagination the most was that of Merleswen's niece. He told how William had "wallowed in the embraces" of the sixteen-year-old daughter of a priest, and recounted that when Matilda found out, she was so enraged that she "sent her packing."[7] According to his account, the queen then exacted a terrible revenge by having the girl hamstrung—an appallingly cruel practice that involved crippling the victim by cutting the tendons of their legs. The tortures that Matilda was said to have inflicted upon the poor girl grew more grisly with time. A later history of William's reign claimed that she had ordered her jaws to be slit. This scandalous story was in turn surpassed by the thirteenth-century chronicler Robert of Gloucester, who told how "the priest's daughter was privily slain by a confidential servant of Matilda, the queen." To such rumors is added the even more outlandish claim "that the Conqueror was so enraged at the barbarous revenge taken by his consort, that, on his return to Normandy, he beat her with his bridle so severely, that she soon after died."[8] He subsequently sent the offending servant into exile.

The idea that Matilda was murdered by her husband is entirely false: her death occurred some years later and is well attested by the sources. Neither is there much reliable evidence to support the rest of Lady Grantmesnil's story. Her slander, and that of Harold's mother, was referred to only in sources considerably later than the period in which it was supposed to have happened. None of the contemporary records mention it: indeed, they consistently praise William's fidelity. Malmesbury himself admitted that the story was "lunacy."[9] Even if the king had forsaken his marriage vows, it is unlikely that a woman of Matilda's dignity and restraint would so far forget herself as to murder a mistress.

It is interesting, though, that both this and the rumor of Matilda's actions toward Brihtric depict her as a ruthless, vengeful queen, capable of inflicting untold cruelty upon any who crossed her. Even if she was innocent of both crimes, it is possible that the chroniclers may have used these stories as a device to portray a darker side to her character.[10]

✦   ✦   ✦

Despite the rumors, and the undercurrents they might suggest, as the 1070s wore on, Matilda was still performing her role with customary aplomb. As usual, whenever an opportunity presented itself for the ducal couple to reinforce their supremacy, she made sure that they took it. They presided at the dedication ceremonies of three magnificent new churches in 1077, including St.-Évreux and William's newly completed abbey of St.-Etienne.[11] According to Orderic Vitalis, the latter ceremony attracted "an immense multitude of people" and the duke was "puffed up with worldly pride."[12] Arguably the greatest of these occasions, though, took place in July that year, when Matilda joined her husband at the head of the galaxy of notables from both sides of the Channel who attended the consecration of Odo's new cathedral at Bayeux. It was a truly dazzling occasion. A man of extravagant tastes, William's half-brother had not stinted in his creation. Towering columns and exquisite monumental carvings made it one of the most magnificent buildings that western Europe had ever seen. With the queen at the height of her powers, this should have been one of the proudest moments of her life. Among the assembled dignitaries were two of her surviving sons, Robert and William.

Although Matilda had dominated her eldest son during their period as coregents of the duchy, it was still expected that he would one day come into his full inheritance. His status as heir was formally acknowledged on at least two further occasions before 1078, and there is evidence to suggest that he was already being styled "duke" or "count" in some quarters well before his father's death.[13] Indeed, William allowed his eldest son to witness charters as "Count Robert" or "Robert Count of the Normans," which might have been meant to appease him lest he grow impatient to take hold of the duchy.[14]

While his titles might for the present have been empty of authority, Robert had little cause to complain. Indeed, he was able to enjoy considerable personal independence during the late 1060s and early 1070s, a period that coincided with his most impressionable teenage years. However, he had built up a military household that included the younger sons of some of the most powerful Norman families. This following, which was described as "a swarm of obsequious sycophants," flattered his vanity and encouraged the more rebellious aspects of his nature.[15]

Moreover, free from the shackles of his father's overbearing authority, Robert was indulging in a life of excess. His court became notorious for dissolution and debauchery, as etiquette and ceremonials gave way to pleasure and lasciviousness. As well as jesters and other entertainers, his entourage included prostitutes of both sexes. Orderic Vitalis decried the loose morals that existed in Robert's court and criticized his followers for their effeminate appearance. Their long hair and extravagant clothes contrasted sharply with the clipped military style of the Conqueror's entourage.[16]

Even though Orderic was fond of harking back to an idealized past, the number of references to Robert's decadent lifestyle suggests that the criticism was at least partly justified. He lavished enormous sums on keeping himself and his courtiers entertained and was said to always accede to requests for money from his "foolish companions."[17] This implies a gullible, easily led side to his nature, which would have fatal consequences in the years to come.

There are also particular stories that hint at Robert's licentious behavior. Among them is an account that tells of a woman who arrived at court one day claiming that she had two bastard sons by him. Robert denied this, but when she continued to press her claim, it was decided that she should prove her case by ordeal. If she was willing to undertake the challenge of holding a red-hot iron with her bare hands and abide by her story even while suffering the intense pain that it involved, then it must be true. The woman duly did so, and was judged to be in the right. Robert was forced to acknowledge that the boys were his, and they were subsequently brought up at court.[18]

By the time William returned to Normandy in 1072, Robert had developed a dangerous streak of arrogance, together with an overblown sense of his own status and authority. Realizing this, his father was determined to slap him down. Far from involving his eldest son in matters of government as a means of preparing him for the task that lay ahead, William determined to keep him from enjoying any real authority in either Normandy or Maine. As Jumièges observes: "The cause of their disagreement was that King William did not allow his son to act according to his own free will in matters concerning the duchy of Normandy, even though he had appointed him as his heir."[19] Robert would inherit upon his father's death, but not before. In the meantime, the only useful function he could serve was as a member of William's military entourage. Robert bitterly resented this, and by the time of the Bayeux consecration in 1077, simmering resentment had turned into open hostility. During one heated exchange, Robert even accused William of treating him like a hired soldier.[20]

That there was tension between William and his eldest son was neither surprising nor unusual. Some of the most vicious conflicts in history have involved an heir impatient for power and a father reluctant to give him any. In Robert and William's case, this friction was heightened by personal antipathy. William had long felt an aversion toward his eldest son, as suggested by the derogatory nickname of "Curthose" that he had coined. This must have rankled with Robert, who was desperate to assert himself as a man to be reckoned with, rather than—as his father seemed to think—a boy to be made fun of.

By contrast, Robert's two surviving younger brothers were "blessed and favoured" by their father.[21] The nine-year-old Henry had been accorded a much higher standard of education than any of his brothers. Meanwhile, by 1077, William Rufus, who was in his late teens, had already been allowed to grant many charters on the duke's behalf. He had perhaps done more to earn this privilege than Robert, for he is portrayed in the contemporary sources as a loyal and compliant son, "always obedient, displaying himself in battle before his [Duke William's] eyes, and walking by his side in peacetime."[22] Such obvious favoritism must have caused Robert considerable annoyance.

The image of Robert that emerges from most of the contemporary sources appears to justify his father's dislike. Moreover, his father's nickname for him seems appropriate: his appearance reflected the rather indulgent lifestyle he enjoyed. As well as being short, he was also rather stocky, and Malmesbury describes him as "pot-bellied."[23] Orderic Vitalis agrees that he was "short and stout," and he was often derided as "Gambaron" (fat legs). He goes on to paint him as an ungrateful child who spurned the opportunities his father had given him, and refers to him as a "proud and foolish fellow" who was "reckless" and "extravagant."[24]

But Orderic was writing with the benefit of hindsight; knowing that Robert's life would end in failure made him exaggerate the deficiencies of his character. By contrast, Jumièges, whose account was compiled in the early 1070s, described him as "brilliantly shining in the blossoming flower of his handsome body and his advantageous age" and added the hopeful prediction "may he, with his noble virtue and his name follow the example of his great ancestors in famous works which we hope to describe in many pages."[25] Even Malmesbury concedes that apart from Robert's small stature, "there was nothing to criticise, for he was neither unattractive in feature nor unready in speech, nor feeble in courage nor weak in counsel."[26] Indeed, Orderic Vitalis at least concedes that he was "talkative . . . with a clear, cheerful voice and a fluent tongue."[27]

It appears, then, that Robert was a complex character: indulged, impetuous, and easily led, he was also gregarious, generous, and brave. All these qualities would have made him popular with the aristocracy—particularly its younger members, many of whom were tired of William's puritanical, avaricious, and overbearing ways. Orderic Vitalis describes the men who joined Robert's circle as being "of noble birth and knightly prowess, men of diabolical pride and ferocity terrible to their neighbours, always far too ready to plunge into acts of lawlessness."[28] They included William fitzOsbern's son and successor, William de Breteuil; Roger, son of Richard fitzGilbert; and Robert of Bellême, the son of William and Matilda's chief adviser, Roger de Montgomery. Robert had therefore effectively established a rival court to his father's, filled with members of the new generation eager to oust the old.

The fact that there was such a marked difference in the temperaments of Robert and his father exacerbated the tension that existed between them. But in one trait the two men were united, and that was their military expertise. Malmesbury asserts that by his early teens, Robert was "already a young man of established prowess ... his courage was proven."[29] William acknowledged his son's ability, and it may well have been the only compliment he ever paid him. Ironically, the one quality that the duke admired in Robert would almost cost him his own life.

Matilda's relationship with her firstborn son formed a dramatic contrast to William's. From the moment of his birth, she doted upon him. Disregarding the flaws in his character and behavior, she looked with fond maternal pride upon his qualities and skills. The fact that in appearance he was very much his mother's son may have strengthened the bond between them. The diminutive stature that his father so derided was probably inherited from her, and his handsome looks and engaging manners also owed more to Matilda than to William. It may have been at least partly due to his mother's indulgence that Robert was able to enjoy such license during the years that his father was in England. If she disapproved of the debauchery and other vices that were reported to her, then she either thought them exaggerated or chose not to act. Certainly her authority as regent on her son's behalf would have enabled her to curb his excesses if she had wished to.

The tenderness that Matilda showed toward Robert indicates a side of her character that had apparently been repressed in her marriage to William, for the qualities that had marked her actions during these years were all somewhat devoid of emotion. Duty, tact, wisdom, and political guile made her an ideal consort, and her husband had been grateful for it, but she had apparently acted with her head rather than her heart. Where Robert was concerned, the reverse was true. Here we see flashes of the rashness and passion that had incited her as a young woman to offer herself in marriage to a Saxon lord and then spurn the advances of the young duke of Normandy. From the late 1070s, it was feelings such as these, rather than her accustomed shrewdness, that would dictate Matilda's actions.

✢   ✢   ✢

In 1077, the first stirrings of serious trouble were felt in William's family. Now in his fiftieth year, the duke's character was firmly set. Determination and strength of will had hardened into intolerance and ruthlessness. He was used to getting his own way and hated the unexpected. Up until now, he had controlled his family as he controlled his domains. In contrast to his recalcitrant subjects in England or his overmighty nobles in Normandy, they had been for the most part compliant. Matilda had set the example for their children with her loyalty and conscientiousness, and William might confidently have expected to see out his days surrounded by a submissive and obedient brood.

However, the disregard that William showed for his eldest son blinded him to the seriousness of his resentment. The duke neither cared about nor respected Robert's wishes with regard to his inheritance. The young man's followers, eager to share in his glory, encouraged him to press for control of the duchy while his father was still alive. They also stoked his resentment against William by claiming that he was forced to live "in wretched poverty" because "your father's minions guard the royal treasure so closely that you can scarcely have a penny from it to give to any of your dependents."[30] Robert, "filled with the hot blood of youth" and "the fatal advice of his comrades," was all too easily fired up by their self-seeking arguments.[31] He therefore sought an audience with his father and begged him to let him assume the title of duke at once so that he might prove his ability to rule. Assuring his father that he was not prepared to be his "hireling" any longer, he continued: "I ask you therefore to grant me legal control of the duchy, so that, just as you rule over the kingdom of England, I, under you, may rule over the duchy of Normandy."[32] He also demanded possession of the county of Maine, which had been promised to him for some time.

Robert was at least partly justified in expecting his requests to be granted: after all, his father was now king of a new domain—one that had required all his energies ever since he had conquered it eleven years previously. But his proposal elicited a furious response from William, who thundered: "It is not to be borne that he who owes his existence to me should aspire to be my rival in mine own dominions." Determined to humiliate his upstart son, he laughed at him for thinking that he was capable of leading the duchy, "driving the young man away with jeers in that terrific voice of his."[33] Robert stormed from the room "in a passion," his mind set upon revenge.[34] If his father would not give him the duchy, then he would take it by force.

Such was William's scorn for his son that, far from taking this encounter as a warning, he apparently dismissed it from his mind. The idea that he should hand over his duchy to him now was ludicrous. It was bad enough that as his eldest son he would one day inherit it. As William himself once said: "Let no one doubt this for a moment: as long as I live I will surrender my duchy to no one, and will allow no living man to share my kingdom with me."[35]

Things came to a head in late 1077 or early 1078, when the ducal family was staying at L'Aigle on the southern border of Normandy.[36] William was there on military business, preparing an assault against the recalcitrant lords of the Corbonnais with the assistance of his eldest son and his followers. Robert, however, had chosen to stay in the house of one Roger Cauchois rather than with his own family, who were lodging with a nobleman named Gunher. It is hard to imagine that the castle was not large enough to house the whole of the duke's family, so this was probably an act of defiance on Robert's part.

Orderic Vitalis describes the events that unfolded in seductively dramatic detail.[37] According to his account, Robert's younger brothers, William and Henry, went to visit him there, accompanied by the group of rowdy young warriors whose company they often kept. Given the uneasy relations between the brothers, it is likely that this visit was paid out of mischief rather than courtesy. Robert stayed out of their way, preferring to remain outside with his companions. William and Henry, however, went into the upper rooms of Cauchois' house, which were reserved for the family and important guests, and began to play dice. Their game soon got out of hand, and their wild antics disturbed the peace of the entire household—and no doubt the surrounding dwellings. Keen to goad their brother into a fight, they threw fetid water or urine onto him and his party below.

Robert was outraged. All the resentment he felt toward these young upstarts came spilling out. His fury was stoked by his companions, who told him that he ought not to tolerate such unruly behavior from his younger brothers and added that their occupation of the upper floor was symbolic of their superior place in his father's favor. "Don't you see what this means?" they urged. "Even a blind man could. Unless you punish this insult without delay it will be all over with you: you will never be able to hold up your head again." Intent upon avenging the insult, Robert tore off upstairs in a "towering rage."[38] A furious row ensued with his brothers. The commotion became so loud that somebody must have raised the alarm, for shortly afterward the duke himself arrived to break it up.

An uneasy filial truce followed, but Robert was by no means appeased. The following night, he and his entourage deserted William's army and stole away from the town. They rode northward to Rouen and attempted to take the castle there by surprise. This was nothing short of treason. Robert's intention was now clearly to wrest control of the duchy from his father by force. However, this attempt on Rouen was foiled by the vigilant castellan, Roger of Ivry, and Robert had little choice but to hurriedly flee Normandy with his followers.[39]

Roger of Ivry immediately sent word to the duke. According to Orderic Vitalis, William "flew into a terrible rage, and ordered all the conspirators to be seized."[40] Malmesbury presents a rather different version of events, claiming that when the duke heard the news, he merely scoffed: "By God's resurrection! He'll be a hero, will our Robin Curthose!"[41] Given the scorn he had always showed toward his eldest son, this is easy to believe. But William would soon have cause to regret his words.

Indeed, Robert had in fact assembled a group of notable allies. Besides the sons of William's leading nobles, who continued to follow his cause in the hope of personal gain, there were followers drawn from within the establishment. For example, William's half-brother Odo, who was at this time regent of England, was rumored to have lent a sympathetic ear to his nephew's complaints. Ever on the lookout for an opportunity to augment his power, Odo surely realized that a division between William and his heir apparent could turn to his own advantage.

Robert also sought the help of his uncle, Count Robert of Flanders. Though Matilda had waged war against her brother when he had usurped the rightful succession, the count now proved a willing ally to her son. He was already one of Duke William's most troublesome enemies, and like King Philip, he was keen to exploit any political weakness in Normandy. Robert went to visit his kinsman in Flanders to secure his support and was delighted when it was swiftly given, for now he could potentially invade Normandy from two of its major frontiers.

News of Robert's rebellion spread rapidly to England. The *Anglo-Saxon Chronicle* notes: "Robert, the son of King William, ran from his father to his uncle Robert in Flanders, because his father would not let him govern his earldom in Normandy which he himself and also the king Philip with his consent had given him; and the best who were in the land had sworn with oaths and taken him as lord."[42] This overstated the case and was perhaps wishful thinking on the part of the author. Despite trawling the courts of Europe—including Germany, Aquitaine, and Gascony—Robert received fair words but no firm promises. According to Orderic, any financial support he did receive was soon "recklessly squandered" on "jongleurs and parasites and courtesans."[43] But help was soon to arrive from an altogether unexpected source.

⁜　⁜　⁜

Exactly what Matilda felt upon hearing that her beloved son had sought the assistance of her relatives can only be imagined. She would already have been grieved at his self-enforced exile, and extremely fearful for his safety if he should launch an attack. Perhaps she regretted not having curbed his waywardness when she had the chance. Now it was too late. Robert's actions had pitted her son and her natal family against her husband. It was a severe case of divided loyalties.

Although society dictated that Matilda should support her husband, it was not as simple as that. Where Robert was concerned, the strength of the maternal bond was greater than her sense of duty and pragmatism. She adored her eldest son and felt a mother's natural protectiveness toward him. By contrast, the feelings that she had toward William seemed more about duty than love. It is also possible that Matilda empathized with Robert's plight. She, too, had had to endure her husband's overbearing nature and implacable will, which grated against her own tact, learning, and ambition, so she would perhaps have understood the frustration her son experienced at being denied his inheritance. What was more, the prospect of having Robert, rather than her husband, as duke of Normandy might well have held an appeal of its own. It would have increased her own influence, given the power dynamic between mother and son established during the various regencies. Even if Robert had wished to gain a greater measure of authority, the closeness of their relationship meant that she would always be guaranteed a share of his power. The dramatic events that unfolded shortly afterward support the idea that her loyalties lay firmly with her son.

Matilda certainly remained in contact with Robert during his exile, and the evidence suggests that she exchanged secret messages with him via trusted servants.[44] The fact that he resided in her native land for a time no doubt made this easier than it would otherwise have been. From this contact, she got to know where her son was and what his plans were, with regard to Normandy. If she tried to persuade him against an invasion, there is no record of it. Instead, she took a step that would shock her contemporaries and tear her family apart: she sent him money to fund the enterprise. According to Orderic Vitalis, she "often used to send him [Robert] large sums of silver and gold and other valuables without the king's knowledge."[45] Although both Orderic and Malmesbury claim that she diverted revenues from the royal estate in order to supply her son with a troop of soldiers, it seems more likely that she used money from her own resources.[46] This would have enabled her to act with the necessary secrecy.

After a quarter of a century of playing the dutiful wife and consort, Matilda had at last shown her true colors. Her loyalty to her husband had crumbled in the face of the love she felt toward her wayward son. The latter had reignited her long-dormant willfulness and passion—and her ambition. William's more permanent presence in Normandy had inevitably lessened the autonomy she enjoyed as regent, and now Robert's rebellion presented her with the chance to carve out a powerful new role for herself. Who knew what authority she might enjoy as the much-beloved mother of the new duke? And if Robert succeeded in wresting control of the duchy, then England might follow. It was treason, but—in Matilda's eyes—it was worth it. Setting aside her accustomed caution, she threw herself behind Robert's cause.

A rebellious son and heir was troublesome but not exceptional; a rebellious wife was deeply shocking in an age when any degree of female independence was problematic. Moreover, there was the deep-seated belief that queens should be responsible for family unity, which was in itself crucial to the successful government of medieval states. The sources are full of familiar idealized images of consorts presiding benevolently over their loving sons, daughters, and husbands. Among them was Matilda's namesake, the wife of Henry I, king of the Germans, who in the previous century took pride of place at a family reunion: "All the royal progeny of either sex gather, brought together by divine mercy and in love at seeing one another . . . and that renowned mother queen Mathilda, rejoicing in the birth of such great children, was received in great honour."[47] But it seems Matilda was tired of bowing to social convention. She had decided to follow her own inclinations.

In the spy-ridden world of the Norman court, it was inevitable that Matilda's treachery would soon be found out.[48] When William heard that his wife had been secretly supporting his upstart son, he was furious and ordered her, "in a passion, never to do such a thing again."[49] Such leniency was surprising, given that Matilda had committed treason, and it no doubt owed much to the strength of his feelings for her. Still, a nineteenth-century account claims that he "flung her from her horse in one of the principal streets of Caen"—although this is not substantiated by any of the contemporary chroniclers.[50]

Matilda's reaction to being upbraided by her husband is not recorded, but it is likely that she vowed not to send any more money to her son—even if she had no intention of keeping this promise. However, the fact that she had so easily escaped punishment seems to have given her confidence, because just a short while later, she was discovered to have "recklessly renewed her offence."[51] In so doing, she had placed both herself and those closest to her in great danger. William was now beside himself with fury that his formerly dutiful wife should betray him so soon after her last transgression. Worse still, she had repeated exactly the same treachery. If he needed any more proof of the superior place his despised son held in her affections, he now had it.

Matilda's younger sons, William Rufus and Henry, may have stirred up their father's anger. They were probably jealous of the obvious favor that their mother showed toward Robert, and the incident at L'Aigle proves that they were capable of spiteful and vindictive scheming. But the duke needed little encouragement. Determined to punish Matilda, he resolved upon humiliating her in front of the entire court. "How very true here and now is the maxim of a certain sage, 'A faithless wife brings ruin to the state,' " he railed. "After this who in this world shall ever find himself a trustworthy helpmate? The wife of my bosom, whom I love as my own soul, whom I have set over my whole kingdom and entrusted with all authority and riches, this wife, I say, supports the enemies who plot against my life, enriches them with my money, zealously arms and succours and strengthens them to my grave peril."[52]

Retaining her composure, Matilda sank to her knees in front of her husband and pleaded for forgiveness—both for herself and for their son. Her words were recorded by one of the leading chroniclers of the time—apparently verbatim:

O my lord, do not wonder that I love my first-born child with tender affection. By the power of the Most High, if my son Robert were dead and buried seven feet deep in the earth, hid from the eyes of the living, and I could bring him back to life with my own blood, I would shed my life-blood for him and suffer more anguish for his sake than, weak woman that I am, I dare to promise. How do you imagine that I can find any joy in possessing great wealth if I allow my son to be burdened by dire poverty? May I never be guilty of such hardness of heart; all your power gives you no right to demand this of me.[53]

This is the only surviving record of the words that Matilda spoke, and it therefore gives us an invaluable insight into her character and state of mind at this time. Even if there are inaccuracies in the account, it still conveys a sense of the fierce love and protectiveness that she felt toward her firstborn son and the desperation with which she pleaded for his life. It portrays her as a woman capable of intense passion, of true and abiding affection.

On the surface, it was a masterly performance. Matilda had betrayed one of the most feared leaders in western Europe, a man notorious for his ruthlessness and brutality. He could well have sent her into exile—or worse. She judged that a display of humble contrition was unlikely to win him over. A natural bully, William scorned weakness in others and would pursue any who displayed it with the same relentlessness that he showed when hunting down a stag in the woods. Rather, she pleaded the strength of her maternal feelings—something that was both expected and admired in a royal spouse—and used these to justify her otherwise treacherous actions. That she dared to turn the tables on William by accusing him of trying to make her forget her motherly duties constituted a level of bravery that few showed when faced with the mighty Conqueror.

That Matilda had the audacity to turn herself from accused into accuser is also a measure both of the confidence that she had in her husband's devotion and of how deftly she thought she could play him. Yet she knew that she had to strike a delicate balance between self-righteous indignation and wifely deference. By delivering her words while kneeling at his feet, she emphasized her position as William's inferior and supplicant. She had played her role to perfection.

William's immediate reaction, however, suggests that she had gravely miscalculated. It seems that until now he had not realized the depth of his wife's feelings toward their eldest son. Confronted with the strength of her affection for Robert and the contrast with her obviously cooler feelings toward himself, he was consumed by jealousy.

Orderic describes how "the stern duke grew pale with anger and, bursting with rage, he commanded one of the queen's messengers named Samson, a Breton, to be arrested and blinded." The force of William's rage suggests that Samson may have been responsible for conveying his mistress's gold to her son. Fortunately, Matilda had her own network of supporters at court, who succeeded in getting word to the poor man before the terrible sentence could be carried out. Samson fled to refuge in the monastery of St.-Évroult, where "at the queen's plea he was received by Abbot Mainer, and prudently adopted the monastic way of life to save both body and soul."[54] While there, he met Orderic Vitalis, a fellow resident of the abbey, which is perhaps why the latter was able to recount the scandal in such detail in his *Ecclesiastical History*.

Apart from being upbraided in front of the court, Matilda escaped further reprisals. The horrific fate that her servant only narrowly escaped no doubt struck terror into her. It certainly seems to have shocked her into obedience, for there is no further evidence of her supporting Robert against her husband. Malmesbury, surely playing things down, recalls that the "small disagreement" between the couple was soon forgotten and claims that it "occasioned no lessening of their affection as man and wife he [William] himself made clear."[55]

But the atmosphere between the royal couple must have been strained. As Malmesbury himself quoted: "Kingship and love make sorry bedfellows and sort but ill together."[56] On the surface, they soon resumed their accustomed cordiality toward each other, but their relationship would never recover. As a result of Matilda's betrayal, William would never again trust her to enjoy the full powers of regency. In future, she would be obliged to act alongside her husband or younger sons. Her days as one of the most powerful women in western Europe seemed to be over.

The stress caused by this rift and consequent demotion seemed to damage Matilda's health. At around the same time as the debacle with her husband and son, this formerly energetic and robust woman sought a cure for lethargy from "Saint" Adelelme, a former soldier who had begun his religious career at La Chaise-Dieu abbey in southern France. She apparently did so in some secrecy, for the sources indicate only that an anonymous English queen made the request. Edward the Confessor's queen, Edith, having died in 1075, it could only have been Matilda.

In the late 1070s, Adelelme had become dissatisfied with the monastic life and had moved to the Spanish court at the invitation of Constance of Burgundy, the wife of Alfonso of León—now emperor of a reunited Spain—to whom Matilda's daughter had once been betrothed. It was while there that he grew famous for performing miracles. Having heard tales of his amazing feats, Matilda dispatched messengers to him pleading that he might bless some bread and send it to her as a cure for her disease. Adelelme resisted at first but eventually sent the bread that she had requested. As soon as Matilda ate it, so the tale goes, she was cured. In gratitude, she tried to reward the abbot with money, but he refused to accept it. She therefore chose a more fitting gift, and sent him a "precious priestly vestment," together with £100 toward the cost of the monks' dormitory—equivalent to around £70,000 today.[57]

✧ ✧ ✧

Left to their own devices, Robert and his followers would probably have languished in exile, frittering away what was left of their money and possessions in a life of excess. But their existence presented an irresistible opportunity for the duke's enemies to make trouble. The rebels had secured a strategically advantageous base, thanks to Robert of Bellême's brother-in-law, Hugh de Châteauneuf, who had offered them the use of his castle at Rémalard, just twenty-five miles south of L'Aigle. From here, they—and any supporters they managed to attract—could easily make raids into Normandy. William was quick to retaliate. He bribed Hugh de Châteauneuf's overlord, Count Rotrou of Mortagne, to support him, and promptly built four fortifications of his own at Rémalard. He also confiscated the estates of his son's followers and used the revenues from them to swell his forces with mercenaries. The contest was finely balanced. "Now one and now another took up arms either for or against the king. Frenchmen and Bretons, men of Maine and Anjou and other peoples vacillated, not knowing which side they ought to support."[58]

But Robert had another ace up his sleeve. Once more, this was thanks to his mother. He approached King Philip of France, with whom he could claim kinship on the strength of Matilda's family connections. The French king was at this time enjoying a resurgence of power and was keen to exploit any opportunity to regain the initiative over his rival, William. He therefore lent a sympathetic ear to Robert's request for assistance. The very fact that the two men entered into negotiations meant that William could now no longer dismiss his eldest son as a powerless fool.

Robert's lobbying with the king of France paid off, and in late 1078 Philip granted him the castle of Gerberoy, which was the most powerful fortress on the frontier with southeastern Normandy.[59] This provided him with a much stronger base from which to plan his campaign, and he soon amassed a considerable body of support from within his father's duchy by promising riches that he did not possess to any man who would fight on his behalf. He proceeded to lead his augmented rebel forces on a series of raids across the Norman frontier: "he ravaged in Normandy far and often, burnt townships, killed people, and caused his father much trouble and worry," recorded one chronicler.[60] Robert's aim was to prove himself a serious contender to his father and thus draw even more supporters to his cause. The tactic was devastatingly effective. "So Normandy was more sorely vexed by her own people than by strangers, and was eaten away by inward sickness."[61]

The duke was characteristically swift to react. He ordered that all the Norman castles close to Gerberoy should be fortified. In the meantime, he opened his own negotiations with King Philip and persuaded him—no doubt with a substantial bribe—to stay out of the quarrel thenceforth. Then, shortly after Christmas 1078 (which he had probably spent with Matilda at Rouen), he gathered his forces and laid siege to his son's fortress. For three long weeks he battered the castle with siege engines and trebuchets until Robert and his garrison sallied forth and engaged the duke's army in battle.

Stoked by fury at his son's treachery, William—by then in his fifties—fought with more stamina and ferocity than his much younger opponents. His horse was shot from under him, "and he who brought up another for him was straightway shot with a cross-bow."[62] Undeterred, William carried on relentlessly, felling opponent after opponent, until he met his match. In the confused mêlée, he encountered one rebel who fought just as fiercely and unyieldingly as himself. Heavily armored, the two men hurled themselves against each other, slashing with their swords. In the struggle, the duke was struck on the hand and fell back, vanquished. His opponent, the first man ever to triumph over the most feared warrior in Europe, was his own son, Robert.

According to the early-twelfth-century chronicler John of Worcester, it was only when William cried out that Robert—horror-struck—grasped the identity of his opponent. He promptly ordered his father to mount his horse "and in this way allowed him to leave."[63] This version of events is possible. Both men would have been heavily armored, and this was the age before heraldic devices identified the major players in a battle. But William was so distinctive by his height, girth (he had grown corpulent in recent years), and overall bearing that it seems inconceivable that his eldest son would have failed to recognize him. Moreover, Robert had been trained by his father since his youth and had fought alongside him in many encounters, so he would have been well used to seeing him heavily clad in armor. Given the by now implacable hatred that he felt toward the man who had taunted him since his youth and restricted his powers in adulthood, the more likely conclusion is that Robert knew full well who his opponent was. But why did he refrain from killing him? That he shrank from the final deed was perhaps due to a dawning realization of the enormity of the act. He would have been murdering not just his father, but his duke and king.[64]

The Battle of Gerberoy marked a turning point in William's reign. It was the first defeat he had suffered, either in Normandy or England, since the revolts of Le Mans and York in 1069. The fact that it was inflicted upon him by his own son made it even harder to bear. It is a testament to the humiliation that William felt that all subsequent accounts of the battle were strictly censored. The authors of the *Anglo-Saxon Chronicle*, for example, went too far. Although claiming, "We do not want, though, to write more here of the harm which he [did] his father," they evidently went on to do so, because that part of the manuscript was cut away.[65] Malmesbury was more tactful, portraying the encounter as an unfortunate blot upon William's otherwise flawless military career. He admits, though, that the duke's troops suffered "heavy casualties."[66] Among the wounded was Robert's younger brother, William Rufus, who had shown his loyalty toward their father by entering the fray on his side. The apparently tight-knit family unit that had once been the envy of Europe had unraveled with alarming speed.

✛   ✛   ✛

In the immediate aftermath of the battle, William retreated to Rouen, while Robert again fled into exile—possibly to his mother's homeland of Flanders. Even though he had won a significant victory over his father, the mighty duke was far from vanquished, and Robert knew that he would be thirsting for his blood. Matilda was deeply distressed by what had happened. If she allowed herself to rejoice secretly at her beloved son's victory over her husband, her joy was overshadowed by the sorrow that she felt at his continued exile. She was also terrified of what the future might hold for him: William, if he were to capture his son, would be fully justified in putting him to death. His reaction to the pleas of his counsels to restore peace suggests that he was quite prepared to do so. "Which of my ancestors from the time of Rollo ever had to endure such hostility from any child of his as I do?" he demanded angrily. "He would not hesitate, if he could, to stir up the whole human race against me and slay me and you as well. According to divine law, given to us through Moses, he is deserving of death."[67]

Orderic claims that after failing to persuade her husband to relent toward Robert, Matilda fretted desperately and resorted to increasingly odd measures to gain reassurance. For instance, shortly after the Battle of Gerberoy, it was rumored that she sent gifts via her messengers to a famous hermit in Germany, held to be a prophet, imploring him to pray for her husband and son and asking him what should befall them.

The hermit whom Matilda had consulted "received the messengers of this great lady courteously" and requested three days to prepare his reply. When the stated time had elapsed, he sent for the men and told them of a troubling vision he had had that augured ill for the future of Normandy. He had seen a meadow, "fairly decked with grass and flowers," in which a "highly-mettled horse" was grazing. All around stood a great herd of cattle, longing to feed from the same meadow, but they were driven off by the horse. However, "the brave and stately steed suddenly fell down dead" and the herd at once rushed in and "greedily devoured its former beauty without fear of the defender." The hermit explained that the meadow signified Normandy and the grass its people, "who enjoy peace and abundance of goods in it." The horse represented William, and the greedy cattle were the French, Bretons, Angevins, Flemings, "and other frontier peoples, who are jealous of the prosperity of Normandy, and are eager to seize some of its riches as wolves their prey." The hermit foretold that after William's death, Robert would succeed to the duchy, whereupon "enemies from all sides" would invade the land and devour its riches, and "disregarding its foolish ruler" would "trample all Normandy contemptuously under foot."

The fate that the hermit predicted for Robert must have grieved his mother sorely. He claimed that the young man would "give himself up to lust and indolence" and would plunder the wealth of the church in order to distribute it among his lecherous followers. "In Robert's duchy catamites[68] and effeminates will govern, and under their rule vice and wretchedness will abound . . . Towns and villages will be burned . . . and many thousands of men will be destroyed by fire and sword." In conclusion, he told Matilda's messengers that under her son's leadership, Normandy, "who once so proudly lorded it over her conquered neighbours will now, under a foolish and idle duke, be despised, and will long and wretchedly lie at the mercy of the swords of her neighbours. The weak duke will enjoy no more than an empty title, and a swarm of nobodies will dominate both him and the captive duchy, bringing ruin to many." The hermit ended by offering Matilda the cold comfort that she herself would not live to see the evils that would befall Normandy, for she would die before her husband. She would therefore be spared "the misfortunes of your son," which would lead to "the desecration of your beloved land."[69]

The existence of the prophet is at best dubious. It is more likely that the whole tale and the reported vision was a means by which Orderic, with hindsight, was able to vent his disapproval of Robert's failings and of the disaster that his later rule would prove to be. None of the other sources refer to Matilda's exchange with the hermit, and it seems unlikely that a woman renowned for her shrewdness and wisdom would resort to such a whimsical strategy. But while the details of the prophecy may owe more to Orderic's poetic license than to reality, it is possible that Matilda did seek the help of mystics during what was arguably the greatest crisis of her life. This was, of course, an age dominated by superstition, and Matilda was by no means immune to it, as had been proved on various occasions in the past—notably when her husband was preparing to invade England. Fortune telling—or divination—was widely used by people at all levels of society who were anxious to perceive, and thus avoid, potential harm to either themselves or a loved one.

For Matilda, Robert's rebellion, and William's unbending refusal to forgive him, was a moment as crucial as the Conquest. It forced her to make a choice between marital and maternal loyalty. The situation was further complicated by the fact that another of her sons, William Rufus, had sided with her husband. It was a scenario for which there was no clear script, and it would take all of Matilda's shrewdness and tenacity to survive the bitter aftermath of the conflict.

15

"Murmurs of Loud and Heartfelt Grief"

atilda's support for her eldest son's rebellion had torn the ducal family apart. Suddenly, one of the most powerful dynasties in the world looked fragile and vulnerable. The system of government that had served William so well ever since his conquest of England had utterly broken down. He could now no longer rely upon either his wife or his eldest son to take care of his dominions during his frequent absences. As well as constituting an immediate crisis, this void also had far-reaching consequences for the succession.

Moreover, the contagion within the ducal family had spread throughout Normandy, bringing it to the brink of civil war. Some of the leading families of the Norman aristocracy were divided by the quarrel, with members of the younger generation supporting Robert and the older members remaining loyal to his father. Worse still, the turmoil had coincided with a time when rival potentates were once again beginning to threaten Normandy's borders, notably King Philip of France and the duke of Anjou. William's alliance with the former was by no means a guarantee of loyalty: medieval rulers were notoriously capricious in their dealings with each other, and alliances often proved all too fleeting.

For Matilda, the crisis was deepened by news from her homeland. Her mother, Adela, died on January 8, 1079, at Messines, the abbey that she had founded in 1057.[1] Twelve years before, in the wake of her husband's death, Adela had traveled to Rome and taken the nun's veil from the hands of Pope Alexander II, residing at the abbey ever since. Indeed, such was her reputation for piety that she was later honored as a saint by the Roman Catholic Church.

The cause of Adela's death is not known, but she would then have been around seventy years old, which was an advanced age for the time. Beyond the influence that Adela exerted upon her upbringing and piety, little is known of Matilda's relationship with her mother. But the reference by Orderic to Matilda's being "overwhelmed with grief" at the thought of Adela's bereavement when her husband, Count Baldwin, died in 1071 suggests a degree of affection.[2] There is no record of Matilda's reaction upon hearing the news of her mother's death, but coming at such a time, it must have aggravated her already troubled state of mind. She who had been famed for her serene and dignified bearing was now so distraught that she "choked on her words because of her tears."[3]

Regardless of the role that she had played in the rift, Matilda was determined to reunite her warring husband and son and thereby reclaim her former position in the powerful family corporation that had ruled its dominions so effectively for more than two decades. She was assisted by a host of high-profile figures, both within Normandy and overseas. They included the former Count Simon of Amiens, Valois, and the Vexin. He was well known to Matilda, having been raised with her elder sons at the ducal court and apparently intended by William for one of her daughters. Even though Simon had given up the political arena two years earlier to become a monk, his biographer records that he held "sweet talks" with both William and Matilda, which suggests that he was as much a mediator between the couple as between the duke and his son.[4]

Matilda's old adviser, Roger de Montgomery, also intervened in the quarrel, and even Pope Gregory VII tried to bring his influence to bear, urging Robert to "wholly banish the counsels of wicked men and in all things agree to the will of your father."[5] Both of these men were on close terms with Matilda, so it was almost certainly at her request that they endeavored to persuade her husband to relent. Unlikely though it seems, she may also have enlisted the support of her nephew, Philip of France, whom Orderic claims sent representatives to join in the entreaties.[6] Of course, the very fact that Matilda was forced to rely upon intermediaries proves the degree to which her own influence over her husband had diminished. They might have resumed cordial relations on the surface, but the memory of her betrayal was still fresh in William's mind. Nonetheless, it was almost certainly through her pacifying influence that the two men were eventually brought to terms. As Orderic observes: "The queen and representatives of the king of France, with noble neighbours and friends, all combined to restore peace."[7]

The occasion of the formal reconciliation between William and Robert was a great assembly held at Rouen in early April 1080.[8] The court had gathered for the traditional Easter celebrations, and as well as a host of Norman magnates, there were also important guests from overseas, including envoys from the Pope. It was an ideal opportunity to send a message to the world that the unity and power of the Norman dynasty had been restored.

The assembled dignitaries were sufficiently convinced of the sincerity of the truce. Pope Gregory's envoys reported back to their master that the rebellion was at an end, and the pontiff subsequently wrote a letter to Robert reminding him of his filial duty.[9] Naturally, it was a carefully stage-managed production, and beneath the apparent cordiality, the old resentments continued to simmer. The duke had only grudgingly agreed to pardon his son. Moreover, Robert would not have returned to Normandy if it had not been for the assurance that he would be restored to his status as heir to the province. William honored this promise, although he must have shuddered at the thought of this upstart's succeeding him one day.

Indeed, after the charade of the ceremony, William "continually poured abuse and reproach on him [Robert] in public for his failings" and missed no opportunity to humiliate and provoke him.[10] The reconciliation seemed more likely to be a temporary cease-fire than a lasting peace. As Orderic Vitalis observed, the "fiendish dispute" was far from over, and it would give rise to "many battles and outrages later."[11]

Robert is next recorded to have been with his family on July 14, 1080, when he and his father were among the witnesses to a charter at Caen. It was also around this time that another opportunity to present a united front arose. Matilda's youngest daughter, Adela, was to marry Stephen, the son and heir of Theobald III, the count of Blois.[12] Blois had for many years proved a hostile region, so the match provided Normandy with a valuable ally who could help to offset the threat posed by the other northern French territories. A formal ceremony of betrothal took place with due pomp at Breteuil, in southwest Normandy, attended by all the ducal family.[13] The choice of location was significant not just because of its proximity to Blois, but because the castellan of Breteuil had been one of Robert's supporters. This was intended as a clear signal that the rebellion was over.

✢ ✢ ✢

Toward the end of 1080, William set sail for England—his first visit in four years. It is a telling indication of his changed feelings toward Matilda that rather than entrust her with the regency, as he had on numerous other occasions, he took both her and their eldest son with him. Although this had the happy side effect of demonstrating family unity, it is likely that the stronger motive was to keep them both firmly under his control. The records do not reveal whom William left in charge of Normandy; it is possible that he conferred that honor upon his favorite son, Rufus. If this was so, then it must surely have rankled with both Matilda and Robert.

The visit began with the usual ceremonials that accompanied the Christmas season, which the royal family celebrated at Gloucester. Matilda and her son then accompanied William to Winchester for the Easter and Whitsun crown-wearings the following year.

During Matilda's sojourn in England, Queen Margaret of Scotland, who had attended her coronation twelve years before, gave birth to a daughter, Edith (who was later known as Matilda). Out of respect for the English queen, Margaret asked Matilda to be a godparent, along with her son Robert, and invited them both to the christening. William might have wished to accompany them, but his attention was required in other parts of his vast domain, and he seems to have judged that the pair could be trusted to make the journey without him. Besides, it suited him to have his eldest son in Scotland. The ever-troublesome King Malcolm III had invaded England the previous year, and William was keen to ensure his loyalty, particularly as a rebellion in Northumbria in the spring of 1080 had seriously weakened the nobility there. The presence of a royal heir in Scotland was intended to instill peace on William's behalf.

Matilda and her son duly attended the baptism. Legend has it that during the ceremony, the infant Edith grabbed at Matilda's veil and tried to pull it toward her own head. This was said to have been taken as an omen by those present, although it was possibly a later embellishment, written with the wisdom of hindsight, for Edith would one day follow in her godmother's footsteps and become a formidable queen consort of England.[14]

It is not clear how long Matilda stayed in England. Her visit took place during a period that is very sparsely covered by the chroniclers, presumably because the situation was relatively peaceful in both England and Normandy. We do know that William held his Pentecost court at Winchester in 1081, and since all of his sons were present, it is likely that Matilda was, too. The charter evidence suggests that the king returned to Normandy that autumn, accompanied by Matilda and their eldest son.[15]

They were certainly back in the duchy before the end of 1081, when Matilda visited the abbey of Évroul in Bayeux. She was "received with honour" by the monks, and it was noted that she behaved with great humility throughout her stay. After placing a gold mark on the altar, the duchess asked to be remembered in their prayers, together with her daughter Constance. It is not clear why she chose to single out this daughter for their devotions. It may indicate that she was the only one still under Matilda's care. Adeliza had died in the late 1070s, and the evidence suggests that the daughter who was named after Matilda might also have died young.[16] Meanwhile, Cecilia was flourishing at La Trinité, and Adela might also have been there during this time. There is no evidence of any matrimonial or other schemes for Constance, which may suggest that she was a favorite of Matilda, who wished to enjoy her company for as long as possible.

Perhaps Matilda was feeling penitential for the part that she had played in her son's rebellion, for she made a number of pious bequests at around the same time. For example, she gave the income from the village of Brixton Deverill in Wiltshire to the abbey of Le Bec. She also granted the village of Frampton in Dorset to her husband's abbey, St.-Étienne in Caen.[17] The queen also maintained a strong interest in her original commission of La Trinité. The archives there include numerous bequests, which show her to have been extraordinarily assiduous in her care of the nuns. They include a grant of wool and precious fabrics, a tithe on wool to pay for their heating and clothes, and another tithe to fund the lighting of their chambers. The nuns must have been among the best fed in any religious house throughout William and Matilda's domains, for many of the bequests concerned their diet. There was a grant of plowlands and mills to supply bread and grain, regular gifts of "animals, bacon and cheeses" from England, and the establishment of an annual fair, the profits of which were to supply even more delicacies for the nuns' table.[18] It has been estimated that the total value of Matilda's donations to La Trinité, excluding the English estates that she gave the abbey, was equivalent to around £650,000 in modern terms.[19]

The following year, 1082, Matilda and her husband visited William's half-brother Odo at Grestain. This was the place where their mother, Herleva, was buried, and out of respect for her, they decided to build an abbey there. The fact that it was more than thirty years since her death suggests that both sons had a true and abiding affection for her.

There was, however, a subtext to the meeting, for William was concerned by the power that Odo had accumulated as regent of England. He was immensely rich, thanks in no small part to the fact that he had plundered the wealth of his adopted country, and he had built up a strong personal following, which could easily have posed a serious threat to the king's authority. Indeed, he was even rumored to have supported Robert in his rebellion. While Odo was also fiercely ambitious, though, his aim was not the crown. Despite showing a blatant disregard for his vows as an archbishop by fathering children, he had his eye on the greatest church office of all: that of pope.

At his meeting with Odo, which Matilda presumably attended, William expressly forbade him to pursue the papacy. Not only would it take him away from England, where his presence was now necessary during the king's absences, but it would also place him in a position of such power that he would no longer be subject to his half-brother's authority. It is a measure of Odo's arrogance that he promptly disregarded William's injunction and prepared to embark for Rome. The duke was one step ahead of him, however, and had Odo arrested as he was about to set sail. He was imprisoned in the Tower of Rouen, where he would remain for the rest of William's reign.

The ruthlessness that William displayed in dealing with his half-brother again highlights just how fortunate Matilda and her eldest son had been. Odo's fate proved that William had no qualms about punishing members of his family just as harshly as he might do an ordinary miscreant. Matilda and Robert had committed a far greater treachery than Odo; although he had overreached himself by setting his sights on the great prize of the papacy, and had flouted William's orders in the process, he had not tried to usurp his half-brother's own position. If it had not been for the love and admiration that the duke felt for Matilda, and to an extent her own skillful manipulation of such fondness, she and her son might well have met a terrible fate.

Throughout this time, Robert Curthose had remained part of his parents' entourage. However, the veneer of unity had now begun to fracture once more. William continued to scoff at his son in public, tormenting him with petty humiliations, and in turn Robert again began to treat William with contempt. Father and son are last recorded as being together at Caen on July 18, 1083, along with Matilda.[20] It seems that, frustrated with being kept under close scrutiny as part of William's entourage, Robert left court soon after. Although he attested another charter with his father on January 9, 1084, this seems to have been a fleeting return, and he subsequently disappears from the records.[21] In self-imposed exile, he was this time accompanied by a much-reduced band of followers. Although Robert had come close to victory at Gerberoy, William had reasserted his authority so effectively that few believed his son to have any real credibility any longer as an opponent.

✣   ✣   ✣

Matilda's health must have begun to seriously deteriorate shortly after that last meeting with her husband and beloved son at Caen in July 1083, for she would never leave that city. The fear and stress caused by the collapse of William and Robert's rapprochement may have hastened her decline—contemporaries certainly believed this to be the case. Another theory is that Matilda fell victim to the plague, which had struck Normandy and was particularly prevalent in Caen.[22] She was now about fifty-two years old—an advanced age at a time when most women died in their thirties. Although she seems to have been of a robust constitution, and had no recorded illnesses, the years of childbearing, travel, and the tumultuous travails of state must have taken their toll.

Orderic claims that Matilda had in fact fallen grievously sick the previous year, at about the time when she and William met Odo at Grestain.[23] This is supported by one of the charters to which she bore witness. Around 1156, her great-grandson restored to St.-Étienne the village of Northam in Devon, which he said had been originally granted to the abbey by Matilda "in her last illness." The charter to which this refers is not dated, but it is likely to have been compiled in around 1082.[24] It was also around this time that Matilda's ecclesiastical endowments increased, perhaps in an attempt to secure eternal salvation. In 1082, she granted the manors of Felsted in Essex and Tarrant Launceston in Dorset to La Trinité in order to provide the nuns with money for wardrobes and firewood. Out of respect for her husband, she also made bequests to three churches in Falaise, the place of his birth.

More conclusive evidence that Matilda knew she was dying in 1082 was the fact that she almost certainly drew up her will in that year. The document survives in the registry of La Trinité, along with an inventory of Matilda's wardrobe and jewels. It is a disappointingly neutral list, with no touching bequests for her loved ones and precious few references to personal belongings that would provide a clue as to what Matilda held dear. She was returning to that typical businesslike approach she had taken toward all affairs of state throughout her reign as duchess and queen. In the carefully crafted piece of statesmanship, she maintained the appearance of a dutiful wife to the last, stressing, "I have made all . . . bequests with the consent of my husband."

The contents of the will also functioned to reiterate Matilda's public image of benevolence and piety. For instance, she left the contents of her chamber, including her crown and scepter and many other precious objects, to her abbey at La Trinité, where she wished to be buried. The bequests give a further clue to the lavish style in which she must have lived, for they included a fine chasuble made by an English noblewoman at

Winchester, "a cloak worked in gold from her chamber which is to be used to make a cope, two gold chains each with a cross, one chain with carved decorations for hanging a lamp in front of the altar, candlesticks made at Saint-Lô . . . a chalice and vestment made in England, with all a horse's accoutrements and all her vases, with the exception of those given away during her lifetime." The trappings for the horses stand out as a peculiar item amongst the rich regalia. It is possible that the nuns of La Trinité had asked Matilda to make this bequest, knowing that they would be useful for the abbess or prioress during visits away from the abbey. Or perhaps they were meant to signal the peripatetic life that Matilda had led as queen and duchess.

The abbey was also granted some property owned by the queen, including the town of Quettehou in Normandy and two houses in England.[25] Lastly, she gave generously to the poor, which seemed to inspire her husband, a witness to her last bequests, to do the same upon his own death four years later.

However, the fact that the lion's share of Matilda's possessions went to her abbey in Caen could indicate that she was influenced not just by a desire for eternal salvation, but also by consideration for her daughter Cecilia, who was now in her mid-twenties and had completed seventeen years' service at the abbey. She was no doubt already of some standing in the hierarchy of La Trinité, and she would go on to achieve a highly successful career there.

With this in mind, then, it could be said that the will to some extent reflected Matilda's character. Functional and businesslike, it displayed her cool grip of statecraft and the importance of a benevolent public image, but it also contained a hint of that underlying, and at times destructive, tenderness toward her family.

The long interim between the will and Matilda's death suggests that the decline was a lingering one. By the onset of winter 1083, she was gravely ill, and in the early hours of November 2, "growing apprehensive because her illness persisted, she confessed her sins with bitter tears and, after fully accomplishing all that Christian custom requires and being fortified by the saving sacrament, she died."[26] William stayed with her throughout. He was consumed with grief at the death of the woman whom he confessed to love "as my own soul," and was said to have wept profusely for many days afterward.[27]

✢   ✢   ✢

Despite its often turbulent nature, William and Matilda's marriage had been one of the most successful partnerships in medieval Europe. Matilda had been instrumental to her husband's success. His mainstay for more than thirty years, she had been one of his most valued advisers, had proved a wise and capable ruler during his long absences in England, and had borne him many children to secure his dynasty. It was her blood-line that had enabled him to pursue so vigorous a claim to the English throne in the first place, and her family connections had helped him to retain both this kingdom and the duchy of Normandy for himself and his heirs. Above all, though, it was her personal qualities that he would miss the most. Her wisdom, shrewdness, and strength of character made her utterly irreplaceable.

According to Malmesbury, William eschewed all other women for the remainder of his days. "For when she died, four years before him, he . . . showed by many days of the deepest mourning how much he missed the love of her whom he had lost. Indeed from that time forward, if we believe what we are told, he abandoned pleasure of every kind."[28] The duke subsequently fell into a profound depression, from which he never truly recovered, and was, according to one historian, "a mourner till the day of his death."[29] The various bequests that he made for the soul of his dead wife reveal the sincerity of his grief.[30]

Upon Matilda's death, the entire duchy was plunged into mourning, and Mass was celebrated for her everywhere, from the great abbeys and cathedrals to the smallest and most remote of its churches. The monastery of St.-Évroult, where the young Orderic Vitalis took up residence two years later, was among those that held special services of remembrance.[31] He and his fellow Anglo-Norman chronicler, Malmesbury, record Matilda's passing with regret and claim that she was greatly missed. Orderic remembered her as "the most amiable, the most courteous, the most intelligent woman of her time; the most chaste, the most devoted to her husband, the most tender towards her children."[32] Her recent transgressions had soon been forgotten. The large number of bequests that were made for her soul by her family and members of her court—even many years after her death—demonstrate the high regard in which she was held as well as her enduring influence.[33]

In an epigram that he wrote to honor the late queen, the poet Fulcoius, Archdeacon of Beauvais, lamented:

> If she could be brought back from death through tears,
> Money, fair or foul means, then rest assured
> There would be an abundance of these things . . .
> Let this be the inscription [on her tomb]:
> "Matilda, queen of the English
> Known for her twofold honour, ruled over the Normans,
> But here rests entombed in good state,
> Blessed in title that nature cannot revoke from her.
> O twofold light of November, it is a little plot,
> A small pile of ash, but nevertheless a source of glory and grace."[34]

A series of other memorial poems followed, all equal in their praise of the late queen. As well as those written by Norman and French poets, there was also a eulogy by Geoffrey of Cambrai, a monk at Winchester—a testament to the respect that Matilda had earned on both sides of the Channel.[35] By contrast, the *Anglo-Saxon Chronicle* affords only the following cursory mention: "And in this same year passed away Matilda, King William's queen, on the day after the Feast of All Saints."[36] This gives a misleading impression of the impact that her death had upon her English subjects, who had just as much cause as the Normans—if not more—to mourn her loss, as the years to come would prove. Indeed, as one contemporary put it: "Her death represents tragedy for both the clergy and the common folk." She would be "wept for by the English and the Normans for many years."[37]

Orderic tells how Matilda's body was conveyed to La Trinité as soon as she had breathed her last. To honor her memory, William ordered "a most splendid funeral" at the abbey, which lasted for two full days. It was attended by scores of monks, abbots, and bishops as well as the nuns of La Trinité.[38] This reinforced the reputation for great piety that Matilda had enjoyed during her lifetime. Likewise, the "great throng of poor people" who came to pay homage to their late duchess served as a testament to her generosity as a benefactress to many charitable causes.[39] One account claimed that "murmurs of loud and heartfelt grief" were heard throughout the land.[40]

The sources do not reveal which, if any, of Matilda's children attended the funeral. By the time of her death, she had three surviving sons—Robert, William Rufus, and Henry—and as many daughters—Cecilia, Constance, and Adela. As a nun of the abbey, Cecilia would certainly have witnessed her mother's body being laid to rest. The close bond that existed between the late queen and her eldest son, Robert, makes it likely that he, too, would have honored her memory by attending, even if it did entail the unsavory prospect of meeting his father. The presence of Cecilia may have provided an added incentive. Judging from the evidence of the charters, Robert felt a strong affection toward her, for he made a number of generous bequests to the abbey when she later became its abbess.[41]

Some time after Matilda's funeral, an exquisite monument, "wonderfully worked with gold and precious stones," was erected over her tomb in the nave of the abbey.[42] However, her remains suffered as turbulent a history as she herself had done in life. Five centuries after her death, her tomb was plundered in the French wars of religion. The marauding Calvinists spared the tombstone, but they smashed the monument and the effigy of the late queen that lay upon it and eagerly searched the tomb for treasure. When Matilda's corpse was uncovered, their leader, Admiral Gaspard of Coligny, spied a gold ring set with a fine sapphire on one of her fingers. It was the ring with which Matilda had been presented at her coronation and which she had worn ever since. No doubt realizing its value, Coligny promptly seized it, but the abbess, Anna de Montmorenci, condemned his desecration with such passion that he was overcome with remorse and presented the ring to her.[43]

In the seventeenth century, amends were made for this violation, and Matilda's bones were reverentially reinterred in a small casket. A new monument was erected in 1708, but this was destroyed during the French Revolution. Her coffin was spared, though, and in 1819, the original eleventh-century tombstone, crafted from black-and-white Tournai marble in honor of her Flemish origins, was restored and moved to pride of place in the middle of the choir, before the high altar, where it can still be seen today.[44] The epitaph, which her husband had ordered to be "lovingly engraved in letters of gold," demonstrates that, to the last, Matilda was immensely proud of her ancestry.[45] It also bears testament to her piety, and the charitable works she undertook during her lifetime:

> *The lofty structure of this splendid tomb*
> *Hides great Matilda, sprung from royal stem;*
> *Child of a Flemish duke; her mother was*
> *Adela, daughter of a king of France,*
> *Sister of Henry, Robert's royal son.*
> *Married to William, most illustrious king.*
> *She gave this site and raised this noble house,*
> *With many lands and many goods endowed,*
> *Given by her, or by her toil procured;*
> *Comforter of the needy, duty's friend;*
> *Her wealth enriched the poor, left her in need.*
> *At daybreak on November's second day*
> *She won her share of everlasting joy.*[46]

This monument, and the eulogies that preceded it, suggest that even in death Matilda maintained her dutiful and pious image. Indeed, she remained a powerful figurehead for the Norman dynasty—perhaps even more so than she had been in life. However, as her grieving family were soon to learn, the loss of her active, physical presence was to cost them dearly.

16

"The Storms of Troubles"

"After the death of his illustrious queen, Matilda, King William, who survived her for almost four years, was continually forced to struggle against the storms of troubles that rose up against him."[1] This was no exaggeration on the part of Orderic Vitalis. The loss of Matilda caused a profound shift in her husband's outlook. Grief turned to bitterness and made him even more intolerant than he had been before. His attitude toward his English dominions underwent a particularly dramatic shift. While Matilda had promoted peace and conciliation, "after her death, he [William] became a thorough tyrant," according to one contemporary chronicler. It was suddenly obvious just how great a restraining influence she must have exercised over her husband in life. Deprived of her wise counsel, he became reckless and tyrannical, undoing much of the good work that Matilda had urged him to in fostering better relations between the Normans and Saxons in England.

Unchecked by Matilda's benign influence, William fell into ever worse excesses. "The king and the principal men greatly loved, and over-greatly, greed in gold and in silver, and did not care how sinfully it was got as long as it came to them," lamented the *Anglo-Saxon Chronicle*. "The greater the talk about just law, the more unlawful things were done. They levied unjust tolls and they did many other unjust things which are difficult to relate."[2] Malmesbury concurs that the king was rightly criticized for his "passion for money, which no scruples restrained him from scraping together by seeking opportunities in all directions, doing and saying much—indeed everything—that was unworthy of so great a monarch, where dawned a glittering hope of gain."[3]

It was at least partly William's covetousness that inspired him to commission the great survey of his kingdom that became known as Domesday Book. The scale of this survey and the level of detail it entailed are staggering. William wanted to know how many hundreds of hides of land there were in each shire, how much land and livestock he possessed, and what annual dues were owed to him from all parts of the country. But his own holdings were only part of it, for he also ordered his surveyors to find out how much land and livestock the other landholders possessed and how much it was all worth. It was with some dismay that the *Anglo-Saxon Chronicle* describes the whole painstaking process: "He had it investigated so narrowly that there was not one single hide, not one yard of land, not even (it is shameful to tell—but it seemed no shame to him to do it) one ox, not one cow, not one pig was left out, that was not set down in his record."[4]

William's avarice was reflected by his growing corpulence. According to Malmesbury, this "gave him an unshapely and unkingly figure" and made him the butt of his enemies' jokes. When he was obliged to take an unaccustomed period of rest at his palace in Rouen, King Philip scoffed: "The king of England lies at Rouen, keeping his bed like a woman who has just had her baby."[5]

For the English, things seemed to go from bad to worse after Matilda's death. The *Anglo-Saxon Chronicle* describes 1087 as "a very heavy and pestiferous year in this land." According to the account:

> Such a disease came on men that very nearly every other man had the worst illness—that is the fever, and so severely that many men died from the illness. Afterwards, through the great bad weather which came as we already told, there came a very great famine over all England, so that many hundreds of men died wretched deaths through the famine. Alas! how wretched and how pitiful a time it was then! Then the miserable men lay well-nigh driven to death, and afterwards came the sharp famine and did for them completely. Who

cannot pity such a time? Or who is so hard-hearted that he cannot weep for such misfortune?[6]

The author of this chronicle was in no doubt that England was being punished for the manifold sins of its people—and its king. Without Matilda there to boost her husband's public image, he was more despised now than he had ever been.

The fate of Matilda's sons—in particular her eldest—would have grieved her if she had lived to witness it. Robert's rebellion against his father had been a source of great anxiety to her, but it was as nothing compared to the bitter infighting between her sons that would bring the empire she and William had created to the brink of ruin. The speed with which their relationships now completely unraveled again hints at the vital unifying role Matilda had played while she was alive.

Without her pacifying influence, the old hostilities between William and Robert flared anew.[7] This time, Robert's resentment was stoked by his father's refusal to make clear his intentions with regard to the English succession. In theory, this should have passed to Robert, along with Normandy and Maine. But William himself had struggled to keep all three dominions under his control, and it was in large part thanks to the able government of his late wife that he had been able to do so. He was understandably reluctant to give England over to a son whose loyalty was highly questionable and whom he regarded as an incompetent fool.

In fact, the enmity was such that William was determined "Curthose" would never set foot on Norman soil again, and he banished him to permanent exile. Robert tried in vain to rally his former supporters within Normandy to his cause; none of them were interested. He had failed the last time, and there was no reason to suppose that this increasingly dissolute and ineffective exile now had either the means or the personal qualities to oust the formidable Conqueror from his duchy. Without their support, Robert was a good deal less appealing a prospect to William's enemies.

With Robert apparently out of the picture, William focused on his younger sons. Having always favored William Rufus and Henry above their eldest brother, he was only too happy to install them in his place.

Orderic Vitalis claims: "William Rufus and Henry who were obedient to their father earned his blessing, and for many years enjoyed the highest power in the kingdom and duchy."[8] The alacrity with which William arranged for the two young men to begin approving charters that would formerly have been Robert's domain suggests that he had long wished (or even planned) to do so. William Rufus and Henry now became involved in the government of both Normandy and England, which made Robert's prospects of inheriting anything seem distant indeed. The ease with which the duke was now able to supplant his eldest son proves just how great a role Matilda had played in protecting Robert's rights. She had been his most powerful advocate at the ducal court, and without her influence, he found himself entirely at the mercy of his father's will.

The life of the ducal family in the immediate aftermath of Matilda's death may have been dominated by the revival of hostility between William and Robert, but there was also cause for celebration. In the autumn of 1086, William and Matilda's daughter Constance was betrothed to Alan IV Fergant, Count of Brittany. The wedding, which took place in either Caen or Bayeux,[9] brought Normandy an extremely valuable ally, for Brittany had long been a thorn in William's side.[10]

But it would prove an all too brief respite. Around the time when his sister was exchanging her vows with the count of Brittany, Robert returned to northern France. It is an indication of just how embattled William now felt that, rather than dismissing his eldest son as ineffective, he immediately went on the offensive. The focus of the duke's attack was the French Vexin, a strategically important region close to Rouen on the Norman border that was under King Philip's authority.[11] In July 1087, his army sacked the town of Mantes, which had been used as a base from which to attack Normandy in the past. The ferocity with which William fought was astonishing for a man of sixty, and he was every bit as brutal—if not more so—as he had been during any of the campaigns he had fought throughout his long career.

However, during the sack, the great warrior was suddenly taken ill. He seems to have sustained an internal injury when his horse tried to leap a ditch and the pommel of his saddle was driven into his heavy stomach, which was protruding over the front.[12] Racked by pain, William was forced to order a retreat. Having left the field of conflict, he gave way to his injuries. Jumièges tells how he was "overcome by nausea; his stomach rejected food and drink, his breathing became increasingly difficult and, shaken by sobs, his strength deserted him."[13] The duke was taken back to his palace at Rouen, where "the malady increased" and he was obliged to retire to bed.[14] A short while later, he was moved to the nearby priory of St.-Gervais. The official reason was that he needed some peace and quiet away from the city, but the choice of a religious house was significant. It was obvious to everyone around him that the great Conqueror was dying.

William himself knew it, and he railed against death as he would the bitterest of enemies.[15] The prospect of what would happen to his dominions once he had gone intensified his anguish, for he lamented "that after his death his homeland of Normandy would be plunged into misery."[16] His rebellious son was no doubt foremost in his mind as he contemplated this gloomy prospect. Rather than halting his campaign upon hearing of his father's illness, Robert was even now attacking Normandy's borders with the aid of King Philip. His younger brothers, meanwhile, were playing the dutiful sons at St.-Gervais.

Summoning the archbishop of Rouen, the dying Conqueror decreed his wishes for the future of his dominions. He ordered that William Rufus should make haste to England to receive the crown. Triumphant at having superseded his elder brother, Rufus embarked for England straightaway. By contrast, the archbishop and the nobles who were present were aghast at William's apparent resolve to deny Curthose his rightful inheritance, and "feared that he [William] would remain implacable towards his eldest son Robert, knowing that a wound frequently cut or cauterized causes sharper pain to the wounded." They urged upon him the fact that they had already sworn oaths of allegiance to the young man, and that these could not be broken without a loss of honor. Eventually, and with great reluctance, William gave in to their persuasions. Mustering his strength, he told the anxious throng: "Because he does not want to come or he spurns to come in order to apologise, I shall do what I think is correct. With you and God as my witnesses I forgive him all the sins he has committed against me, and I grant him all the duchy of Normandy."[17]

Shortly after making this bequest, in the early hours of September 9, the mighty Conqueror conceded defeat in this, his last earthly battle.[18] Orderic describes how the late duke's chamber was robbed by his servants, and his corpse was left "almost naked" on the floor.[19] Such disrespect would never have been allowed if Matilda had been alive.

William had decreed that his final resting place should be his abbey of St.-Étienne in Caen. A country knight named Herluin[20] took on the task of organizing the funeral out of kindness, but it was hardly the lavish occasion that might be expected for such a formidable ruler. The duke's body was conveyed "without any ceremony . . . in a small boat down the Seine." Even the place that was chosen for the internment was disputed by a "yokel" named Ascelin fitzArthur, who claimed that William had stolen the land from him.[21] Ascelin was pacified only when William's youngest son, Henry, recompensed him for the loss.

The occasion fell woefully short of the dignity and honor that should have been accorded the late king. It was attended by scores of ecclesiastics but, according to Malmesbury, very few laymen. Neither was his family well represented. William Rufus was already on his way to England, "thinking it more to the purpose to secure his own future interests than to attend the burial of his father's body."[22] Robert had not yet returned from waging war against Normandy. Only their younger brother, Henry, was at the ceremony.

As well as being poorly attended, the funeral also degenerated into the same chaos that had marked William's coronation more than twenty years before. During the ceremony, one of the houses in the city caught fire, "sending up great balls of flame."[23] The blaze quickly spread to neighboring houses, and the congregation of St.-Étienne was seized with panic. Many of the guests fled, leaving the monks to lay their late ruler hastily to rest.[24] Then, as they attempted to force William's bloated corpse into a sarcophagus that was too small, the body suddenly burst open, emitting "an intolerable stench that soon filled the entire church." The presiding ecclesiastics hastily concluded the last rites and took flight. In describing these events, Orderic mused that this once all-powerful Conqueror was reduced to nothing by such indignities.[25] Without Matilda, the calm and brilliant controller of public spectacle, William's funeral had been a woeful ceremony, wholly unfit for a king.

✣   ✣   ✣

Within weeks of the Conqueror's death, Normandy was on the brink of civil war, and the fragile cross-Channel realm that he and Matilda had created looked set to collapse. Robert soon justified his father's misgivings by proving a dissolute and ineffective ruler in Normandy, and his authority was easily circumvented by the nobility. Although he and William Rufus had reached an uneasy truce by agreeing to be each other's heir, upon the latter's untimely death in 1100, their younger brother Henry seized the crown of England. Robert made a number of unsuccessful attempts to claim what he saw as his rightful inheritance, but he could barely keep hold of Normandy, let alone wrest England from his much more capable brother.

The rapid disintegration of William's regime during the last years of his life and in the immediate aftermath of his death reveals its underlying fragility. But this regime had been the envy of the world during Matilda's lifetime. Her efficacy as regent of Normandy and queen of England had been essential to William's exercise of power on both sides of the Channel. She was the vital ingredient in his success, and without her, the balance that was so crucial to his power broke down irretrievably. If Matilda had outlived her husband, it seems almost certain that his final years and the future of his domains would have been more secure.

Epilogue

"Mother of Kings"

Matilda's achievements as duchess of Normandy and queen of England had been considerable. She had carved out a position of power and influence in the male-dominated political arena of both countries, and in so doing had confounded the conventional stereotypes of women. Far from being a meek and submissive wife and consort, subject entirely to her husband's will, she had wielded authority in her own right and had enjoyed an independence of action matched by few of her contemporaries.

In the dangerous, brutal world of conquest and rebellion, fragile alliances and bitter familial rivalries, Matilda had possessed all the attributes required for a woman to thrive. Her impeccable lineage, combined with her loving, pious, and loyal nature, had made her a paragon of fidelity and motherhood. But strength, intelligence, and ambition were also prerequisites to survive in such an environment. This side of her character, coupled with a fiercely independent nature, had made her essential to William's rule, giving her unparalleled influence over the king. She had proved such an able and effective ruler that he had come to rely upon her completely.

Matilda's ambition and strength of will had ultimately contributed to the fracturing of the Norman dynasty. But without the unifying influence that she had exerted for so long, this fracturing would arguably have occurred much sooner. It should not therefore detract from the extraordinary achievement of this remarkable woman—an achievement that would prove an inspiration both to her immediate successors and for hundreds of years to come.

Matilda's influence was particularly apparent in the lives of two of her daughters. Cecilia made a resounding success of her career at the abbey of La Trinité, rapidly gaining renown for her virtue and dedication. The noted intellectual Baudri of Bourgueil, the archbishop of Dol, wrote in praise of her, as did the poet Hildebert of Le Mans. To them, she was "a queen, a goddess and a royal virgin married to a heavenly husband."[1] Cecilia lavished care and attention upon the abbey that she seemed to have come to love as much as her mother had, and she commissioned a number of improvements. She also played a leading role in the administration of La Trinité, acting as coadjutor to its long-lived abbess, Matilda. Her efforts were rewarded in 1113, when she was appointed abbess upon the death of her superior. That same year, she granted her first charter—an indication of her newfound power.[2] She held that exalted position until her death fourteen years later, at the age of sixty-eight.[3]

While Cecilia inherited her mother's piety, her youngest sister, Adela, echoed her political achievements. Of all Matilda's children, Adela seems to have been the closest to her in appearance, character, and spirit. The amorous archbishop of Dol, who seemed to be a little in love with her, praised her "beauty, dignity and grace" and claimed that she had "the brilliance of a goddess."[4] At the time he wrote these words, Adela would have been in her forties. It is interesting to consider whether she inherited her lasting good looks from Matilda, whose beauty had been praised even in middle age and who had held William in thrall for most of their marriage.

Adela certainly inherited her mother's extraordinary fecundity, giving birth to as many as eleven children during the course of her marriage to Stephen of Blois, including a daughter whom she named after Matilda.[5] Having been inspired by the education that her own mother had given her, she paid as much attention to their studies. Like Matilda, Adela was strong-willed and politically astute, and she ruled her husband every bit as effectively. Malmesbury describes her as "a powerful woman with a reputation for her worldly influence."[6] This was demonstrated most forcefully in 1098, when her husband returned from the siege of Antioch, a key encounter in the First Crusade. Rather than welcoming him home like a dutiful wife, Adela promptly ordered him back to rejoin the crusade.[7] At first Stephen shrank from the idea of returning to the danger and hardships of the crusading life, but Adela eventually wore him down with "these speeches and many more like them."[8]

Continuing the similarity to her mother's life, Adela acted as regent for her husband while he was abroad on campaign. Orderic praised her competence: "This noble lady governed her husband's county well after his departure on crusade."[9] Judging from her reaction to his return from Antioch, she evidently relished the role just as much as Matilda had. Thanks to her insistence that he return to the Holy Land, she had the chance to exercise her authority to the full, because her husband met his death on this crusade in 1102. Their eldest son, William, would probably then have been old enough to inherit his father's title, but he was deemed unfit to rule. His mother therefore had him married off to a lady of her household and gave him lands in the north of the principality, well away from court.

This left Adela free to seize the reins of power herself. She proved more than equal to the task, and her shrewd political judgment and wise government were widely praised. Jumièges observed that she "ruled the country nobly for some years," while Orderic lauded her as a "wise and spirited woman" who ably led the province until her sons had reached maturity.[10] The archbishop of Dol, meanwhile, claimed that although she was a countess, she was "worthy rather of the name of queen."[11] Having learned from her mother's example, Adela became active in every sphere of government, wielding authority over political, ecclesiastical, and military matters as well as the administration of justice.

In 1107, Adela's second son, Theobald, was invested as count of Blois. Theobald was much more stable than his elder brother. He was also entirely subject to his mother's authority. Just as Matilda had ruled on behalf of her son Robert, so Adela retained power even after Theobald had been made count. Only when she was confident that he would continue the work that she had begun did she gradually cede authority to him.

Even then she remained at the heart of government, advising her son and keeping him firmly under her control—just as Matilda would have done if she had outlived her husband.

It was no doubt at Adela's instigation that Theobald intervened on her brother Henry's behalf when he attempted to take Normandy from Robert Curthose in 1106. As the two youngest siblings, Adela and Henry shared a natural affinity, and the countess certainly favored him over their reckless elder brother. On September 28, 1106, forty years to the day since their father had embarked for the conquest of England, Henry defeated his elder brother in the Battle of Tinchbrai and became duke of Normandy, thus reuniting the Norman empire. It was fitting that, through the influence of Adela, the spirit of Matilda had played a part in such a reunification.

In April 1120, Adela finally relinquished the political life and entered the nunnery of Marcigny-sur-Loire. Like her sister Cecilia, she possessed her mother's piety and would thrive in the religious arena. Jumièges wrote admiringly that she "served God in a praise-worthy manner till the end of her life."[12] Adela also shared her elder sister's longevity, and was in her seventieth year when she died in 1137.

Matilda would have taken great pride in Henry's restoration of the might of the Norman dynasty, even though he had ousted her favorite son from power. Yet her influence over the English monarchy would far outlive her youngest son. Her bloodline would continue for more than a thousand years. Indeed, all sovereigns of England and the United Kingdom, including the present queen, are directly descended from this remarkable woman.

But Matilda's legacy extends beyond even this extraordinary feat. The first crowned queen of England to be formally recognized as such, she had established a model of female rule that would last for hundreds of years. Thenceforth, the consorts of kings would expect to do far more than fulfill the conventional role of producing heirs. For instance, because the tradition had been set by the first Matilda, her daughter-in-law, Edith-Matilda, the wife of Henry I, was the natural choice for regent when her husband was away. Moreover, Henry subsequently bequeathed his throne to his daughter, even though his nephew Stephen had a stronger claim in the eyes of most of his subjects; clearly, his mother's example had inspired a confidence in female rulers that few of his contemporaries shared. In so doing, he became the first English king to put down in written form the right of a daughter to inherit land.[13] Farther afield, other female consorts, such as the formidable Eleanor of Aquitaine, or Isabella the "She-Wolf" of France, the wife of Edward II, would aspire to the same authority and influence over their husbands and their kingdoms that Matilda had exercised to such brilliant effect.

It is a legacy of which Matilda, whose formidable skills of leadership and political guile have been overshadowed by the achievements of her conqueror husband, would heartily have approved.

NOTES

ASC   *Anglo-Saxon Chronicle*

GG   *Gesta Guillelmi,* William of Poitiers

GRA   *Gesta Regum Anglorum,* William of Malmesbury

GND   *Gesta Normannorum Ducum,* William of Jumièges, Orderic Vitalis, and Robert of Torigni

OV   *Ecclesiastical History,* Orderic Vitalis

INTRODUCTION

1. Barlow, *William I,* p. 185; Clay.
2. C.N.L. Brooke, " 'Both Small and Great Beasts': An Introductory Study," in Baker, p. 1.
3. OV, I, p. 35; III, p. 213.
4. Musset, *Les actes de Guillaume le Conquérant,* p. 38. It was customary for a scribe to distinguish between the crosses by writing the name of the witness next to each one.

1: "OF KINGLY LINE"

1. The spelling of names was by no means consistent in the eleventh century. Baldwin was also known as Baudouin, and Adela as Adelais.
2. Jumièges began his account, *Gesta Normannorum Ducum* (*The Deeds of the Norman Dukes*), in the 1050s and completed it in 1070–71. Although it is of great value as the earliest and most detailed of the eleventh-century histories, the *Gesta* is not wholly reliable and exaggerates the Normans' achievements. Despite its short-

comings, Jumièges's account became one of the most influential of the Norman period. It was subsequently added to and revised by other chroniclers, notably Orderic Vitalis and Robert of Torigni, and was widely available in the Middle Ages. No fewer than forty-seven manuscript copies exist in libraries and archives across Europe.

3. OV, II, p. 281. Orderic lists the children as Robert the Frisian, Arnulf, Baldwin, Odo Archbishop of Trier, Henry the clerk, Matilda, and Judith, wife of Earl Tostig. But Orderic's account of Flemish affairs is riddled with mistakes, and he had no direct experience of events there. In fact, Judith was the daughter of Baldwin IV, Arnulf was the son of Baldwin VI, and there is no record of an Odo of Trier among Baldwin and Adela's offspring.
4. Ibid., p. 105.
5. Ducarel, p. 64, provides an illustration of Matilda's Flemish and French descent, tracing her ancestors back to the seventh century.
6. The name took various forms, including Mathilde, Mahtild, Mahault, Molde, and Maud. Matilda herself was often referred to as Maud.
7. D. Nicholas, p. 89.
8. Ibid.
9. Hilton, p. 22.
10. R. A. Brown, pp. 31–32.
11. D. Nicholas, p. 51.
12. GG, pp. 31, 33.
13. GRA, I, p. 437. The *Gesta* was an extraordinarily ambitious work, spanning more than eleven hundred years: from the Roman invasion of England to the last decade of Henry I's reign. The account is riddled with scandal and hearsay, but is still invaluable as a source of social and political history, and the fact that the author was born of Anglo-Norman parents made his history more balanced. Malmesbury was one of the few chroniclers who lived and worked in England. He was also one of the youngest: he was just twenty-nine or thirty years old when the *Gesta* was completed.
14. Strickland, p. 22.
15. A. Campbell, p. 47.
16. Barlow, *Life of King Edward*, p. 83.
17. ASC, pp. 160–61; A. Campbell, p. 47.
18. Hilton, p. 26.
19. Ibid., p. 27.
20. OV, II, p. 225; Aird, *Robert Curthose*, p. 36.
21. Hilton, p. 25.
22. Corinthians 7:13.
23. Cowdrey, *Register of Pope Gregory VII*, pp. 219–20. Gregory later wrote in the same vein to Matilda. See below, pp. 173–74.

24. GG, p. 33.

25. Cowdrey, *Register of Pope Gregory VII*, p. 228.

26. GG, p. 33.

27. ASC, p. 134.

28. Starkey, p. 80.

29. ASC, p. 154.

30. GRA, I, p. 323.

31. ASC, p. 158. Much doubt was cast by contemporary chroniclers upon Harold's legitimacy. The author of the Abingdon Manuscript for the year of his accession claims that he was in fact the bastard son of a shoemaker. Jumièges, meanwhile, claims that Harold was Cnut's bastard son by his concubine, Aelfgifu. GND, II, p. 105.

32. ASC, p. 160. This was not the first time that Emma had been forced to flee her adopted country. Following a raid upon London by Sweyn "Forkbeard" in 1013, after which he usurped the throne, she had "turned across the sea" to her brother Richard II, the duke of Normandy. GRA, I, p. 305. Her then husband, King Aethelred, had dispatched their sons Edward and Alfred across the Channel soon afterward. ASC, p. 144; GND, II, p. 7.

33. GRA, I, p. 337.

34. ASC, pp. 160–61; A. Campbell, p. 47.

35. ASC, pp. 160–61; A. Campbell, pp. 51, 53.

36. ASC, p. 161.

37. The *Anglo-Saxon Chronicle* implies it was poison: "Harthacnut died as he stood at his drink, and he suddenly fell to the earth with an awful convulsion." ASC, p. 162.

38. Ibid., pp. 162–63.

39. Ibid., p. 172.

40. Most English exiles who sought refuge in Flanders were accommodated first at St.-Omer because it was the closest major town to the Channel coast. This was the case when Tostig again sought refuge in Flanders shortly before the Norman invasion of England in 1066.

41. Barlow, *Life of King Edward*, p. 37.

42. The two brothers spent the next ten years in Flanders, and they would remain friends with Matilda for the rest of her life. Both men fought on Duke William's side in the Battle of Hastings and were rewarded richly for it. When she became queen of England, Matilda gave Baldwin thirty acres of land in Shalford, Essex. He married Emma, a kinswoman of William's, who was evidently acquainted with Matilda, because she appeared in charters relating to La Trinité, the abbey that Matilda later founded.

43. OV, II, p. 225. In common with other monastic chronicles, the *Historia* began as a history of Orderic's own religious house, St.-Évroult in southern Normandy, but it rapidly grew into a work of staggering ambition that encompassed the entire

history of the Norman dynasty. The range and vibrancy of the material that it contains is truly remarkable. As well as drawing upon earlier histories, documentary sources, and oral traditions, Orderic also included some of his own memories from his childhood in England. The result is a rich and engaging narrative that brings the Norman period vividly to life. Admittedly, at times Orderic is too prone to peddling anecdotes, rumors, and legends, and it is not always clear whether he has based these upon a lost source or simply hearsay. But the fact that, like Malmesbury, he was born of Anglo-Norman parentage gave him a greater objectivity than the likes of Poitiers and Jumièges, and as he wrote his account during the reign of William and Matilda's youngest son, Henry, he evidently felt at liberty to explore the more shadowy aspects of his protagonists' lives.

44. GRA, I, p. 437.
45. Burgess and Holden, p. 199.
46. Strickland, p. 24.
47. GND, II, p. 129.
48. Delisle, *Receuil de Travaux d'Érudition*, pp. 223–24, 224–25.
49. Ibid., pp. 223–24 (author's translation).
50. Laing, III, p. 76.
51. *Chronique Rimée de Philippe Mouskes*, p. 174. See also Lair, p. 15.
52. This was carried out by Professor Dastugue, director of the anthropology laboratory of the Regional University Hospital in Caen.
53. A thegn was a recognized grade of nobility in eleventh-century England. It described a wealthy landowner who was a dependent of the king or an earl and who was wealthy enough to support a prestigious estate and a retinue of men. Brihtric and his peers were referred to in pre-Conquest sources as optimates ("best men") or procures ("chief men"). His great-grandfather may have been Aelfgar, "the king's kinsman," a Devon landowner whose death in 962 is recorded in the *Anglo-Saxon Chronicle*.
54. "A West-Country Magnate of the Eleventh Century: The Family, Estates and Patronage of Beorhtric son of Aelfgar," in Keats-Rohan, *Family Trees*, p. 50. A hide was a measurement used to calculate the amount of land tax due from its owner. There is no precise definition of the size of a hide. In Anglo-Saxon times, it simply meant enough land to support a household.
55. Freeman, *History of the Norman Conquest*, III, p. 86. Strickland, p. 23, claims that his surname of "Meaw" or "Snaw" may have derived from his fairness.
56. Dugdale, II, p. 60; Turgis, p. 11.

2: WILLIAM THE BASTARD

1. One of the foremost authorities on William and the Norman Conquest, D. C. Douglas, states that it was most likely in the autumn of 1028. He bases this upon

the early narrative *De Obitu Willelmi*, which claims that in September 1087, William was in the fifty-ninth year of his life. This, together with the broad agreement by contemporary chroniclers that William was in his eighth year when his father died, has led Douglas to this conclusion. Douglas, *William the Conqueror,* p. 368. For an alternative view, see Planché, I, pp. 77–82.

2. Malmesbury rejects as "very doubtful" the theory that Robert's later pilgrimage to Jerusalem was in repentance for this evil deed. GRA, I, p. 309.

3. GND, II, pp. 39 and 41.

4. Also known as Herleve, Arlette, Arletta, and Arlotte.

5. A useful analysis of the subject is provided by Houts, "Origins of Herleva."

6. GRA, I, p. 427.

7. Another version has Herleva dreaming that a tree grew out of her womb and stretched out over Normandy and England. Burgess and Holden, p. 167.

8. GRA, I, p. 427. This tale is repeated in Burgess and Holden, p. 167.

9. GRA, I, p. 427.

10. Adelaide married Enguerrand II, count of Ponthieu; Lambert II, count of Lens; and Odo II of Champagne.

11. See, for example, GND, II, p. 96n.

12. Herleva also had at least two daughters by Herluin (Muriel and Isabella), and possibly two others. However, the evidence for their lives is sketchy.

13. GND, II, p. 97. He also referred to him as "William the Bastard" in his *Ecclesiastical History.* See OV, IV, p. 111.

14. Poitiers was archdeacon of Lisieux, one of the most important cathedrals in Normandy. As such, he was well acquainted with the ducal family and the workings of the Norman court. Like Jumièges, he was writing at the same time as the events that he described, but his account, the *Gesta Guillelmi Ducis Normannorum et Regis Anglorum (The Deeds of William, Duke of the Normans and King of the English),* which was completed in around 1077, was hardly a balanced appraisal. Written at the duke's command, it was little more than a propaganda piece to praise—and, more important, to justify—William's actions.

15. GRA, I, p. 427.

16. GND, II, p. 81. Although William's date of birth is most often assumed to be 1027 or 1028, Robert of Torigni claims that he was only five years old when his father left him in charge of the duchy. It seems unlikely that Robert would have entrusted his kingdom to one quite so young.

17. Ibid.

18. Malmesbury claims that Robert's servant, Ralph Mowin, had poisoned him in the hope of assuming control of the duchy. However, when Mowin returned to Normandy, the truth came to light and he was "universally rejected as a monster and departed into lifelong exile." GRA, I, p. 309.

19. Malmesbury asserts that in 1086, shortly before William's own death, he sent a

mission to reclaim his father's remains from Nicaea so that he could have them reburied in his native Normandy. The envoys succeeded in recovering Robert's body, but had only reached as far as Apulia in Italy when they learned of William's death and therefore decided to bury Robert in Italy. GRA, I, pp. 505, 507. Further evidence of William's veneration of his late father is provided by Professor Bates, who points to the fact that William founded an abbey in 1063 and dedicated it to St. Stephen. This saint had been uncelebrated in Normandy until Duke Robert acquired one of his fingers during his pilgrimage to Jerusalem. The relic was sent back to Normandy after the duke's death and sparked a major cult. Bates, *William the Conqueror,* p. 43.

20. GRA, I, p. 427.
21. GND, II, p. 97.
22. OV, IV, p. 83.
23. Le Vaudreuil was on the river Seine south of Rouen.
24. GND, II, p. 91.
25. Ibid., p. 121.
26. GRA, I, p. 335.
27. GND, II, p. 91.
28. GRA, I, p. 451.
29. Ibid., p. 477.
30. ASC, p. 219.
31. Southern, *Life of St. Anselm,* p. 56.
32. GND, II, p. 125.
33. The stigma of William's birth would still be felt by his successors a century later. His great-grandson, Henry II, snubbed the bishop of Lincoln at a picnic one day because they had quarreled. The king was mending a leather bandage on his finger with a needle and thread. Seeing this, the bishop quipped: "How like your cousins of Falaise you do look." Luckily for him, Henry appreciated the joke. Bates, *William the Conqueror,* p. 58.
34. ASC, p. 219; Forester, p. 217.
35. GND, II, p. 121; GG, p. 9. See also Searle, *Chronicle of Battle Abbey,* pp. 41, 93.
36. GND, II, p. 189. This is corroborated by Malmesbury, who claims that William was "a practising Christian as far as a layman could be, to the extent of attending mass every day and every day hearing vespers and matins." GRA, I, p. 493.
37. Clover and Gibson, p. 61.
38. OV, II, p. 239.
39. ASC, p. 219.
40. GRA, I, p. 507.
41. According to Malmesbury, the two men were of very different character. He describes Robert of Mortain as "dense and slow-witted," whereas Odo "was a

man of much livelier mind" who was "a great double-dealer and showed great cunning." GRA, I, p. 507.

42. The eighteenth-century historian Rapin claims that there were reports that William was "very much addicted to women in his youth," but there are no contemporary sources to corroborate this. Rapin, p. 81.

43. Ibid.

44. GRA, I, p. 501.

45. GND, II, p. 189.

46. Bates, *William the Conqueror*, p. 137.

47. GND, II, p. 189.

48. GRA, I, p. 509.

49. Bates, *William the Conqueror*, pp. 138–39.

50. GND, II, p. 189.

51. GRA, I, p. 511.

52. Ibid., p. 509.

3: THE ROUGH WOOING

1. GND, II, p. 129.

2. GG, p. 31.

3. Ibid.

4. GND, II, p. 129.

5. Fauroux, pp. 275–77.

6. GND, II, p. 129; Blaauw, p. 109.

7. Strickland, p. 26.

8. *Chronicon Turonense*, p. 348.

9. "Cronique attribuée à Baudoin d'Avesnes," p. 559.

10. *Chronicon Turonense*, p. 348.

11. "Cronique attribuée à Baudoin d'Avesnes," p. 559.

12. Indeed, another account claims that on a later occasion he killed her instantly by kicking at her from his horse and driving his spur into her breast. See p. 77.

13. Philippe Mouskes and Baldwin of Avesnes, *Chronique Rimée de Philippe Mouskes*, pp. 175–77; "Cronique attribuée à Baudoin d'Avesnes," p. 559.

14. Strickland, p. 25.

15. "Interdixit et Balduino comiti Flandrensi, ne filiam suam Willelmo Normanno nuptui daret; et illi, ne eam acciperet." Mansi, col. 742.

16. Robert had also repudiated his first wife, Rozala of Italy, when she failed to give him an heir. Ironically, his third wife, Constance of Arles, gave him the sons he had hoped for but incited them to rebel against their father.

17. Douglas, *William the Conqueror*, p. 76.

18. Ibid.

19. GND, II, p. 147.

20. Blaauw, pp. 109–10, certainly believes this was the case and asserts it strongly. See also Mason, *William II*, p. 27.

21. Prentout, pp. 14–29, provides a useful précis of this argument. See also Boüard, *Guillaume le Conquérant*, pp. 163–65; Douglas, *William the Conqueror*, p. 380.

22. This theory was put forward by the mid-nineteenth-century medievalist Thomas Stapleton, in "Observations in Disproof." See also Freeman, *History of the Norman Conquest*, III, pp. 86–87, 651–60, and Appendix O; Freeman, "Parentage of Gundrada"; Blaauw; Lair, pp. 25–26; Planché, pp. 134–35; Prentout, pp. 9–14; Waters; Guérard, p. 201; H.W.C. Davis, I, p. 52.

23. Also referred to as "Gundrada" and "Gundred."

24. There is no direct reference to Matilda's being the mother of Gerbod and Frederic; this is inferred from contemporary evidence about Gundreda's brothers. Orderic Vitalis claims that Gundreda was the sister of Gerbode, a Fleming, to whom Duke William later gave the earldom of Chester. His account is confirmed by a reference in the chronicle of Hyde Abbey to "Gerbodo" from Flanders, brother of a countess. A number of references contained within Domesday Book to a man named Frederic from Flanders led Stapleton to conclude that he, too, was a brother of Gundreda—and therefore a son of Matilda. Another nineteenth-century historian claims that there was a third son, Richard Guett, who was listed as the brother of "the Countess of Warren" in a bequest to Bermondsey Abbey, although the evidence for this is flimsy. OV, II, p. 221; Edwards, pp. xcvii, 296; Morris, vol. XVIII, no. 18:7; Clay, pp. 44–45; Planché, pp. 136–37, 144.

25. This is supported by another Lewes charter, which records that the manor of Carleton in Norfolk was given to the priory by "Matilda, mother of the Countess Gundred." Clay, pp. 43, 61; Freeman, "Parentage of Gundrada," p. 681; M.A.E. Green, I, pp. 73n, 77.

26. Clay, pp. 40–41, 44, 56–57; M.A.E. Green, I, pp. 74–75. Strickland, pp. 97–98, accepts this theory and confidently names Gundreda as the "sixth and youngest daughter of the Conqueror and Matilda." The belief that Gundreda was the daughter of William and Matilda evidently still prevailed in the sixteenth century. The British Library contains a sketch from around the time of Henry VIII's reign that shows the couple with three of their sons and three of their daughters. Gundreda is included among the latter. BL Harleian 1449 fo.6b. The badly damaged tombstone that bore Gundreda's epitaph was discovered at Isfield Church near Lewes in 1774 by the antiquary Sir William Burrell, who reerected it in St. John's Church, Southover. In 1845, her lead coffin was discovered by workmen during the construction of the Lewes and Brighton railway. It bore the inscription "Gundrada" and lay alongside that of her husband, William of Warenne, in the grounds of St. Pancras Priory, Lewes, which they had founded. The coffins were later rein-

terred in a specially constructed chapel at the priory. H.W.C. Davis, I, p. 52; Clay, pp. 40–41, 44.

27. If they were not mother and daughter, Matilda and Gundreda do seem to have been well acquainted. Gundreda shared Matilda's Flemish descent and might have been affiliated to her father's court. The evidence suggests that she was of noble birth, and the intriguing inscription on her tomb implies that she was part of the ducal family itself. It is possible that she was a daughter of one of Matilda's brothers. There is no Gundreda listed among their children, but the records concerning female offspring are notoriously sketchy during this period, and she could in any case have been illegitimate. Alternatively, she may have been a member of Matilda's household—the duchess retained a number of Flemish ladies in her service throughout her life. It has even been suggested that Gundreda was adopted by Matilda and William as a child. Certainly, the couple seem to have held her in some esteem, for they granted various estates to her and her husband. Gundreda, for her part, was grateful to Matilda, for she later gave her the manor of Cariton in Cambridgeshire as a gift. Clay, pp. 43, 54–55, 56–57, 59–62. See also H.W.C. Davis, I, p. 52.

28. OV, II, p. 105.

29. This had been a controversial marriage. According to one account, Richildis had proved as unwilling a bride as Matilda, and had refused to marry Robert for fear of offending the emperor. This had prompted Count Baldwin to take matters into his own hands. He gathered a troop of soldiers together and took Richildis by force to Flanders, where she was married to his son before any further protests could arise. Lair, pp. 21–22.

30. Round, p. 421; Smet, p. 552; Fauroux, pp. 254, 284–86, 293–95, 302–3; *Chronicon Turonense*, p. 348. For a more recent discussion of the subject, see Davis, "William of Jumièges," pp. 603–4; Barlow, *William Rufus*, p. 8n; Douglas, *William the Conqueror*, pp. 379–80.

31. GG, p. 33. Presumably Matilda would also have been presented with lavish gifts by her husband-to-be, as this was traditional. An old English poem prescribed: "A king shall buy a queen with goods, with cups and with bracelets." Stafford, *Queens, Concubines and Dowagers*, p. 57.

32. Bates, *William the Conqueror*, p. 42.

33. Licquet claims that it was celebrated at Rouen: Turgis, p. 22n. Wace, meanwhile, asserts that the venue was Eu: Burgess and Holden, p. 199.

34. Turgis, p. 23.

35. "Cronique attribuée à Baudoin d'Avesnes." See also Strickland, pp. 27–28.

36. GND, II, p. 131.

37. Bates, *Normandy Before 1066*, pp. 199–201. See also Bates, *William the Conqueror*, pp. 55–56; GND, II, p. 148n. A recent biography of Lanfranc supports this theory, and cites a letter from Pope Nicholas to Lanfranc implying that the prelate had

not visited Rome during the early part of 1059, when the ban was lifted. Gibson, pp. 69n, 109–10.

38. They were Robert Champart, abbot of Jumièges, and Jean de Ravenne, abbot of Fécamp.

39. Freeman, *History of the Norman Conquest*, III, pp. 105–6.

40. GRA, I, p. 495.

4: BIRTH OF A DYNASTY

1. GND, II, pp. 129, 131.

2. GG, p. 33.

3. OV, III, p. 36.

4. Bates, *William the Conqueror*, p. 56.

5. Burgess and Holden, p. 199.

6. Not to be confused with the chronicler William of Jumièges, with whom there was apparently no connection.

7. Wulfnoth and Haakon would remain in Normandy for the next thirteen years. Another theory is that they were there as part of a bargain struck between Earl Godwine and King Edward. The English king had apparently demanded that the two men be placed under Duke William's guardianship to ensure that the earl would not rebel against him.

8. GRA, I, p. 355.

9. Ibid., p. 417.

10. Brown, *Normans and the Norman Conquest;* Wright, *Chronicle of Pierre de Langtoft,* I, p. 413.

11. Bradley, p. 348.

12. Bates, *William the Conqueror*, p. 137.

13. The date of Richard's birth is cited as c. 1055 in GND, II, pp. 216n, 290–91. This is the earliest account to mention Matilda's second son. One source claims that William Rufus was born as early as 1056. However, his biographer, Professor Barlow, places his date of birth at around 1060. He quotes Malmesbury's statement that William's death occurred when he was *major quadragenario* (above the age of forty), although he admits that this phrase may have simply meant that William was no longer young. Barlow, *William Rufus*, p. 3n. William's nickname is assumed to refer to his red hair, which may have recurred in his father's family due to its Viking ancestry. But contemporary writers agree that his hair was "yellow" or "blond," and variously claim that it was his red beard or ruddy complexion that earned him his nickname. See, for example, GRA, I, pp. 566–67. This is discussed further in Mason, *William II*, pp. 9–11.

14. OV, II, p. 225.

15. The exception is Orderic Vitalis, who, in his revision of the *Gesta Normannorum Ducum,* completely ignored Jumièges's paragraph about William and Matilda's offspring and the succession. This may have been a tactful omission because he was conscious of the turbulent relationship between William and his eldest son.

16. GND, II, p. 131. In his later revision of this work, Robert of Torigni provides a little more detail, saying that Matilda's children by William included "Robert, who after him held the duchy of Normandy for some time, and William who ruled the kingdom of England thirteen years, and Richard who died in his youth . . . and four daughters." Torigni, who was writing in the 1130s, was a methodical and conscientious historian, more concerned with recording the information as he found it than with dramatizing it for the benefit of his audience. As prior of Le Bec and later abbot of Mont-Saint-Michel, he played a much more active role in the secular world than either Jumièges or Orderic had been able to, and the insights that he provides into the political world of Normandy are therefore of value.

17. GND, II, pp. 261, 263; GRA, I, p. 505; OV, II, pp. 105, 225; IV, p. 351; GG, pp. 59, 61, 95, 96, 157; Burgess and Holden, pp. 199, 223. Historians have differed almost as much as contemporary chroniclers in their accounts of William and Matilda's daughters. Some of the most useful analyses include Barlow, *William Rufus,* pp. 88–92, Appendix A; Freeman, *History of the Norman Conquest,* III, pp. 666–70; D. C. Douglas, *William the Conqueror: The Norman Impact upon England* (London, Folio Society, 2004), Appendix C; OV, III, pp. 114–15n; Barlow, *William Rufus,* pp. 441–45; Pryde et al., *Handbook of British Chronology,* p. 31. See also Madden, p. 31.

18. Also referred to as Adelais, Adelida, and Aelgiva.

19. OV, IV, p. 351.

20. See, for example, Douglas, *William the Conqueror,* p. 383; Bates, *William the Conqueror,* p. 151.

21. The only account that contradicts this is the nineteenth-century poem written in Matilda's honor by H. M. Carey. She claims that "several of Matilda's children died in their infancy" and cites Orderic Vitalis as her source, even though there is nothing in his account to substantiate it. Carey, p. 16n.

22. The ministrations of doctors often did more harm than good. For example, the treatment advocated for a woman who suffered excessive bleeding after childbirth was to bleed her first from one ankle and then the other. Leyser, p. 281.

23. R. V. Turner, p. 21.

24. The names that were chosen for William and Matilda's daughters cast further doubt upon the separate existence of Agatha. There is no known source for this name from either side of the family, nor does it have any other obvious connections. Indeed, its absence from most contemporary sources suggests that it was a

highly unusual name. Only Orderic Vitalis refers to it: once as the name of William and Matilda's daughter, and once as a third-century virgin and martyr who was commemorated at Catania in Sicily. OV, III, p. 86.

25. Barlow, *William Rufus*, p. 14. See also James, pp. 13–23. The theory continues that youth was from twenty-nine to fifty; dignity from fifty-one to seventy; and thereafter was old age.

26. Delisle, pp. 224–25.

27. Fauroux, pp. 434–35, 409–15.

28. GRA, I, p. 543.

29. Strickland, p. 80, claims that Roger de Beaumont had played a role in the education of William and Matilda's children, but there is no contemporary evidence to substantiate this.

30. Migne, p. 156; Houts, "Norman Conquest Through European Eyes." The two might have been related through Matilda's mother, Adela. Matilda also witnessed a grant to Rouen cathedral by Simon in 1075. Bates, *Regesta Regum*, pp. 720–21.

31. Migne, p. 156; Houts, *Normans in Europe*, p. 199.

32. GRA, I, p. 543.

33. Bates, *Regesta Regum*, pp. 94–96; Fauroux, no. 141; Round, p. 421.

34. Other notable examples of mothers advising their sons on political affairs included Berthe de Blois, who upon the death of her husband, Hugh IV of Maine, advised their young son Herbert to ingratiate himself with Duke William. Meanwhile, Harold Godwinson would have done well to heed his mother Gytha's advice not to do battle with William at Hastings in 1066. Truax, "From Bede to Orderic Vitalis," pp. 49–50.

35. For example, William of Poitiers mentions a daughter of William and Matilda who was betrothed to Count Herbert of Maine. GG, pp. 59, 61.

36. Foreville, pp. 92, 120.

37. It has been suggested that William Rufus was close in age to Cecilia and that his parents may therefore have intended to commit him to the duke's abbey of St.-Étienne at the same time that Cecilia entered her mother's foundation at La Trinité in 1066. Barlow, *William Rufus*, p. 22.

38. Round, p. 108.

39. OV, V, p. 177. He was also known as "Arnulf the grammarian" and was later appointed chaplain and chancellor to Matilda's eldest son, Robert. He taught Cecilia at La Trinité, the abbey that Matilda founded at Caen, where he was also schoolmaster and chaplain to the other nuns. David, p. 219; GND, II, p. 53n.

40. For praise of Cecilia and Adela's beauty, see Abrahams, pp. 199, 255.

41. K. A. LoPrete, "Adela of Blois as Mother and Countess," in Carmi Parsons and Wheeler, p. 319.

42. They included "Ilgerius, pedagogue of Robert," who is listed among the witnesses to a charter that was confirmed by William shortly before he departed for

the invasion of England. Fauroux, pp. 437–38; Aird, *Robert Curthose*, p. 37; K. A. LoPrete, "Adela of Blois as Mother and Countess," in Carmi Parsons and Wheeler, p. 315.

43. GRA, I, p. 493. All the chroniclers attest to Lanfranc's exceptional intellect and ability. Orderic Vitalis hails him as "remarkably well-versed in the liberal arts, a man full of kindness, generosity, and piety, who devoted much time to alms and other good works." He also claims that "By intellect and learning Lanfranc would have won the applause of Herodian in grammar, Aristotle in Dialectic, Cicero in rhetoric, Augustine, Jerome, and the other commentators on the Old and New Testaments in scriptural studies." OV, II, pp. 147, 251. Eadmer, meanwhile, describes him as "a man of energetic character and possessed of outstanding knowledge in studies both sacred and secular." Eadmer, p. 10.

44. OV, III, p. 101.

45. GRA, I, p. 701.

5: DUCHESS OF NORMANDY

1. Bates, *Regesta Regum*, pp. 638–39.
2. Bates, *William the Conqueror*, p. 149.
3. Ibid., p. 147.
4. Ibid., p. 29.
5. GND, I, p. 5.
6. ASC, p. 221. As king of England, William would be widely criticized for the draconian measures that he introduced to protect game. Malmesbury condemned him for the destruction that was entailed in creating his favorite hunting ground, the New Forest, and Orderic claimed that sixty parishes were laid waste in the process, although this was an exaggeration. William, he said, had "replaced the men with beasts of the forest so that he might hunt to his heart's content." OV, V, p. 285. See also Forester, p. 217.
7. Forester, p. 217.
8. GND, II, p. 147. The Lateran Councils of the Roman Catholic Church were so named because they were held in the Lateran Palace, a former papal residence, in Rome between the seventh and the eighteenth centuries.
9. GND, II, pp. 147, 149.
10. Burgess and Holden, pp. 199, 201.
11. Ibid. The full verse runs:

    Before their union was allowed
    A hundred prebends they endowed:
    A hundred poor men clothed and fed,
    To sick and crippled gave their bread

At Cherbourg and at Rouen,
At Bayeux too, no less than Caen–
These pious gifts are with us still
As founded by the ducal will.

12. The same stone was later used for building work in England, notably the choir of Canterbury Cathedral.

13. GND, II, p. 149. The date of La Trinité's foundation depends upon the length of Abbess Matilda's tenure. For this we must rely upon Orderic Vitalis, but his accounts leave room for doubt. In the *Gesta Normannorum Ducum,* he claims that Abbess Matilda ruled for forty-eight years, but in his *Historia Ecclesiastica* he says it was forty-seven years. There is some confusion as to when he dated her tenure from—i.e., when the abbey was first operational in 1059, or when it was dedicated in June 1066. GND, II, pp. 148–49n; OV, IV, p. 47. For a further discussion on this point, see Musset, "La Reine Mathilde," pp. 191–210.

14. Musset, *Les Actes de Guillaume le Conquérant,* p. 15.

15. GG, p. 85.

16. Freeman, *History of the Norman Conquest,* III, p. 109.

17. Bates, *William the Conqueror,* p. 90. Orderic Vitalis inaccurately claims that William built both churches, completely overlooking Matilda's role in commissioning La Trinité. OV, II, pp. 11, 191. It is true that William had more involvement in the foundation of La Trinité than Matilda did in St.-Étienne, judging from the frequency of his name on its charters. But the sources make it abundantly clear that La Trinité was very much Matilda's project.

18. OV, II, p. 11.

19. OV, VI, p. 451. This would be completed by her youngest son, Henry, who turned it into the priory of Le Bec. His heart was later buried there, which may have been intended as a compliment to his mother. The rest of his remains were buried at his father's abbey of St.-Étienne in Caen.

20. Bates, *Regesta Regum,* p. 93.

21. The wording used was *"Hoc viderunt Guillelmus Rex et Mathildis regina."* Bates, *Regesta Regum,* pp. 183–87, 271–95, 302, 530–33, 625–27, 750–51, 767–69; Round, pp. 141, 429, 431; Davis, *Regesta Regum Anglo-Normannorum,* I, pp. 8, 30, 33, 41.

22. Bates, *Regesta Regum,* pp. 176–78, 632–33, 643–46, 722–23, 750–51, 759–62, 774–75; Fauroux, pp. 343–44, 375–76, 377–78, 396–98, 408–9, 442–46.

23. The lands included Bures-en-Bray, Maintru, and Osmoy-St.-Valéry. For the contention that Matilda was comparatively poor before the Conquest, see Musset, "La Reine Mathilde," p. 193. As well as the dowry that a woman brought to her marriage, which represented her share of her family's inheritance, she was also endowed with dower rights in her husband's lands.

24. Bates, *Regesta Regum*, pp. 530–33.
25. Musset, *Les Actes de Guillaume le Conquérant*.
26. OV, III, pp. 135–39.
27. GRA, I, p. 501.
28. Strickland, p. 37.
29. Carey, p. 79.
30. Round, pp. 341–42; Fauroux, p. 432.
31. GRA, I, p. 501.
32. Ibid.
33. OV, III, pp. 103, 105.
34. Round, p. 425.
35. Carey, p. 16.
36. Turgis, p. 10 (author's translation).
37. There was also a portrait of Matilda's future husband, William, and their sons, Robert and William. She commissioned the paintings when the abbey was built. They survived until the seventeenth century, when the room in which they were housed was demolished. The engravings were reproduced in a work by the French Benedictine monk Bernard de Montfaucon, in *Les monuments de la monarchie française,* 5 vols. (Paris, 1729–33).
38. Turgis, p. 10n.
39. GG, p. 149; GRA, I, p. 501.
40. GRA, I, p. 277.
41. Laing, III, p. 94.
42. Morris, vol. V, no. 67:1. This is corroborated by the mortuary roll of Abbess Matilda of the abbey of La Trinité, Caen, which includes a request that prayers be said for Duchess Matilda and three of her daughters, including the younger Matilda. Delisle, *Rouleaux des Morts,* pp. 181–82. If William and Matilda had as many daughters as the sources imply, it would have been unusual if none of them had shared their mother's name, so this lends the accounts credibility.
43. Fauroux, Hilton, p. 38.
44. GG, p. 63.
45. GRA, I, p. 441.
46. GND, II, p. 151; GRA, I, p. 441.
47. GRA, I, p. 337.

6: EARL HAROLD

1. GRA, I, p. 417.
2. An excellent summary of the unification of England is given in Bates, *William the Conqueror,* p. 91. See also Fletcher, pp. 13–24.

3. Loyn, p. 315.

4. GRA, I, p. 419. Eadmer, meanwhile, attests that Harold and his men were stripped of all their most valuable possessions before being released. Eadmer, p. 6.

5. GRA, I, p. 417.

6. GG, p. 69.

7. Eadmer, p. 6.

8. GRA, I, p. 419.

9. GND, II, p. 161.

10. GRA, I, p. 441.

11. OV, II, p. 137.

12. Barlow, *Life of King Edward*, p. 49.

13. Laing, III, p. 76.

14. Carey, p. 14.

15. Laing, III, p. 76.

16. Ibid.

17. GG, p. 71.

18. OV, II, pp. 135, 137.

19. Eadmer, p. 7.

20. GRA, I, p. 419. Eadmer, p. 7, also mentions this, but does not name the girl. There is a great deal of confusion among the contemporary sources about which daughter was betrothed to Harold. The girl's name is variously given as Agatha, Adela, Adeliza, and Adelida. The chroniclers differ not only from each other, but also within their own accounts. In his *Ecclesiastical History,* Orderic Vitalis refers to the girl as Agatha, but as Adelaide in his additions to the *Gesta Normannorum Ducum:* OV, III, p. 114n, 115. Wace's account is more confused still. He claims that Matilda had just two daughters, Cecilia and Adela, and he is the only chronicler who attests that Adela was betrothed to Harold: Burgess and Holden, pp. 199, 223. We can be reasonably certain that Adeliza, Adelida, and Agatha were one and the same girl, and given that Adela was not even born when Harold visited Normandy, his intended bride must have been Adeliza. As William and Matilda's eldest daughter, she was the most suitable candidate for a betrothal of this significance.

21. Laing, III, p. 76. See also Forester, p. 206.

22. Eadmer, p. 7.

23. Laing, III, p. 76.

24. Hill, pp. 24–26; Grape, p. 40. An earlier proponent of this theory is Turgis, pp. 41–42.

25. Andrew Bridgeford provides a compelling account of this mystery, alongside a myriad of others that the tapestry poses, in his excellent study.

26. GND, II, p. 161.

27. Eadmer, p. 8.

28. Ibid.
29. Carey, p. 46.
30. GRA, I, p. 447.
31. Eadmer, p. 8.

7: CONQUEST

1. OV, II, p. 137.
2. ASC, p. 194.
3. GND, II, p. 167; OV, II, p. 171.
4. GRA, I, p. 447.
5. OV, II, p. 145.
6. GRA, I, p. 449.
7. Strickland, p. 45.
8. Their sons Robert, Richard, and William witnessed the document confirming Cecilia's entry. Musset, *Les Actes de Guillaume le Conquérant*, p. 53; Fauroux, pp. 442–46; Dugdale, p. 1072.
9. Around twenty young girls entered La Trinité with Cecilia that day. The endowments that they brought with them made the abbey so prosperous that it was able to survive with no other income until the French Revolution.
10. Freeman, however, argues that Cecilia must have been William and Matilda's firstborn daughter for their relinquishing of her to the abbey to have been a sufficient sacrifice. None of the contemporary sources corroborate this theory, and the evidence is stronger that Adeliza was the eldest. Freeman, *History of the Norman Conquest*, III, p. 385. Meanwhile, M.A.E. Green, I, p. 5, asserts that Cecilia did not enter the cloister until 1074, and that the ceremony in 1066 was merely to pledge her as a future novice of the abbey. "In the summer of 1075, after completing a year's trial, the girl expressed her steadfast desire to take the monastic vows." However, Green probably confused this with the fact that in 1075 Cecilia took her vows as a fully ordained nun, having spent the previous nine years as a novice in the abbey.
11. GND, III, p. 149. See also OV, III, p. 9; IV, p. 47.
12. OV, III, pp. 9, 11; IV, p. 47. Orderic cites the date of Cecilia's entry to La Trinité as 1075. OV, III, p. 9n; Walmsley, p. 429.
13. GND, II, p. 261.
14. The tapestry depicts ten men in the ship, but this was undoubtedly representative of many more.
15. Another account describes the sails as being painted in several places with three lions—the device of the Norman ensign—although this is doubtful, because armorial ensigns were not introduced until much later.
16. The figure was also thought to represent their third son, William Rufus. Burgess

and Holden, p. 239. See also Houts, "The Ship List of William the Conqueror"; Houts, *Normans in Europe,* pp. 130–31.

17. GG, pp. 175, 177, 181; Houts, "The Echo of the Conquest in Latin Sources," pp. 149–51. Figureheads had long been believed to have a magical as well as a symbolic function. For this reason, it was customary to remove them from ships before they arrived at their destination, because the inhabitants of the land that received them were afraid of being cursed. The Bayeux Tapestry shows that this happened with the ships of William's fleet when it arrived on England's shores.

18. Other theories for the ship's name include "foolish" or "foolish woman," a less common meaning derived from the Latin translation. This could have been a jest implying that Matilda was unwise to let her husband embark upon such a risky enterprise. Houts, "The Ship List of William the Conqueror," p. 172.

19. The evidence suggests that Matilda chose one of her own servants to captain the ship. Orderic Vitalis names him as Stephen, son of Airard. This may have been the same man who is listed as "Stephanus seruiens comitisse" in the foundation charter of the duchess's abbey at Caen, La Trinité. Ibid., pp. 172–73. Fifty-four years later, Stephen's son commanded the White Ship when it was shipwrecked off the coast of Normandy. Among those lost was Matilda's grandson, the heir to England, and her granddaughter Matilda, daughter of Adela.

20. Burgess and Holden, p. 235.

21. ASC, p. 194. This "star" was Halley's comet, and the Bayeux Tapestry represents it as coinciding with Harold's coronation, which was a case of dramatic license, for it could only have been seen in England between April 24 and 30. For other English commentaries on the phenomenon, see Riley, pp. 137–38; Darlington and McGurk, II, p. 601.

22. GND, II, pp. 162n, 163.

23. OV, II, p. 135. In a similar vein, Jumièges claimed "it portended, as many said, a change in some kingdom." GND, II, pp. 162n, 163.

24. GG, p. 103. Edward III took ten thousand men to France in 1346, and Henry V's force in 1415 probably comprised around fifteen to twenty thousand men.

25. Jumièges also cites this figure, although Douglas claims that it was more likely to have been around one thousand at most: *William the Conqueror,* pp. 183–4n. Brown's estimate is more conservative still, at six or seven hundred: *Normans and the Norman Conquest,* p. 130. See also Barlow, *Carmen de Hastingae Proelio,* pp. xv–xvi.

26. GND, II, pp. 165, 167. See also OV, II, p. 145.

27. Thorpe, II, p. 12; OV, II, p. 356; III, pp. 98, 112; IV, p. 92; GND, I, Appendix; ASC, pp. 213–14. See also OV, II, p. 357; IV, p. 93.

28. A recent source claims that Matilda and Anne of Kiev were friends and that their sons Robert and Philip played together as children. Beguiling though this image is, there is no evidence for it in the contemporary sources. Fettu, p. xx.

29. Stafford, *Queen Emma and Queen Edith*, p. 186.
30. Bates, *Normandy Before 1066*, p. 151.
31. Truax, p. 117.
32. Strickland, p. 42.
33. William held at least three great councils as he made his preparations to invade England: one at Lillebonne, another at Bonneville-sur-Touques, and a third at Caen. It is not clear at which of these Matilda's position as regent was confirmed, but given that the Caen council did not take place until June, the former two are more likely.
34. Foreville, p. 261; GG, p. 179.
35. OV, II, p. 263.
36. A reference by Orderic Vitalis implies that Montgomery was coregent, but this is not substantiated elsewhere and would hardly have been consistent with William's policy of empowering family members above his nobles. There has in fact been some debate as to whether Montgomery was among those who stayed behind when the duke embarked upon his enterprise. Whereas both William of Poitiers and Orderic Vitalis assert that he was one of Matilda's advisers, Wace goes into some detail about the pivotal role that Montgomery played at the Battle of Hastings. However, the former chroniclers were closer to the events, both in time and geography, so their accounts are more reliable. Similarly, it has been suggested that Hugh d'Avranches, who hailed from a powerful noble family in southwest Normandy, accompanied William to England in 1066 rather than playing a more political role back in the duchy. He seems, though, to have been confused with his father, Richard, who is known to have fought at Hastings, and there is compelling evidence that Hugh did not go to England until the following year. GND, II, p. 267n; OV, II, p. 211; Bates, "Origins of the Justiciarship," pp. 6–9; Planché, pp. 181–84; II, pp. 16–17.
37. GG, p. 179.
38. OV, III, p. 99.
39. ASC, pp. 195, 197.
40. According to his account, the two men were "close friends" because they had married two sisters, Judith and Matilda. In fact, Judith was Matilda's aunt.
41. OV, II, p. 141.
42. Malmesbury refers to Hardrada as "Harold Fairhair, king of Norwegians." GRA, I, p. 421.
43. Ibid. See also ASC, pp. 197–98.
44. GRA, I, p. 449. See also Barlow, *Carmen de Hastingae Proelio*, p. 7.
45. GRA, I, p. 449. See also OV, II, p. 171.
46. GND, II, p. 165.
47. Brown, *Normans and the Norman Conquest*, p. 133.
48. GRA, I, p. 451. Wace gives a slightly different account of the incident, and credits

William himself with the quickness of thought: "When the duke first disembarked, he fell forward on to the palms of his hands; at once a loud cry arose and everyone said: 'This is a bad sign!' But he cried out to them: 'My lords, by the splendour of God! I have taken possession of the land in my two hands.' " Burgess and Holden, p. 241. This account is corroborated by Searle, *Chronicle of Battle Abbey,* p. 35.

49. Strickland, p. 49.

50. ASC, pp. 199–200. See also OV, II, p. 173.

51. GG, p. 131. For a similar account, see OV, II, p. 175.

52. GRA, I, p. 457; GG, p. 135; Barlow, *Carmen de Hastingae Proelio,* pp. 27, 29.

53. Barlow, *Carmen de Hastingae Proelio,* p. 27; GG, p. 133.

54. GRA, I, p. 455.

55. Wace claims that Harold continued fighting after his eye was "put out" by an arrow and was subsequently felled by a blow to the thigh, whereupon "there was such a throng . . . that I cannot say who killed him." Burgess and Holden, p. 287. There was little of Harold's body left to identify when his grief-stricken mistress, Edith "Swanneck," later walked through the carnage of the battlefield in the hope of rescuing her lover's remains for burial. A grisly account of his slaughter is provided by Guy, bishop of Amiens: Barlow, *Carmen de Hastingae Proelio,* p. 33.

56. GG, pp. 137, 139.

8: "A FATAL DISASTER"

1. GRA, I, p. 457.

2. GND, II, pp. 169, 169n.

3. Searle, pp. 39, 41.

4. OV, II, p. 179. For a similar account, see GG, pp. 139, 141.

5. ASC, pp. 199–200.

6. Barlow, *Carmen de Hastingae Proelio,* p. 35.

7. OV, II, p. 179. His account is taken from William of Poitiers: GG, p. 141. A similar version is provided by Guy, bishop of Amiens: Barlow, *Carmen de Hastingae Proelio,* p. 35. They are contradicted by Malmesbury, who claims that William agreed to release his rival's body for an honorable burial: GRA, I, p. 461.

8. GRA, I, p. 423.

9. Fauroux, p. 27; Ducarel, p. 36.

10. OV, II, p. 225.

11. Some doubt has been cast upon whether Guy of Amiens was Matilda's chaplain. He is cited as such by Orderic Vitalis, but Professor Barlow has questioned whether a French bishop would have attended a duchess of Normandy. True, Matilda had strong family connections with France, and Guy was also descended from the French royal family. But he was routinely to be found at the court of the

French king and regularly witnessed charters there, whereas he is not known to have witnessed any charters in Normandy or England, including the two charters that were granted on the day of Matilda's coronation. Barlow, *Carmen de Hastingae Proelio*, p. xvii.

12. Orderic Vitalis claims that Guy had already written the poem when he came to England with Matilda in 1068. Some scholars believe the poem was not his work at all and that it was written much later. However, Professor Barlow has put forward convincing evidence to support Orderic's claim. Particularly convincing is the fact that William of Poitiers almost certainly made use of it when writing his history. Barlow also believes that it was written to further the cause of Eustace of Boulogne rather than at Matilda's prompting. Matilda was not mentioned in the prologue, as might be expected if she had commissioned it, but it is possible that her name appeared at the end of the work, which has since been lost. See also Barlow, *Carmen de Hastingae Proelio;* OV, II, p. 369; Houts, "Latin Poetry," pp. 53–56; Bridgeford, pp. 22–23.

13. Barlow, *Carmen de Hastingae Proelio*, p. 3.

14. William's apologist, William of Poitiers, was also fond of comparing him to Caesar, but he went further than Guy of Amiens by claiming that he was superior to the celebrated Roman emperor. See, for example, GG, pp. 155, 169, 171, 173, 175.

15. B. de Montfaucon, *Les monuments de la monarchie française*, vol. II (Paris, 1730), p. 2. See also Bridgeford, pp. 30–31.

16. Strickland, pp. 64–65.

17. Bridgeford, p. 156.

18. GG, p. 177.

19. Bridgeford, pp. 9, 165.

20. Andrew Bridgeford puts forward a convincing case for this.

21. Bridgeford, p. 162.

22. GG, p. 143.

23. Barlow, *Carmen de Hastingae Proelio*, p. 39.

24. GG, p. 149; Barlow, *Carmen de Hastingae Proelio*, p. lxxxix. See also Wright, *Chronicle of Pierre de Langtoft*, I, p. 413.

25. Barlow, *Carmen de Hastingae Proelio*, p. 45.

26. OV, II, p. 185. For another account of the incident, see GG, p. 151.

27. GG, pp. 260, 179; Fauroux, p. 197.

28. William did not grant her the county of Kent as he had promised, but instead gave it to his half-brother Odo. The reason for this is not clear.

29. Strickland, p. 87.

30. It is possible that Matilda did not conceive until William's return from the Conquest in spring 1067. But by this reckoning, she would have given birth in early 1068, which would have allowed a very short (though not impossible) gap between this birth and that of her last child, Henry.

31. Houts, "Echo of the Conquest," pp. 145–46. See also Fettu, p. 17.

32. This idea is explored by Houts, "Echo of the Conquest," pp. 147–49.

33. Hilton, p. 33.

34. Darlington and McGurks, III, p. 27.

35. ASC, p. 200.

36. The English tend to be referred to as the "native" population when comparisons are drawn with the conquering Normans, but this term is misleading. In fact, England was made up of a complex patchwork of nationalities reflecting the many invasions that she had suffered over the centuries.

37. OV, II, p. 199; GG, p. 181; GRA, I, pp. 459, 461.

38. GRA, I, p. 461.

39. Ibid., p. 471.

40. OV, II, p. 191.

41. Clover and Gibson, pp. 31,33. Matilda had added her voice to the many who urged Lanfranc to take the post and had let it be known that she had prayed he would relent. Freeman, *History of the Norman Conquest,* pp. 344–45.

42. Riley, p. 142.

43. OV, II, p. 267. Orderic Vitalis claims that William's daily revenue was £1,061 10s and 3 halfpence. Although this is a very precise estimate, it is likely to be exaggerated. Ibid., p. 267n.

44. Stevenson, *Chronicon Monasterii de Abingdon,* p. 491.

45. OV, II, p. 269.

46. Ibid., p. 271.

47. Riley, p. 142.

48. Ibid.

49. OV, II, p. 257.

50. Ibid., p. 269.

51. Loyn, p. 324. See also Leyser, pp. 74–90.

52. GRA, I, pp. 415, 417.

53. OV, II, p. 257.

54. ASC, p. 220. This is corroborated by Orderic Vitalis, OV, II, p. 193, and William of Poitiers, GG, pp. 159, 161.

9: QUEEN OF ENGLAND

1. Douglas, p. 85.

2. OV, II, p. 91.

3. Ibid., IV, p. 83.

4. GG, pp. 33, 179.

5. Abrahams, pp. 255–56.

6. Boüard, *Guillaume le Conquérant,* pp. 403–4. This legend has left its mark on the

topography of modern-day Caen, for the Rue Froide still exists, and some claim that a collection of crosses in the city marks the spot where Matilda's "Croix Pleureuse" used to stand.

7. Turgis, p. 47.

8. Matilda later granted the manor to Roger de Busci.

9. Dugdale, II, p. 60. See also Freeman, *History of the Norman Conquest,* IV, Appendix O.

10. H.W.C. Davis, I, p. 7.

11. Morris, vol. V, no. 1:8; VI, no. 17:1, VII, no. 1:15–29, 17:1, 54:8, 56:19; VIII, no. 17:8; IX, no. 1:57–72, 13a:2, 24:1, 27:1, 40:4; 52:25 and 30; X, no. 1:13–19; XIII, no. 52; XV, no. 1:47, 69:6–7; XXII, EG2:3; XXXI, no. 68:30; XXXII, no. 1:11, 60:3, 82:1, B3:j.

12. These Gloucestershire lands reverted to the crown after Matilda's death and were then granted by William to their third son, William Rufus.

13. An excellent analysis of Brihtric's landholdings and what became of them is provided by Ann Williams in "A West-Country Magnate of the Eleventh Century." The lands that Matilda retained are as follows: (Gloucestershire) Tewkesbury, Old Sodbury, Avening, Fairford, Thornbury; (Dorset) Frome St. Quintin, Cranborne, Ashmore; (Devon) Northlew, Halwill, Clovelly, Bideford, Littleham, Langtree, Iddesleigh, Winkleigh, Ashreigny, Lapford, Irishcombe, High Bickington, Morchard Bishop, Holcombe Burnell, Halberton, Ashprington; (Cornwall) Connerton, Coswarth, Binnerton, Trevalga, Carwogie.

14. Strickland, pp. 90–91. Strickland cites her source as a charter dated 1082. There are two charters involving bequests from Matilda to La Trinité that year, but neither mentions Nailsworth: Bates, *Regesta Regum,* pp. 287–88, 292–95. It is possible—but unlikely—that Strickland had access to a charter that has eluded the editors of later collections.

15. FitzOsbern also seized a number of Brihtric's other possessions, including the revenues of Hanley Castle and Forthampton and land at Bushley in Worcestershire. He may have been given these as a reward for the part that he played in quashing the rebellion. Williams, "West-Country Magnate of the Eleventh Century," p. 62.

16. Sancho had inherited Castile and Garcia had inherited Galicia.

17. Jumièges, Orderic Vitalis, and Robert of Torigni all concur that the daughter who was betrothed to Alfonso was the same one who had earlier been allied to Harold of England. Only Malmesbury claims that they were two different girls, although he admits that he cannot remember their names. William of Poitiers, on the other hand, refers to a daughter of William who was fought over by two kings of Spain, but he fails to name her altogether. GND, II, pp. 160–61, 263; GRA, I, pp 419, 505; OV, III, pp. 114n, 115; GND, II, pp. 160–61, 262–63; GG, p. 95. See also Freeman, *History of the Norman Conquest,* IV, pp. 852–53.

18. OV, III, p. 115.
19. Foreville, p. 143; OV, III, p. 114n. See also Douglas, pp. 381–82; Houts, *Normans in Europe*, p. 198n. There is some confusion as to the identity of the two Spanish kings because there were three brothers to whom Ferdinand I bequeathed his Spanish dominions. Although Alfonso is most often cited as the king who eventually triumphed, one historian has cast doubt upon this. In her translation of Orderic's *Ecclesiastical History*, Marjorie Chibnall claims that Orderic referred to Adeliza's betrothed simply as "rex Galicie" and probably did not mean Alfonso because he usually called him "Hildefonsus." However, she concludes that there is a "strong case" for Alfonso's being the man involved, even if Orderic did not believe that this was so. OV, III, pp. 114–15n. The plans for a Spanish marriage for William and Matilda's daughter may have begun as early as 1064, with the siege of Barbastro in northern Spain, at which a contingent of Norman soldiers was present.
20. OV, III, p. 115.
21. Ibid.
22. The circumstances of this match are not known, and there is some room to doubt whether it ever took place. However, Strickland argues that it was more likely to have been Edwin rather than the late king Harold to whom Adeliza was so attached that she eschewed all others. She argues that they were closer in age and that Edwin "had, in all probability, been privileged with some intimacy with the princess." There is no evidence for this in the contemporary sources, however. Strickland, pp. 96–97.
23. GG, p. 179. Easter fell on April 8 that year.
24. OV, II, p. 141.
25. GG, pp. 175, 177.
26. Ibid., p. 175.
27. OV, II, p. 199.
28. GG, p. 181.
29. OV, II, p. 199.
30. Ibid., p. 285.
31. Ibid., pp. 211, 285. For a contrasting view, see GND, II, p. 179.
32. OV, II, p. 215.
33. Ibid.
34. Wright, *Chronicle of Pierre de Langtoft*, I, p. 411.
35. Bates, *Regesta Regum*, pp. 594–601, 863–65; Domesday Book, vol. V, no. 67:1.
36. ASC, p. 402.
37. Strickland, p. 22.
38. There is some debate as to whether Matilda was already pregnant when she arrived in England, because the chroniclers cite different dates for the birth. Orderic

Vitalis simply states that the child was born "within a year of her coronation": OV, II, p. 215. The *Winchester Chronicle*, meanwhile, reports that the birth occurred "not many days" after her coronation: "Annales monasterii de Wintona," in Luard, vol. XXXVI, part I, p. 27.

39. J. L. Nelson, p. 70.
40. Ibid.
41. Strickland, pp. 62–63, claims that William was recrowned at the same ceremony, but there is no contemporary evidence for this.
42. The name "Whit" probably derives from the white garments that were traditionally worn on this day. ASC, p. 202n. See also Darlington and McGurk, III, p. 7.
43. There is some suggestion that the coronation took place at Winchester rather than Westminster. The sources are frustratingly ambiguous, but given the importance of the occasion and the need to make it as high-profile as possible, Westminster seems more likely. This also ensured continuity with William's coronation. Luard, vol. II, p. 27; vol. III, p. 424.
44. Laudes were ritual chants sung during Mass at great religious festivals. They honored the powers wielding authority in heaven and on earth, and were therefore entirely appropriate for such an occasion. The argument that they were first used in England at Matilda's coronation can be found in Cowdrey, "Anglo-Norman Laudes regiae," pp. 50ff. See also Gathagan, "Trappings of Power."
45. Hilton, p. 34.
46. Wright, *Chronicle of Pierre de Langtoft*, I, p. 413.
47. Strickland, pp. 63–64.
48. Ibid., p. 63. The grant was on the condition that the manor provide this dish at future coronations in perpetuity.
49. A list of the witnesses to the charter regarding St.-Martin-le-Grand is provided by Keynes, pp. 242–43.
50. They embarked at the city of St.-Omer. Darlington and McGurk, III, p. 7. Orderic Vitalis inaccurately states that they went to France, even though St.-Omer was part of Flemish territory at this time. OV, II, p. 225.
51. Hilton, p. 34.

10: "THE ENGLISH TUMULTS"

1. ASC, p. 202.
2. GND, II, p. 183.
3. This estimate is provided by Douglas, *William the Conqueror*, p. 210.
4. Tomkeieff, p. 29. It is not clear where William and Matilda stayed while this palace was under construction. Work had begun on a new castle in Winchester at about the same time, and if this was finished first they might well have taken up resi-

dence there temporarily. Even though the kitchens tended to be separate from the main palace in order to minimize the risk of fire, William's new palace at Winchester fell victim to this fate in 1140 and was never rebuilt.

5. Abrahams, pp. 255–56. A transcript of the section of the poem that describes the tapestry can be found in S. A. Brown, Appendix III. See also Houts, *Normans in Europe*, pp. 125–28.

6. *Beowulf*, lines 994–96.

7. See, for example, Bates, *Regesta Regum*, pp. 247, 276, 287, 293.

8. OV, II, p. 215.

9. GRA, I, p. 711.

10. Stevenson, *Historical Works of Simeon of Durham*, p. 550.

11. According to Eadmer, "Lanfranc had the ear of King William, not merely as one of his advisers but rather as his principal adviser." Eadmer, p. 12.

12. GRA, I, pp. 709, 711. See also OV, II, p. 215. When he became king, Henry gave greater attention to the education of his daughter, the future empress Matilda, than was usual for the time, and she reached such a standard of intellect that she was able to understand government documents in Latin. Hilton, p. 159.

13. OV, II, p. 233.

14. GRA, I, p. 363. See also OV, II, pp. 219, 221.

15. OV, IV, p. 95.

16. Ibid., II, pp. 231, 233.

17. Stevenson, *Historical Works of Simeon of Durham*, p. 551.

18. GND, II, p. 181.

19. Sweyn did have a valid claim to the English throne, because he was the son of King Cnut's sister and the cousin of King Harthacnut.

20. She was there in time for the Easter celebrations at Winchester, but it is not clear how soon before that she arrived.

21. OV, II, pp. 222–23n.

22. Round, p. 21.

23. GRA, I, p. 509.

24. Stafford, *Queen Emma and Queen Edith*, p. 107.

25. Stafford, *Queens, Concubines and Dowagers*, p. 101.

26. Biddle, p. 57.

27. Strickland, p. 63.

28. Carey, p. 14n.

29. Domesday Book, vol. VI, no. 24p.

30. Strickland, p. 87. The cost of feeding the royal court rose even higher during the reign of William and Matilda's son, William Rufus, whose notorious excesses put an unbearable pressure on the rural economy. Caring nothing for the hardships that his people suffered as a result, he and his followers plundered the land through which they passed. What they could not eat, they burned, and to show

their disdain for the local populace, they washed their horses' feet in the leftover wine and ale.

31. Delisle, *Receuil de Travaux d'Érudition,* pp. 224–25.

32. Bates, *Regesta Regum,* p. 296. See also Musset, *Les Actes de Guillaume le Conquérant,* p. 112.

33. Morris, vol. VI, no. 67:86.

34. Strickland, p. 67.

35. OV, II, p. 223.

11: "MUTUAL AND LASTING HOSTILITY"

1. Orderic Vitalis cites these dates, and his estimate is supported by two charters for the abbey of St.-Gabriel in Calvados, which were attested by Matilda at Valognes. Douglas, p. 211n.

2. Bates, *Regesta Regum,* pp. 634–35. For a related grant, see pp. 638–39.

3. According to Orderic Vitalis, this marriage had resulted from a rift between Robert and his father. He claims that they had had such a serious quarrel when Robert was a young man that Baldwin had disowned him and sent him into exile. Robert had sought refuge with his father's enemy, Florence, duke of Frisia, who had given him his daughter in marriage. Upon hearing of this, Baldwin "flew into a violent rage" and disinherited Robert, making his younger brother Arnulf heir instead. OV, II, pp. 281, 283. In fact, Arnulf was the son of Baldwin's eldest son and heir (also called Baldwin), who became Count Baldwin VI in 1067 upon his father's death. Baldwin V had not been at all opposed to Robert's marriage.

4. GND, II, pp. 225, 227.

5. GRA, I, p. 475.

6. OV, II, p. 281; GND, II, p. 147. Orderic Vitalis claims that fitzOsbern had been instructed to act as coregent with Matilda, but this is not supported by any other source. Neither is his assertion that the English king went in person to Flanders to take up arms on Arnulf's behalf, although it is likely that William returned to Normandy for a brief spell around that time.

7. OV, II, pp. 215, 217, 218. Malmesbury claims that fitzOsbern was eager to undertake the mission because he hoped to marry the widow Richildis, for whom he had a consuming passion. However, his account of the revolt as a whole is severely flawed, and his claim is not corroborated by any other contemporary source. GRA, I, p. 475. Nevertheless, Douglas asserts that there was some truth in it. He claims that it was Richildis who sought fitzOsbern's aid, offering herself in marriage to him and placing her son Arnulf in his wardship. According to his account, her offer was accepted with alacrity. Douglas, *William the Conqueror,* p. 217.

8. GND, II, p. 225.

9. OV, III, pp. 215, 217.

10. The tale of Agatha's betrothal to Edwin is told by the nineteenth-century poet H. M. Carey in *Matilda of Normandy*, p. 42n. Turgis also relates that Agatha was betrothed to Edwin, "beau frère d'Harold," whom she loved deeply, and that when he was killed in the revolt, she was so inconsolable that she rejected any further talk of matrimony by taking the veil. Turgis, p. 41.

11. OV, II, pp. 280–82.

12. Ibid, p. 285. The reference to "another brother" is a mistake. Orderic Vitalis claims that Arnulf was Robert's brother, whereas he was in fact his nephew.

13. Ibid.

14. GRA, I, p. 481. This took place in the autumn of 1085 and posed such a threat to William's rule that he drafted in "a larger force of mounted men and foot soldiers from France and Brittany than had ever come to this country, so that people wondered how this country could maintain all that army." Chibnall, *Anglo-Norman England*, p. 37. All his preparations were for nothing: Cnut was murdered before any invasion force could be launched.

15. OV, II, p. 285.

16. Bates, *William the Conqueror*, p. 37.

12: "MATILDA, WEALTHY AND POWERFUL"

1. GND, II, p. 183.

2. Bates, *William the Conqueror*, p. 164.

3. These were exclusive to England, because the Norman dukes did not have crowns—this was the prerogative of their nominal overlord, the king of France. Even so, William and Matilda did bend the rules slightly by wearing their English crowns at great occasions of state in Normandy.

4. As such, William followed a similar pattern to his predecessor, who had tended to celebrate these festivals at the same locations. The annals of Winchester claim that the Christmas crown-wearings took place at Worcester, but most other sources concur that they were usually at Gloucester. Stevenson, "Annals of the Church of Winchester," p. 356. An excellent analysis of these gatherings, including their origins, is provided by M. Biddle, "Seasonal Festivals and Residence: Winchester, Westminster and Gloucester in the Tenth to Twelfth Centuries," vol. VIII (1985), pp. 51–72.

5. ASC, p. 402.

6. Bates, *William the Conqueror*, p. 168.

7. Bates, *Regesta Regum*, pp. 247, 276, 287, 293. The most elaborate of these is *coniunxque sua reginarum nobilissima, Baldoini incliti ac strenuissimi Flandrensium comitis filia regisque Francorum Henrici neptis clarissima*. See also H.W.C. Davis, I, p. 41.

8. See, for example, Farrer, vols. I–III, nos. 559, 1002; vol. IV, no. 1; vol. VI, no. 1; Stafford, "Women and the Norman Conquest," pp. 244–45.

9. W. W. Skeat (ed.), *Aelfric, Lives of the Saints,* Early English Text Society, vol. II (London, 1900), p. 6.

10. A useful analysis of Domesday Book's references to the queen's household before and after 1066 is provided by Stafford, *Queen Emma and Queen Edith,* Appendix II, pp. 306–23.

11. Morey and Brooke, p. 538.

12. Wright, *Anglo-Latin Satirical Poets.*

13. Bates, *William the Conqueror,* p. 145.

14. Stafford, *Queens, Concubines and Dowagers,* p. 98.

15. Van Caenegem, p. 157.

16. Gathagan provides an excellent analysis of Matilda's judicial role in the context of her predecessors and contemporaries in chapter 4, "Embodying Power," pp. 145–73.

17. Riley, pp. 189–91; Clover and Gibson, pp. 45, 47, 49.

18. Bates, *Regesta Regum,* pp. 307–14; Stevenson, *Historical Works of Simeon of Durham,* p. 555.

19. Bates, *William the Conqueror,* p. 152.

20. Bates, *Regesta Regum,* p. 869. For another example, see pp. 619–20.

21. Ibid., pp. 201–9, 463–65, 594‑601, 603–4, 863–65. The grant for St.-Martin-le-Grand was one of the first English charters in which Matilda was involved, for it was confirmed at her coronation in 1068. Matilda's signum is also found on a diploma relating to Worcester Cathedral, but as this has been reliably dated to 1067, her signature must have been added after her arrival in England. Ibid., pp. 987–90.

22. Eadmer, p. 12.

23. OV, II, p. 239.

24. Ibid., IV, pp. 45, 47.

25. Gundulph had a talent for architecture as well as religious observance. William employed his skill in the construction of various key Norman buildings, most notably the Tower of London.

26. See, for example, Morris, vol. V, no. 53:2; XXIII, no. 3:4.

27. Strickland, pp. 9, 57.

28. When they refused, Thurstan summoned armed retainers, who "shot cruel arrows in their midst," killing several monks. OV, II, p. 271.

29. GRA, I, p. 727.

30. Morris, vol. XV, no. 1:24.

31. Houts, *Normans in Europe,* p. 199.

32. GRA, I, p. 351.

33. GG, p. 115.

34. Stafford, *Queen Emma and Queen Edith,* p. 55.

35. While a queen or consort might be afforded some attention in contemporary chronicles, farther down the social scale the lives of women in the early medieval

period are typically obscure. The rise of monasticism afforded them some distinction, but only if they enjoyed particular longevity or were extraordinarily generous in their benefactions. A cousin of Matilda named Beatrice of Valenciennes was among those considered worthy of note. She married Gilbert, son of Richard of Heugleville, who shared kinship with Duke William. According to Orderic, he was a great-grandson of William's uncle, Duke Richard II. This made the two men cousins, albeit distant. Richard had established a town at Auffay in the region of Talou, Normandy, and founded a priory of secular canons there, which was linked to the influential monastery of St.-Évroult. His son Gilbert gained renown as a soldier in William's forces, but was evidently a pious man. Although he took part in the Norman invasion of England in 1066, he refused to take his share of the spoils and instead focused his energies upon developing the priory of Auffay. His wife was no less devout, and it was at her suggestion that the secular canons were replaced by monks in 1079. OV, III, pp. xix–xx.

36. Hilton, p. 420, provides an excellent analysis of the role of women in *Beowulf.*

13: A "WHOLLY WRETCHED MOTHER"

1. ASC, p. 209.
2. Eadmer, p. 26.
3. He was referred to as duke in a number of charters, and by his father's biographer, Jumièges. Bates, *William the Conqueror,* p. 152.
4. Bridgeford, p. 209. It has been estimated that Odo's total fortune in England was worth £43.2 billion in modern money. Ibid.
5. ASC, p. 219; Eadmer, p. 17.
6. OV, II, p. 265.
7. Ibid., pp. 203, 205.
8. Ibid., p. 202n. By contrast, Poitiers praises their "wise vigilance" and strong sense of justice and claims that the English rebelled without provocation. GG, pp. 181, 183.
9. Pelteret, p. 83.
10. The document was a confraternity agreement signed by Wulfstan, bishop of Worcester, and various other important English ecclesiastics sometime between 1075 and 1078. It included a declaration of loyalty to William and Matilda. Mason, "Wulfstan of Worcester."
11. Delisle, *Receuil de Travaux d'Érudition,* pp. 223–24.
12. Rudborne, *Historia Major,* cited in Strickland, p. 99.
13. ASC, p. 212.
14. GRA, I, p. 503.
15. Ibid.

16.   Cowdrey, *Register of Pope Gregory VII,* p. 75.

17.   Ibid., pp. 357–58.

18.   GND, II, p. 71. See also Crispin.

19.   Bates, *Regesta Regum,* pp. 564–65.

20.   Ibid., pp. 621–23.

21.   It is not clear who Hugolin of Cherbourg was, or what his offense had been. Round, p. 425; Bates, *Regesta Regum,* pp. 638–39.

22.   Riley, p. 194.

23.   GRA, I, p. 505.

24.   OV, III, p. 115.

25.   Less credibly, in his original text, Malmesbury claims that Richard "caught some sickness from breathing the foggy and corrupted air." There was an outbreak of malaria in Hampshire at that time, but the fact that most sources refer to an accident involving hunting makes this the more likely cause of death. GRA, I, p. 505. See also GND, II, p. 216n; Bates, *William the Conqueror,* p. 159; Strickland, pp. 76–77.

26.   OV, III, p. 115.

27.   According to the educational traditions of the day, boys were dubbed a knight between the ages of thirteen and twenty-two, after emerging from childhood. Barlow, *William Rufus,* pp. 13, 13n, 16. This means that Richard might have been even younger when he died. Aird points out that Richard's brothers were all knighted in their mid- to late teens, and therefore asserts that Richard's death could well have been as early as 1069. Aird, *Robert Curthose,* pp. 56–57. Robert of Torigni, one of the more reliable of the early medieval chroniclers, claims that Richard was killed in 1074, when he was about nineteen. GND, pp. 251, 279.

28.   OV, III, p. 115.

29.   Williams, *The English and the Norman Conquest,* pp. 79n, 80. See also Stafford, *Queen Emma and Queen Edith,* p. 312. It is not known why Matilda chose Eadgifu for this benefaction. The woman may have been known to her through her chamberlain, Humphrey, from whom Eadgifu held her lands. William made a similar bequest in Richard's memory by granting the town of Tewin in Hertfordshire to a man named Halfdane.

30.   Musset, "La Reine Mathilde," p. 193.

31.   Round, p. 26; Bates, *Regesta Regum,* pp. 737–38. For another example, see Davis, *Regesta Regum Anglo-Normannorum,* I, p. 35.

32.   GRA, I, p. 505.

33.   Migne, cols. 1215–16; Barlow, *William Rufus,* p. 443; M.A.E. Green, I, pp. 35–38.

34.   Migne, p. 156; Houts, *Normans in Europe,* pp. 197–99.

35.   Coulton and Swinton, p. 33. According to this account, Simon had converted to the religious life after having his late father's remains disinterred. Upon seeing

"the wasted body of him who had been his powerful and daring father," he realized the futility of the political world and resolved to turn his back on it for good. Ibid., p. 33.

36. Abrahams, pp. 255–56. The editor of this work surmises that the sister in question could have been Constance, but there is no evidence for this. See also Barlow, *William Rufus,* p. 444.

37. OV, III, p. 115.

38. Southern, *Saint Anselm: A Portrait in a Landscape,* pp. 92–93.

39. Elisabeth van Houts has shed new light upon the careers of Matilda's daughters, in particular Adelida, and she provides an excellent analysis of their varying fates in "The Echo of the Conquest in Latin Sources."

40. Barlow, *William Rufus,* p. 13. A similar theory was put forward in the early twentieth century by Turgis, p. 43, who claimed that the girl was named Alice, was very beautiful and virtuous, and died when she reached puberty.

41. Delisle, *Rouleaux des Morts,* pp. 181–82. The legend that Adeliza was buried at Bayeux (which originated with Orderic) is still repeated by the cathedral guides today.

42. GRA, I, p. 505. Jumièges concurs that Adelida "died as a girl of marriageable age": GND, II, p. 263. William of Poitiers does not mention her death at all, which is interesting, as he was writing at the time that it would have occurred. This has led Professor Barlow to suspect that her tragic death en route to Spain was "merely a romantic story": *William Rufus,* p. 443.

43. Houts, *Normans in Europe,* pp. 132–33; Houts, "Echo of the Conquest in Latin Sources," pp. 139–40.

44. Barlow, *William Rufus,* p. 31.

45. Abrahams, p. 198. William evidently did not mind being superseded by his daughter in this respect. Langtoft claims that she was a favorite with her father, who "loved [her] so much." Wright, *Chronicle of Pierre de Langtoft,* I, p. 433.

14: "A FAITHLESS WIFE"

1. Abrahams, pp. 198–99, 255–56.

2. Morris, vol. V, no. loW7:3 and 8; W. Dugdale, *The Baronage of England* (London, 1675). See also Planché, pp. 72–74.

3. Planché, p. 73.

4. Turgis, pp. 44–46.

5. OV, II, pp. 219, 221.

6. Strickland, pp. 71–72. Another theory is that the tale derived from the story of King Eadwig's wife or mistress by Osbern or Eadmer. Freeman, *History of the Norman Conquest,* III, p. 662.

7. GRA, I, pp. 501, 503.

8. Cited in Strickland, p. 72.

9. GRA, I, pp. 501, 503.

10. Turgis claims that the ducal couple also argued frequently over money because William was miserly and his wife was generous. However, there is no mention of this in any of the original sources, and the charters attest to the fact that the duke made at least as many bequests as did his wife.

11. OV, III, p. 11. The abbey church of Bec was also dedicated that year, but William and Matilda did not attend the ceremony.

12. Ibid., pp. 13,15.

13. GND, I, Appendix. Douglas points out that in two charters issued in 1096, Robert seems to date his tenure of the duchy from 1077 or 1078. Douglas, *William the Conqueror*, pp. 228–29. See also Bates, *Regesta Regum*, pp. 94–96.

14. Davis, "William of Jumièges," pp. 597–606.

15. OV, II, p. 359.

16. Bates, *William the Conqueror*, pp. 146–47.

17. GRA, I, p. 701. For a similar account, see OV, IV, pp. 115, 119.

18. Robert would sire a host of illegitimate children during his lifetime. But he would be superseded in this respect by his youngest brother, Henry, whose promiscuity was notorious. He took a string of English mistresses and fathered numerous bastards before he married Edith-Matilda of Scotland in 1100.

19. GND, II, p. 195.

20. OV, III, p. 99.

21. Ibid., p. 115.

22. GRA, I, p. 543.

23. Ibid., p. 701.

24. OV, II, p. 357; IV, p. 93.

25. GND, II, p. 185.

26. GRA, I, p. 703.

27. OV, II, p. 357.

28. Ibid., III, p. 103.

29. GRA, I, p. 701.

30. OV, III, pp. 97, 99.

31. GRA, I, p. 701; OV, II, p. 357.

32. OV, III, p. 99.

33. GRA, I, p. 701. Orderic Vitalis claims that William had reacted in a more considered way, and that only after reflecting carefully upon the matter did he refuse his son's request, persuading him "to wait for a more opportune time to acquire them." He contrasts William's reasonable behavior with Robert's petulance, claiming that in response to his father's calm refusal, Robert cried: "I did not come here to listen to a lecture, for I have had more than enough of these from my schoolmasters . . . I will no longer fight for anyone in Normandy with the

hopeless status of a hired dependent." OV, II, p. 357; III, pp. 99, 101. However, Orderic—more than Malmesbury—made use of hindsight in his account, which reads as a moralizing indictment against filial insubordination. From what we know of William and Robert's relationship, Malmesbury's account seems more credible.

34. GRA, I, p. 701; OV, III, p. 101.

35. OV, III, p. 101. A similar quote is cited on p. 99.

36. The town was known as Laigle in the eleventh century, and Orderic Vitalis claims that its name derived from the fact that an eagle's nest was found in an oak tree during the building of the castle. OV, II, p. 357.

37. Although Orderic tended to combine rumor with fact in his account, the story of what happened at L'Aigle might well be true in most details. The town lay just ten miles from the abbey of St.-Évroult, in which he wrote his history, so he would have been able to draw upon local knowledge of the event. Professor Bates doubts that Matilda's youngest son, Henry, played the part assigned to him, because he would have been nine years old at the time. Bates, *William the Conqueror*, pp. 237–38. But this was in an era when children—particularly those in noble households—were treated as adults from a much younger age than is the case today. Henry's father, William, had been a year younger when he assumed control of the duchy. It is therefore possible that Henry did collude with his brother William in goading Robert into rebellion, as Orderic claims. OV, II, pp. 357, 359.

38. Ibid., p. 359.

39. A castellan was a caretaker or governor of a castle.

40. OV, II, p. 359.

41. GRA, I, p. 701.

42. ASC, pp. 213–14.

43. OV, III, p. 103.

44. Ibid., pp. 104n, 105. The role of messenger was extremely important. Often the letters they conveyed would contain only information that would not necessarily be damning if discovered, the more sensitive part of the communication being left to the messenger to convey orally. Little wonder that they were among the most trusted servants at court.

45. OV, III, p. 103.

46. Ibid.; GRA, I, p. 503.

47. Stafford, *Queens, Concubines and Dowagers*, pp. 109–10.

48. Strickland, pp. 80–81, claims that Roger de Beaumont was the informant and cites Malmesbury as her source, but the latter contains no reference to this. Her statement that William was in England when he received the news is also unlikely, given that most sources place him in Normandy at this time.

49. OV, III, p. 103.

50. Carey, p. 77n. Carey claims that Matilda erected a "Calvaire" (prayer station) at the spot afterward, no doubt in penance for her disobedience.

51. OV, III, p. 103.

52. Ibid., pp. 103, 105.

53. Ibid., p. 105.

54. Ibid. Samson, described as "shrewd and eloquent and chaste," proved well suited to the monastic life and spent the next twenty-six years there. William evidently forgave him for his involvement in the family rift, because it is alleged that he offered him the see of Le Mans in 1082. Barlow, *William I and the Norman Conquest*, p. 182.

55. GRA, I, p. 503.

56. Ibid., p. 439. The quote is taken from the Roman poet Ovid's celebrated work *Metamorphoses*. Although Malmesbury was referring to the personal history of Count Fulk IV of Anjou, it was apt for William and Matilda at this point of their marriage.

57. Beech, pp. 352–53. There is a legend that still persists at La Chaise-Dieu that an English queen was buried in the abbey. The four main candidates are King Harold II's wife and mistress, Edith of Mercia and Edith "Swanneck" respectively; Edward the Confessor's wife, Edith; and Matilda. The first three had no known connections with the abbey, whereas Matilda had known of it since its inception in 1052 because her husband had witnessed the foundation charter. Fauroux, pp. 297–99. Beech also points to the fact that the bequest made to the abbey was very similar to those Matilda made to other religious houses, notably Caen and St.-Évroult. Beech, pp. 368–69. However, although it is almost certain that Matilda was the anonymous queen who sought Adelelme's assistance, there is no reason to suppose that she was buried there. The evidence to support her burial at Caen is irrefutable.

58. OV, II, p. 361.

59. The contemporary spelling was Gerberoi.

60. Darlington and McGurk, III, p. 31.

61. OV, III, p. 109.

62. ASC, pp. 213–14. According to Malmesbury, it was Robert who had shot his father's horse, although this is not mentioned by any other source. GRA, I, p. 477.

63. Darlington and McGurk, III, p. 33.

64. It is interesting that in the contemporary sources and the debates by recent historians, all the focus has been on whether Robert knew that he was fighting his father. Whether William had recognized his son has apparently not been considered. The assumption seems to have been that Robert would have been harder to recognize among the swell of other young warriors who fought that day. Yet he, like his father, was of a distinctive bearing, and his diminutive height should have

made him easy to identify—particularly by the man who had so frequently made fun of it. If the duke had knowingly slain Robert, this would have been a lesser crime: his son was a rebel for whom death would have been a just punishment. But if he had gained the upper hand in the struggle, would he, like Robert, have flinched from striking the final blow? From what we know of his cruelty and ruthlessness, it is hard to believe that he would.

65. ASC, pp. 213–14.

66. GRA, I, p. 477.

67. OV, III, p. 113.

68. A catamite is a young man who is involved in a sexual relationship with an older man.

69. OV, III, pp. 105, 107, 109.

15: "MURMURS OF LOUD AND HEARTFELT GRIEF "

1. Adela was buried at the abbey.

2. OV, II, p. 285.

3. Migne, p. 156.

4. Matilda never forgot the effort that Simon had made on her behalf. Upon his death in 1084, she dispatched a monk to Rome laden with gold and silver "to pay for the burial of the man of God," and she ordered a magnificent tomb to be erected there. Ibid.; Houts, *Normans in Europe*, p. 199.

5. Cowdrey, *Register of Pope Gregory VII*, pp. 358–59.

6. OV, III, p. 113.

7. Ibid.

8. Round, p. 22; OV, III, p. 112. Easter fell on April 12 that year.

9. Bates, *William the Conqueror*, p. 241.

10. OV, III, p. 113.

11. Ibid., II, p. 357; III, p. 113.

12. This may have been Adela's second betrothal. There is evidence to suggest that as a child she was promised to Simon Crispin, the count of Amiens, but that this fell through when he chose the monastic life instead.

13. The marriage itself was celebrated at Chartres, although the exact date is uncertain. The marriage negotiations seem to have been quite protracted, and the ceremony might not have taken place until as late as 1085, when Adela's name first appears in a charter as Stephen's wife. OV, III, pp. 116n, 117; Morey and Brooke, p. 78n.

14. Morey and Brooke, pp. 65–66; Hilton, p. 40. Edith married Matilda's youngest son, Henry, who took her as his wife after he became king in 1100. She became known as Matilda upon her marriage to Henry, which might have been out of

respect for his late mother. The description provided by the *Anglo-Saxon Chronicle* of her mother, Margaret, with regard to her marriage to King Malcolm of Scotland could equally have applied to Matilda and William: "The apostle Paul, teacher of all nations, declared: 'The unbelieving man is saved through his believing wife' . . . that is in our language: 'Very often the unbelieving man is sanctified and saved through a righteous wife' . . . This aforesaid queen afterwards performed many useful works in that land to the glory of God, and also throve well in the royal estate, just as was natural to her." ASC, pp. 201–2.

15. Bates, *Regesta Regum*, pp. 636–37.
16. The reference to the younger Matilda that appears in Domesday Book implies that she was no longer living, which would place her death before 1086, when the survey was compiled. The idea that she died young is supported by the fact that she soon disappears from the contemporary sources.
17. Bates, *Regesta Regum*, pp. 559–62; Morris, vol. VI, no. 17:1; vol. VII, no. 17:1.
18. Musset, *Les Actes de Guillaume le Conquérant*, no. 12; Stafford, *Queen Emma and Queen Edith*, p. 157n; Bates, *Regesta Regum*, pp. 292–95.
19. Gathagan, "Embodying Power," p. 206.
20. Davis, *Regesta Regum Anglo-Normannorum*, I, pp. 49–50.
21. Bates, *Regesta Regum*, pp. 763–64.
22. Turgis, p. 50.
23. OV, IV, p. 45. Freeman asserts that Matilda had suffered a "long sickness" but does not substantiate his claim: *History of the Norman Conquest*, IV, p. 651.
24. Round, p. 157; Bates, *Regesta Regum*, pp. 258–62.
25. Bates, *Regesta Regum*, p. 296. See also Musset, *Les Actes de Guillaume le Conquérant*, p. 112.
26. OV, IV, p. 45. Orderic inaccurately states that Matilda died on November 3. He was probably confusing the date with the celebration of her funeral at St.-Évroult the day after her death: ibid., p. 45n. John of Worcester specifies that November 2 was a Thursday: Darlington and McGurh, III, p. 41.
27. Most sources imply that William was at his wife's side when she died. It has been suggested by a later source that he was in England when he heard the news that she was dying, and that he left for Normandy with all haste but arrived too late. However, there is no evidence for this in the contemporary records. Turgis, p. 50; OV, III, pp. 103, 105.
28. GRA, I, p. 503.
29. Freeman, *History of the Norman Conquest*, IV, pp. 651–52.
30. See, for example, William's gifts to Edmund's in Northamptonshire. Morris, vol. XXI, no. 8:4.
31. OV, IV, pp. 44–46.
32. Lair, p. 28.

33. See, for example, Round, pp. 106, 112, 123, 142, 167, 233, 436.

34. *Certe si fortis,* in Delisle, *Receuil de Travaux d'Érudition,* pp. 223–24. Fulcoius continued the theme in another poem dedicated to her memory, *Tempore quae nostro.*

35. The eulogy was entitled *Consilii virtus decor.*

36. ASC, p. 215.

37. Delisle, *Receuil de Travaux d'Érudition,* pp. 224–25.

38. GRA, I, p. 503; OV, IV, p. 45.

39. OV, IV, p. 45.

40. Carey, p. 79.

41. Davis, *Regesta Regum Anglo-Normannorum,* I, p. 85; M.A.E. Green, I, p. 11.

42. OV, IV, p. 45.

43. Ducarel, p. 65; Strickland, p. 104. The abbess gave the ring to her father, the constable of France, when he received Charles IX at Caen in 1563, the year after the riots. It is not clear what became of it afterward. Ducarel, p. 66, claims that "a very curious manuscript" preserved at La Trinité contained an account of Matilda's wardrobe, jewels, and "toilette," but noted with some regret that he was not permitted to make a copy of it. This may be the same list referred to above (p. 43), which is still preserved in the abbey today.

44. The tomb measures three feet high by six feet long. Ducarel, p. 63.

45. OV, IV, p. 45.

46. Ibid. pp. 45, 47. Orderic's version of the epitaph is faithful to the original, with the exception of a few minor variations of spelling. See also Boüard, *Histoire de la Normandie,* plate 13; Douglas, *William the Conqueror,* opp. p. 341; Bates, *William the Conqueror,* p. 153.

16: "THE STORMS OF TROUBLES"

1. OV, IV, p. 47.

2. ASC, p. 218.

3. GRA, I, p. 509.

4. ASC, p. 216. See also Riley, pp. 159–60. Domesday Book consists of two volumes—"Great Domesday" and "Little Domesday." "Great" comprises a survey of all the counties of England south of a line from the river Tees to the river Ribble in North Yorkshire and Lancashire. The land above that line was evidently still too autonomous for the survey to be completed. This larger volume excludes Essex, Suffolk, and Norfolk, which are covered by "Little."

5. GRA, I, p. 509. See also Burgess and Holden, p. 291. Orderic Vitalis agrees that William grew "very corpulent" in his later years. OV, IV, p. 79.

6. ASC, pp. 217–18.

7. As Marjorie Chibnall states: "The death of Queen Matilda on 2 November 1083 probably removed the only influence capable of preventing conflict between the

two." OV, III, p. 112n. In a similar vein, Professor Barlow comments: "Queen Matilda's death on 2 November 1083 probably removed his [Robert's] last friend at court." Barlow, *William Rufus*, p. 38.

8. OV, III, p. 115.

9. Orderic Vitalis cites both places at different points of his narrative. OV, II, p. 352; III, p. 115.

10. Orderic Vitalis claims that the marriage had taken place some ten years earlier, following William's attack on the province. When he had been unable to take it by force, the "statesman king . . . devised another plan to profit himself and his heirs. He made a treaty of friendship with Alan Fergant and gave him his daughter Constance in marriage with great ceremony at Caen." OV, II, pp. 351, 353. However, Orderic's account of Breton affairs is very confused, and none of the other sources give this date for the marriage. Indeed, Alan Fergant did not become count until 1084. It is possible that Constance had been betrothed to him in 1076, when she was still a child, but there is no evidence to suggest that this was the case. Jumièges differs slightly from the commonly accepted date of 1086, claiming that the marriage took place the following year. GND, II, pp. 254, 261. Although Orderic claims that Constance "lived with her husband as a faithful wife for fifteen years," she was countess of Brittany for a fraction of that time. Her reign was brought to an abrupt end by her premature death in 1090.

11. The Vexin was divided into two parts: the Norman Vexin, which lay between the rivers Epte, Andelle, and Seine, and the French Vexin, situated between the Epte, the Seine, and the Oise.

12. GRA, I, p. 511; GND, II, p. 193. Orderic claims that the duke "fell ill from exhaustion and heat." OV, IV, p. 79.

13. GND, II, p. 185.

14. GRA, I, p. 511.

15. Malmesbury asserts that William "filled the house with complaints that death should overtake him when he had long been planning to reform his life." GRA, I, p. 511. By contrast, Jumièges writes that the duke accepted his fate calmly. GND, II, p. 185. From what we know of William's character, it seems unlikely that he would have been so philosophical, and the image of him fighting death as he would any opponent is more believable. He may have lain in this state for as much as six weeks.

16. GND, II, p. 185.

17. Ibid., p. 189.

18. John of Worcester attests that William, like Matilda, died on a Thursday. Darlington and McGurk, III, p. 47.

19. OV, IV, pp. 101–3.

20. It is not clear whether this Herluin was related to the man of the same name who married William's mother, Herleva. Strickland, p. 101, asserts that it was "in all

probability" William's stepfather himself, although this is unlikely. Quite apart from the fact that he would have been of a very advanced age by 1087, if it had indeed been the original Herluin who arranged William's funeral, the chroniclers would have named him as such.

21. Eadmer, p. 26; Burgess and Holden, p. 297.

22. GRA, I, p. 511.

23. OV, IV, p. 105.

24. Burgess and Holden, p. 295.

25. OV, IV, pp. 101–9.

EPILOGUE: "MOTHER OF KINGS"

1. Houts, "Echo of the Conquest," p. 139; Houts, "Latin Poetry and the Anglo-Norman Court," pp. 46–47; Abrahams, pp. 198–99, 255–56.

2. Round, p. 142.

3. Cecilia died on July 13, 1127. GND, II, p. 149n; OV, III, p. 11; IV, pp. 46n, 47. Jumièges implies that Cecilia's tenure was rather longer than this, for he claims that she "governed the abbey for many years after the death of Matilda the first abbess of the house." GND, II, p. 261. GRA, II, cites the date of her death as July 13, 1127 (p. 154). Another source claims that Cecilia was in her seventieth year when she died, although this is not substantiated by any of the contemporary sources. Planché, I, p. 83.

4. Abrahams, pp. 198–99, 255–56.

5. Jumièges incorrectly states that Adela bore four sons and one daughter; GND, II, p. 263. Orderic Vitalis also lists four sons (William, Theobald, Stephen, and Henry): OV, III, p. 117. Another account states that she had six sons (William, Theobald, Odo, Stephen, Philip, and Henry) and five daughters (Lucia, Agnes, Eléanore, Alix, and Lithuise). Her biographer, Kimberly LoPrete, claims she had between six and eight children, and she names Theobald, Odo, Stephen, Henry, and Agnes. Carmi Parsons and Wheeler, p. 317.

6. GRA, I, p. 505.

7. OV, V, p. 325.

8. Ibid.

9. Ibid., VI, p. 43.

10. GND, II, p. 263; OV, V, p. 325.

11. Abrahams, pp. 198–99, 255–56.

12. GND, II, p. 277.

13. Stafford, "Women and the Norman Conquest," pp. 226–27.

BIBLIOGRAPHY

PRIMARY SOURCES

Abrahams, P. (ed.). *Les Oeuvres Poétiques de Baudri de Bourgueil, 1046–1130* (Paris, 1926).

Barlow, F. (ed. and trans.). *The Carmen de Hastingae Proelio of Guy, Bishop of Amiens* (Oxford, 1999).

—— (ed.). *The Letters of Arnulf of Lisieux.* Royal Historical Society, Camden, third series, vol. LXI (London, 1939).

——. *The Life of King Edward Who Rests at Westminster* (Oxford, 1992).

Bates, D. (ed.). *Regesta Regum Anglo-Normannorum: The Acta of William I, 1066–1087* (Oxford, 1998).

Boüard, M. de. *Documents de l'Histoire de la Normandie* (Toulouse, 1972).

Burgess, G. S., and A. Holden (ed. and trans.). *Wace, the Roman de Rou* (Jersey, 2002).

Campbell, A. (ed. and trans.). *Encomium Emmae Reginae,* Camden Society, third series, vol. LXXII (London, 1949).

Chibnall, M. (ed. and trans.). *The Ecclesiastical History of Orderic Vitalis,* 6 vols. (1968–78).

Christiansen, E. (trans.). *Dudo of St. Quentin: History of the Normans* (Woodbridge, 1998).

Chronicon Turonense, in M. Bouquet (ed.), *Recueil des Historiens des Gaules et de la France,* vol. XI (Paris, 1876).

Chronique Rimée de Philippe Mouskes, vol. II (Brussels, 1838).

Clarke, A., J. Caley, F. Holbrooke, J. W. Clarke, and T. Hardy (eds.). *Foedera, Conventiones, Literae et Cujuscumque Generis Acta Publica 1066–1383,* 4 vols. (London, 1816).

Clover, H., and M. Gibson (eds.). *Letters of Lanfranc* (Oxford, 1979).

Constable, G. (ed.). *The Letters of Peter the Venerable,* 2 vols. (Cambridge, Mass., 1967).

Coulton, G. G., and C. C. Swinton (ed. and trans.). *The Autobiography of Guibert, Abbot of Nogent-Sous-Coucy* (London, 1925).

Cowdrey, H.E.J. (ed. and trans.). *The Epistolae Vagantes of Pope Gregory VII* (Oxford, 1971).

——— *The Register of Pope Gregory VII, 1073–1085* (Oxford, 2002).

Crispin, G. "Vita Herluini," in A. Sapir-Abulafia and G. R. Evans (eds.), *The Works of Gilbert Crispin, Abbot of Westminster* (London, 1986), pp. 183–212.

"Cronique attribuée à Baudoin d'Avesnes," in Baron Kervyn de Lettenhove (ed.), *Istore et croniques de Flandres, d'après les textes de divers manuscrits*, vol. II (Brussels, 1880), pp. 555–696.

Darlington, R. R., and P. McGurk (eds.). *The Chronicle of John of Worcester*, vols. II and III (Oxford, 1995).

Davis, H.W.C. (ed.). *Regesta Regum Anglo-Normannorum, 1066–1154*, vol. I: *Regesta Willelmi Conquestoris et Willelmi Rufi, 1066–1100* (Oxford, 1913).

Davis, R.H.C., and M. Chibnall (eds.). *The "Gesta Willelmi" of William of Poitiers* (Oxford, 1998).

Delisle, M. L. (ed.). *Receuil de Travaux d'Érudition dédiés a la memoire de Julien Havet, 1853–1893* (Geneva, 1972).

———. *Rouleaux des Morts du IXe au XVe Siècle*, Société de l'Histoire de France (Paris, 1866).

Douglas, D. C., and G. W. Greenaway. *English Historical Documents, AD 1042–1189*, vol. II (London, 1961).

Duchesne, H.N.S. (ed.). *Historiae Normannorum Scriptores Antique* (Paris, 1619).

Dugdale, W. *Monasticon Anglicanum: A History of the Abbeys and Other Monasteries, Hospitals, Frieries, and Cathedral and Collegiate Churches, with Their Dependencies, in England and Wales*, 6 vols. (London, 1846).

Eadmer. *Historia Novorum in Anglia*, translated by G. Bosanquet (London, 1964).

Edwards, E. (ed.). "Chronica Monasterii de Hida Juxta Wintoniam," in *Liber Monasterii de Hyda*, Rolls series (London, 1886), Appendix A, pp. 283–321.

Fahlin, C. *Étude sur le Manuscrit de Tours de la Chronique des Ducs de Normandie par Benoit* (Uppsala, 1937).

Fauroux, M. (ed.). *Recueil des Actes des Ducs de Normandie (911–1066)*, Mémoires de la Société des Antiquaires de Normandie, vol. XXXVI (Caen, 1961).

Forester, T. *The Chronicle of Henry of Huntingdon* (Felinfach, 1991).

Foreville, R. (ed.). *Guillaume de Poitiers: Histoire de Guillaume le Conquérant* (Paris, 1952).

Frölich, W. (trans.). *The Letters of Saint Anselm of Canterbury* (Kalamazoo, 1900).

Grierson, P. (ed.). *Les Annales de Saint-Pierre de Gand et de Saint-Amand* (Brussels, 1937).

Guérard, M. *Cartulaire de l'Abbaye de Saint-Bertin* (Paris, 1841).

Holden, J. (ed.). *Wace, Roman de Rou, Soc. Anc. Textes Français*, 3 vols. (Paris, 1970–73).

Houts, E. van (ed.). "The Brevis Relatio de Guillelmo nobilissimo comite. Normannorum, Written by a Monk of Battle Abbey," in *Chronology, Conquest and Conflict in Medieval England*, Camden Miscellany XXXIV, Camden Society, fifth series, vol. X (Cambridge, 1997), pp. 1–48.

————. *The Gesta Normannorum Ducum of William of Jumièges, Orderic Vitalis, and Robert of Torigni*, 2 vols. (Oxford, 1992–95).

Howlett, R. (ed.). *Chronicles of the Reigns of Stephen, Henry II, and Richard I*, vol. IV: *The Chronicle of Robert of Torigni* (London, 1889).

Laing, S. (ed.). *The Heimskringla: or, Chronicle of the Kings of Norway*, translated from the Icelandic of Snorro Sturleson, 3 vols. (London, 1844).

Legg, L.G.W. (ed.). *English Coronation Records* (London, 1901).

Licquet, T. *Histoire de Normandie*, 2 vols. (Rouen, 1835).

Luard, H. R. (ed.). *Annales Monastici*, 5 vols., Rolls series (London, 1864–69).

Madden, F. (ed.). *Historia Anglorum by Matthew Paris*, 3 vols., Rolls series (London, 1866–69).

Mansi, G. D., et al. (eds.). *Sacrorum Conciliorum Nova et Amplissima Collectio*, vol. XIX (Venice, etc., 1759).

Maseres, F. (ed.). *Historiae Anglicanae Circa Tempus Conquestus Angliae à Gulielmo Notho, Normannorum Duce* (London, 1807).

Michel, F. (ed.). "Chronique des Ducs de Normandie par Benoit," in *Collection de Documents Inédits sur l'Histoire de France*, 3 vols. (Paris, 1836–44).

Migne, J. P. (ed.). "Vita B. Simonis," in *Patrologia Latina*, clvi (1853).

Morey, A., and O.N.L. Brooke (eds.). *The Letters and Charters of Gilbert Foliot* (Cambridge, 1967).

Morris, J. (general editor). *Domesday Book*, 38 vols. (Chichester, 1982).

Musset, L. (ed.). *Les Actes de Guillaume le Conquérant et de la Reine Mathilde pour les Abbayes Caënnaises*, Mémoires de la Société des Antiquaires de Normandie, vol. XXXVII (Caen, 1967).

Mynors, R.A.B., R. M. Thomson, and M. Winterbottom (ed. and trans.). *William of Malmesbury, Gesta Regum Anglorum: The History of the English Kings*, vols. I and II (Oxford, 1998–99).

Nelson, L. H. (ed. and trans.). *Herman of Tournai: The Restoration of the Monastery of Saint Martin of Tournai* (Washington, D.C., 1996).

Nichols, J. (ed.). *A Collection of All the Wills, Now Known to Be Extant, of the Kings and Queens of England* (London, 1780; reprinted New Jersey, 1999).

Pelteret, D.A.E. *Catalogue of English Post-Conquest Vernacular Documents* (Woodbridge, 1990).

Riley, H. T. *Ingulphus's Chronicle of the Abbey of Croyland* (London, 1908).

Round, J. H. (ed.). *Calendar of Documents Preserved in France, Illustrative of the History of Great Britain and Ireland*, vol. I: *AD 918–1216* (London, 1899).

Searle, E. (ed. and trans.). *The Chronicle of Battle Abbey* (Oxford, 1980).

Smet, J. J. de (ed.). *Corpus Chronicorum Flandriae*, in *Recueil des Chroniques de Flandre*, vol. I (Brussels, 1837).

Southern, R. W. (ed. and trans.). *The Life of St. Anselm, Archbishop of Canterbury*, by Eadmer (London, 1962).

Stevenson, J. (ed.). "Annals of the Church of Winchester from the Year 633 to the Year 1277. By a Monk of Winchester," in *The Church Historians of England,* vol. IV, part I (London, 1856).

———. *Chronicon Monasterii de Abingdon,* 2 vols., Rolls series (London, 1858).

——— (ed. and trans.). *The Historical Works of Simeon of Durham, The Church Historians of England,* vol. III, part II (London, 1855).

Swanton, M. (ed.). *The Anglo-Saxon Chronicles* (London, 2000).

Thorpe, B. (ed.). *Florentii Wigorniensis Monachi Chronicon ex Chronicis,* 2 vols. (London, 1848–49).

Van Caenegem, R. C., *English Lawsuits from William I to Richard I,* vol. I (London, 1990).

"Vita B. Lanfranci," *Patrologia Latina* 150 (1854), pp. 29–58.

Wright, T. (ed.). *Anglo-Latin Satirical Poets and Epigrammatists of the Twelfth Century.* Rolls series, vol. LI (London, 1872).

———. "The Chronicle of Pierre de Langtoft," in *French Verse, from the Earliest Period to the Death of King Edward I,* 2 vols. (London, 1866–68).

Wright, W. A. *The Metrical Chronicle of Robert of Gloucester,* 2 vols., Rolls series 86 (London, 1887).

SECONDARY SOURCES

Aird, W. "Frustrated Masculinity: The Relationship Between William the Conqueror and His Eldest Son," in D. M. Hadley (ed.), *Masculinity in Medieval Europe* (London and New York, 1999), pp. 39–55.

———. *Robert Curthose, Duke of Normandy* (Woodbridge, 2008).

Ashley, M. *The Life and Times of William I* (London, 1973).

Bailey, M. D. *Magic and Superstition: A Concise History from Antiquity to the Present* (Maryland, 2007).

Baker, D. (ed.) *Medieval Women: Studies in Church History,* Subsidia vol. I (Oxford, 1978).

Barlow, F. "The Carmen de Hastingae Proelio," in K. Bourne, K. Watt, and D. C. Watt (eds.), *Studies in International History* (London, 1967), pp. 35–67.

———. *Edward the Confessor* (London, 1997).

———. *The English Church, 1066–1154* (London, 1979).

———. *William I and the Norman Conquest* (London, 1965).

———. *William Rufus* (London, 1983).

Barré, P. Y., et al. *La Tapisserie de la Reine Mathilde, comédie, en un acte, en prose, mêlée de vaudevilles* (Paris, 1804).

Bates, D. "The Character and Career of Odo, Bishop of Bayeux (1049/50–1097)," *Speculum,* vol. 50 (Massachusetts, 1975).

———. *Normandy Before 1066* (London, 1982).

———. "The Origins of the Justiciarship," *Anglo-Norman Studies: Proceedings of the Battle Conference,* vol. IV (Bury St. Edmunds, 1981), pp. 1–12, 167–71.

————. "Rouen from 900–1204: From Scandinavian Settlement to Angevin 'Capital,' "
in J. Stratford (ed.), *Medieval Art, Architecture and Archaeology at Rouen*, The British
Archaeological Association Conference Transactions for the Year 1986 (Leeds,
1993), pp. 1–11.

————. *William the Conqueror* (Stroud, 2004).

Bates, D., and A. Curry. *England and Normandy in the Middle Ages* (London, 1994).

Bates, D., and E. Hallam. *Domesday Book* (Stroud, 2001).

Baylé, M. *La Trinité de Caen: Sa Place dans l'histoire de l'Architecture et du Décor Romans*
(Geneva, 1979).

Beech, G. T. "Queen Mathilda of England (1066–83) and the Abbey of La Chaise-Dieu
in the Auvergne," *Frühmittelalterliche Studien*, vol. 27 (Berlin and New York, 1993),
pp. 350–74.

Bentley-Cranch, D. *Royal Faces* (National Portrait Gallery, London, 1990).

Biddle, M. "Seasonal Festivals and Residence: Winchester, Westminster and Gloucester
in the Tenth to Twelfth Centuries," *Anglo-Norman Studies: Proceedings of the Battle
Conference*, vol. VIII (Bury St. Edmunds, 1985), pp. 51–72.

Birdsall, J. "The Abbey of La Trinité at Caen in the 11th and 12th centuries," unpublished PhD dissertation, Harvard (1925).

Blaauw, W. H. "Remarks on Matilda, Queen of William the Conqueror, and Her Daughter Gundrada," *Archaeologia* XXXII, December 1846 (London, 1847), pp. 108–25.

Blamires, A. *The Case for Women in Medieval Culture* (Oxford, 1997).

Boüard, Michel de. *Guillaume le Conquérant* (Paris, 1984).

————. *Histoire de la Normandie* (Toulouse, 1984).

————. "La Reine Mathilde," Conférence Donnée le 14 mai 1985 à Bernay, *Les Amis de
Bernay: Societé Historique et Archéologique*, vol. XXVI (July 1989), pp. 13–29.

Bouchard, C. B. "Consanguinity in Noble Marriages in the Tenth and Eleventh Centuries," *Speculum*, vol. 61 (Massachusetts, 1981), pp. 268–87.

Boucher, François. *A History of Costume in the West* (London, 2004).

Bradbury, J. *The Battle of Hastings* (Stroud, 1998).

Bradley, S.A.J. *Anglo-Saxon Poetry: An Anthology of Old English Poems in Prose*, translation
with introduction and headnotes (London, 1982).

Bridgeford, A. *1066: The Hidden History of the Bayeux Tapestry* (London, 2004).

Brooke, C.N.L. *The Medieval Idea of Marriage* (Oxford, 1989).

Brooke, C.N.L., and D. M. Smith. *A History of England*, vol II: *From Alfred to Henry III,
871–1272* (Edinburgh, 1960).

Brooke, I. *English Costume of the Early Middle Ages* (London, 1936).

Brown, R. A. *English Medieval Castles* (London, 1954).

————. *The Normans and the Norman Conquest* (Woodbridge, 1985).

Brown, S. A. *The Bayeux Tapestry: History and Bibliography* (Woodbridge, 1988).

Campbell, M. W. "Queen Emma and Aelfgifu of Northampton: Canute the Great's
Women," *Medieval Scandinavia* IV (1971), pp. 66–79.

Carey, H. M. *Matilda of Normandy: A Poetical Tribute to the Imperial Academy of Caen* (London, 1859).

Carmi Parsons, J. (ed.) *Medieval Queenship* (Stroud, 1994).

Carmi Parsons, J., and B. Wheeler (eds.). *Medieval Mothering* (New York and London, 1996).

Chambers, J. *The Norman Kings* (London, 1981).

Chandler, V. "Intimations of Authority: Notes on Three Anglo-Norman Countesses," *Indiana Social Studies Quarterly*, vol. XXXI, no. 1 (1978), pp. 5–17.

Chibnall, M. *Anglo-Norman England* (Oxford, 1986).

———. *The Debate on the Norman Conquest* (Manchester, 1999).

———. "Women in Orderic Vitalis," *Haskins Society Journal*, vol. 2 (London, 1990), pp. 105–21.

———. *The World of Orderic Vitalis* (Oxford, 1984).

Clanchy, M. T. *Early Medieval England* (London, 1997).

Clay, C. *Early Yorkshire Charters*, vol. VIII (Wakefield, 1949).

Clover, C. "Regardless of Sex: Men, Women and Power in Early Northern Europe," *Speculum*, vol. 68 (1993).

Cotman, J. S. *Architectural Antiquities of Normandy*, 2 vols. (London, 1822).

Cowdrey, H.E.J. "The Anglo-Norman Laudes Regiae," *Viator*, vol. XII (1981), pp. 37–78.

———. "Towards an Interpretation of the Bayeux Tapestry," *Anglo-Norman Studies: Proceedings of the Battle Conference*, vol. X (Bury St. Edmunds, 1987), pp. 49–65.

Crouch, D. *The Normans: The History of a Dynasty* (London and New York, 2002).

Darby, H. C. *Domesday England* (Cambridge, 1977).

David, O. W. *Robert Curthose, Duke of Normandy* (Cambridge, Mass., 1920).

Davis, R.H.C. "William of Jumièges, Robert Curthose and the Norman Succession," *English Historical Review*, vol. XCV (London, 1980), pp. 597–606.

———. "William of Poitiers and His History of William the Conqueror," in R.H.C. Davis et al. (eds.), *The Writing of History in the Middle Ages: Essays Presented to Richard William Southern* (Oxford, 1981), pp. 71–100.

DeAragon, R. "In Pursuit of Aristocratic Women: A Key to Success in Norman England," *Albion* 14 (1982).

Di Clemente, K. "The Women of Flanders and Their Husbands," *Essays in Medieval Studies*, vol. XXIII (2006).

Dodwell, O. R. "The Bayeux Tapestry and the French Secular Epic," in *Burlington Magazine*, vol. CVIII (London, November 1966).

Douglas, D. C. "Companions of the Conqueror," *History*, vol. XXVIII (1943).

———. *The Norman Conquest and British Historians* (Glasgow, 1946).

———. *William the Conqueror: The Norman Impact upon England* (London, Folio Society, 2004).

Duby, G. *Love and Marriage in the Middle Ages*, translated by J. Dunnett (Oxford, 1994).

Ducarel, A. C. *Anglo-Norman Antiquities: Considered in a Tour Through Part of Normandy* (London, 1767).

Duckett, G. F. "Gundreda de Warenne: Final and Conclusive Evidence," *Yorkshire Archaeological Journal,* vol. XV (Leeds, 1900), pp. 428–33.

———. "Observations on the Parentage of Gundreda, Countess of Warenne," *Yorkshire Archaeological Journal,* vol. IX (Leeds, 1886), pp. 421–37.

Duggan, A. J. (ed.) *Queens and Queenship in Medieval Europe* (Woodbridge, 1997).

Erler, M., and M. Kowaleski (eds.). *Women and Power in the Middle Ages* (Athens and London, 1988).

Evergates, T. (ed.). *Aristocratic Women in Medieval France* (Philadelphia, 1999).

Facinger, M. "A Study of Medieval Queenship: Capetian France, 987–1237," *Studies in Medieval and Renaissance History,* vol. V (Lincoln, NE, 1968).

Farmer, S. "Persuasive Voices: Clerical Images of Medieval Wives," *Speculum,* vol. 61 (Massachusetts, 1986).

Farrer, W. *Early Yorkshire Charters,* vols. I–III (1914–16), vol. IV (1935), vol. VI (1939).

Fell, C. *Women in Anglo-Saxon England* (Oxford, 1984).

Fernie, E. *The Architecture of Norman England* (Oxford, 2000).

Ferrante, J. M. "The Education of Women in the Middle Ages in Theory, Fact and Fantasy," in P. H. Labalme (ed.), *Beyond Their Sex: Learned Women of the European Past* (New York, 1980).

Fettu, A. *Queen Matilda* (Cully, 2005).

Fletcher, R. *Bloodfeud: Murder and Revenge in Anglo-Saxon England* (London, 2003).

Fradenburg, L. O. *Women and Sovereignty* (Edinburgh, 1992).

Freeman, E. A. *The History of the Norman Conquest of England,* 6 vols. (Oxford, 1870).

———. "The Parentage of Gundrada, Wife of William of Warren," *English Historical Review,* vol. III (London, 1888), pp. 680–701.

Garlick, B., S. Dixon, and P. Allen (eds.). *Stereotypes of Women in Power: Historical Perspectives and Revisionist Views* (New York and London, 1992).

Gathagan, L. L. "Embodying Power: Gender and Authority in the Queenship of Mathilda of Flanders," unpublished PhD dissertation, City University of New York (2002).

———. "The Trappings of Power: The Coronation of Mathilda of Flanders," *Haskins Society Journal,* vol. 13 (Woodbridge, 1999), pp. 21–39.

George, R. H. "The Contribution of Flanders to the Conquest of England," *Revue Belge de Philologie et d'Histoire,* vol. V (Brussels, 1926).

Gibson, M. *Lanfranc of Bec* (Oxford, 1978).

Golding, B. *Conquest and Colonisation: The Normans in Britain* (Basingstoke, 2001).

Grape, W. *The Bayeux Tapestry* (Munich and New York, 1994).

Green, J. A. *The Aristocracy of Norman England* (Cambridge, 1997).

Green, M.A.E. *Lives of the Princesses of England,* vol. I (London, 1849).

Grierson, P. "The Relations of England and Flanders Before the Norman Conquest," *Transactions of the Royal Historical Society,* fourth series, vol. XXIII (London, 1941).

———. "A Visit of Earl Harold to Flanders in 1056," *English Historical Review,* vol. LI (London, 1936), pp. 90–97.

Hallam, E. *Domesday Book Through Nine Centuries* (London, 1986).

Hanawalt, B. "Medievalists and the Study of Childhood," *Speculum* 77 (2002), pp. 440–60.

Haskins, C. H. *Norman Institutions* (New York, 1967).

Herlihy, D. "Life Expectancies for Women in Medieval Society," in R. T. Morewedge (ed.), *The Role of Women in the Middle Ages* (New York, 1975).

———. *Women, Family and Society in Medieval Europe* (Providence and London, 1995).

Hill, D. "The Bayeux Tapestry and Its Commentators," *Medieval Life* 11 (1999).

Hilton, L. *Queens Consort: England's Medieval Queens* (London, 2008).

Hollister, O. W. *Henry I* (New Haven and London, 2001).

———. *Monarchy, Magnates and Institutions in the Anglo-Norman World* (London and Roncevert, 1986).

Houts, E. van. "The Echo of the Conquest in Latin Sources: Duchess Matilda, Her Daughters and the Enigma of the Golden Child," in P. Bouet, et al., *The Bayeux Tapestry: Embroidering the Facts of History* (Caen, 2004), pp. 135–53.

———. "Latin Poetry and the Anglo-Norman Court 1066–1135: The Carmen Hastingae Proelio," *Journal of Medieval History,* vol. XV, no. 1 (Amsterdam, 1989), pp. 39–62.

———. *Memory and Gender in Medieval Europe* (Basingstoke, 1999).

———. "The Norman Conquest Through European Eyes," *English Historical Review,* vol. CX (London, 1995), pp. 832–53.

———. *The Normans in Europe* (Manchester, 2000).

———. "The Origins of Herleva, Mother of William the Conqueror," *English Historical Review,* vol. CI (Oxford, 1986), pp. 399–404.

———. "The Ship List of William the Conqueror," *Anglo-Norman Studies: Proceedings of the Battle Conference,* vol. X (Bury St. Edmunds, 1987), pp. 159–83.

Hudson, J. "The Abbey of Abingdon, Its Chronicle and the Norman Conquest," *Anglo-Norman Studies: Proceedings of the Battle Conference,* vol. XIX (Bury St. Edmunds, 1996), pp. 181–202.

Humphrys, J. *Clash of Arms: Twelve English Battles* (English Heritage, 2006).

Huneycutt, L. L. *Matilda of Scotland: A Study in Medieval Queenship* (Woodbridge, 2003).

James, E. "Childhood and Youth in the Middle Ages," in P.J.P. Goldberg and F. Riddy (eds.), *Youth in the Middle Ages* (York, 2004), pp. 11–23.

John, E. "Edward the Confessor and the Norman Succession," *English Historical Review,* vol. XCIV (1979), pp. 241–67.

Johnson, P. D. *Equal in Monastic Profession: Religious Women in Medieval France* (Chicago, 1991).

Keats-Rohan, K.S.B. *Domesday People: A Prosopography of Persons Appearing in English Documents 1066–1166,* vol. I: *Domesday Book* (Woodbridge, 1999).

——— (ed.). *Family Trees and the Roots of Politics: The Prosopography of Britain and France from the Tenth to the Twelfth Century* (Woodbridge, 1998).

Keynes, S. "Giso Bishop of Wells," *Anglo-Norman Studies: Proceedings of the Battle Conference,* vol. XIX (Bury St. Edmunds, 1996), pp. 203–71.

Kirshner, J., and S. F. Wemple. *Women of the Medieval World: Essays in Honour of John H. Mundy* (Oxford, 1985).

Klapisch-Zuber (ed.). *A History of Women in the West,* vol. II: *The Silences of the Middle Ages* (Cambridge, Mass., and London, 1992).

Klein, S. S. *Ruling Women: Queenship and Gender in Anglo-Saxon Literature* (Notre Dame, Ind., 2006).

Kliman, B. "Women in Early English Literature, 'Beowulf' to the 'Ancrene Wisse,' " *Nottingham Medieval Studies,* vol. XXI (1977).

Lair, M. J. *La Reine Mathilde dans la légende: Extrait du Bulletin de la Société des Antiquaires de Normandie* (Caen, 1897).

Lane Pool, A. *From Domesday Book to Magna Carta* (Oxford, 1951).

Larson, L. M. *The King's Household in England Before the Norman Conquest* (Madison, Wis., 1904).

Lawson, M. K. *The Battle of Hastings* (Woodbridge, 2002).

Leyser, H. *Medieval Women: A Social History of Women in England, 450–1500* (London, 1995).

LoPrete, K. A. *Adela of Blois, Countess and Lord* (Dublin, 2001).

———. "Adela of Blois and Ivo of Chartres: Piety, Politics and the Peace in the Diocese of Chartres," *Anglo-Norman Studies: Proceedings of the Battle Conference,* vol. XIV (Bury St. Edmunds, 1991), pp. 131–52.

———. "The Anglo-Norman Card of Adela of Blois," *Albion,* vol. XXII (1990), pp. 569–89.

Loyn, H. R. *Anglo-Saxon England and the Norman Conquest* (London, 1970).

Mason, E. *William II: Rufus, the Red King* (Stroud, 2005).

———. "Wulfstan of Worcester: Patriarch of the English?" in S. Keynes and A. P. Smyth (eds.), *Anglo-Saxons: Studies Presented to Cyril Roy Hart* (Portland, Ore., 2006), pp. 114–26.

McLynn, F. *1066: The Year of the Three Battles* (London, 1998).

McNamara, J. A., and S. Wemple. "The Power of Women Through the Family in Medieval Europe," in M. Erler and M. Kowaleski (eds.), *Women and Power in the Middle Ages* (Athens, Ga., and London, 1988), pp. 83–101.

Meyer, M. A. "Queen's Demense," in J. C. Holt (ed.), *Domesday Studies* (Woodbridge, 1987).

———. "Women's Estates in Later Anglo-Saxon England: The Politics of Possession," *Haskins Society Journal,* vol. III (London and Rio Grande, 1991), pp. 111–29.

Musset, L. (ed.). "La Reine Mathilde et la Fondation de la Trinité de Caen (Abbaye aux Dames)," *Mémoires de l'Académie Nationale des Sciences, Arts et Belles Lettres,* vol. XXI (Caen, 1984).

Nelson, J. L. "The Queen in Ninth-Century Wessex," in S. Keynes and A. P. Smyth (eds.), *Anglo-Saxons: Studies Presented to Cyril Roy Hart* (Portland, Ore., 2006), pp. 69–77.

Nicholas, D. *Medieval Flanders* (London and New York, 1992).

Nicholas, K. S. "Countesses as Rulers in Flanders," in T. Evergates (ed.), *Aristocratic Women in Medieval France* (Philadelphia, 1999), pp. 111–37.

Nip, R. "The Political Relations Between England and Flanders (1066–1128)," *Anglo-Norman Studies: Proceedings of the Battle Conference,* vol. XXI (1998), pp. 145–67.

Orme, N. *Medieval Children* (New Haven and London, 2001).

Oxford Dictionary of National Biography.

Planché, J. R. *The Conqueror and His Companions,* 2 vols. (London, 1874).

Powicke, F., E. B. Pryde, D. E. Greenway, S. Porter, and I. Roy (eds.). *Handbook of British Chronology* (Cambridge, 1997).

Prah-Pérochon, A. *La Reine Mathilde: Essais* (Paris, 1980).

———. "Rôle Officielle de Mathilde, Femme de Guillaume le Conquérant, 1053–1083," unpublished thesis, Aix-Marseille (1973).

Prentout, H. "Le mariage de Guillaume," in *Études sur Quelques Points d'Histoire de Guillaume le Conquérant: Mémoires de l'Académie Nationale de Caen,* vol. VI (Caen, 1931), pp. 3–30.

Rapin. *An Abridgement of the History of England,* vol. I (London, 1747).

Renn, D. F. *Norman Castles in Britain* (London and New York, 1973).

Rowley, T. *The Norman Heritage, 1066–1200* (London, 1984).

Rudborne, T. *Historia Major de Fundatione et Succession Ecclesiae Wintoniensis* (1691).

Schramm, P. E. *A History of the English Coronation,* translated by L.G.W. Legg (Oxford, 1937).

Searle, E. "Women and Legitimisation of Succession at the Norman Conquest," *Anglo-Norman Studies: Proceedings of the Battle Conference,* vol. III (Woodbridge, 1981).

Shahar, S. *Childhood in the Middle Ages* (London and New York, 1990).

Slocombe, G. *Sons of the Conqueror* (London, 1960).

Smith, R.A.L. "The Place of Gundulf in the Anglo-Norman Church," *English Historical Review,* vol. LVIII, no. 231 (London, 1943).

Southern, R. W. *Saint Anselm: A Portrait in a Landscape* (Cambridge, 1990).

Stafford, P. "Chronicle D: 1067 and Women: Gendering Conquest in Eleventh-Century England," in S. Keynes and A. P. Smyth (eds.), *Anglo-Saxons: Studies Presented to Cyril Roy Hart* (Portland, Ore., 2006), pp. 208–23.

———. "The King's Wife in Wessex 800–1066," *Past and Present,* vol. XCI (1981), pp. 3–27.

———. *Queen Emma and Queen Edith: Queenship and Women's Power in Eleventh-Century England* (Oxford, 1997).

———. *Queens, Concubines and Dowagers: The King's Wife in the Early Middle Ages* (London, 1983).

————. "Women and the Norman Conquest," *Transactions of the Royal Historical Society*, sixth series, vol. IV (London, 1994), pp. 221–49.

Stapleton, T. "Observations in Disproof of the Pretended Marriage of William de Warren, Earl of Surrey, with a Daughter Begotten of Matildis, Daughter of Baldwin, Comte of Flanders, by William the Conqueror, and Illustrative of the Origin and Early History of the Family in Normandy," *Archaeological Journal*, vol. III (London, 1846), pp. 1–26.

Starkey, D. *The Monarchy of England*, vol. I: *The Beginnings* (London, 2004).

Stenton, F. M. *Anglo-Saxon England* (Oxford, 1962).

————. *The Bayeux Tapestry* (London, 1957).

————. *The English Woman in History* (London, 1957).

Strickland, A. *Lives of the Queens of England*, vol. I (London, 1840).

Tanner, H. J. *Families, Friends and Allies: Boulogne and Politics in Northern France and England, c. 879–1160* (Leiden, 2004).

Thomas, H. M. *The English and the Normans: Ethnic Hostility, Assimilation, and Identity 1066–c. 1220* (Oxford, 2003).

Thompson, S. *Women Religious* (Oxford, 1991).

Tomkeieff, O. G. *Life in Norman England* (London and New York, 1967).

Truax, J. A. "Anglo-Norman Women at War: Valiant Soldiers, Prudent Strategists or Charismatic Leaders?," in D. J. Kagay and L.J.A. Villalon (eds.), *The Circle of War in the Middle Ages* (Woodbridge, 1999), pp. 111–25.

————. "From Bede to Orderic Vitalis: Changing Perspectives on the Role of Women in the Anglo-Saxon and Anglo-Norman Churches," *Haskins Society Journal*, vol. III (London and Rio Grande, 1991), pp. 35–51.

Turgis, S. *La très véridique histoire de la bonne Mathilde de Flandre, Duchesse de Normandie, Reyne d'Angleterre, Femme de Guillaume le Conquérant, auteur de la tapisserie-broderie de Bayeux* (Paris and Bayeux, 1912).

Turner, R. V. "The Children of Anglo-Norman Royalty and Their Upbringing," *Medieval Prosopography*, vol. XI, no. 2 (Kalamazoo, 1990), pp. 17–52.

Verlinden, C. *Robert I le Frison* (Antwerp and Paris, 1935).

Walker, D. *The Normans in Britain* (Oxford, 1995).

Walker, I. W. *Harold: The Last Anglo-Saxon King* (Stroud, 1997).

Walmsley, J. "The Early Abbesses, Nuns and Female Tenants of the Abbey of Holy Trinity, Caen," *Journal of Ecclesiastical History*, vol. XL, part III (Cambridge, 1997), pp. 425–44.

Waters, C. "Gundrada de Warenne," *Archaeological Journal*, vol. XLI (Exeter, 1884).

Weir, A. *Britain's Royal Families: The Complete Genealogy* (London, 1996).

White, G. H. "The Household of the Norman Kings," *Transactions of the Royal Historical Society*, fourth series, vol. XXX (Cambridge, 1948), pp. 127–55.

Williams, A. *The English and the Norman Conquest* (Woodbridge, 1995).

————. "A West-Country Magnate of the Eleventh Century: The Family Estates and Patronage of Beorhtric Son of Aelfgar," in K.S.B. Keats-Rohan (ed.), *Family Trees and the Roots of Politics: The Prosopography of Britain and France from the Tenth to the Twelfth Century* (Woodbridge, 1998), pp. 41–68.

Wilson, D. M. (ed.). *The Bayeux Tapestry* (London, 1985).

INDEX

ABOUT THE AUTHOR

TRACY BORMAN studied and taught history at the University of Hull and was awarded a PhD in 1997. She is now Chief Executive of the Heritage Education Trust and also works for Historic Royal Palaces. Her previous books include *Henrietta Howard: King's Mistress, Queen's Servant; Elizabeth's Women: Friends, Rivals, and Foes Who Shaped the Virgin Queen;* and *The Ring and the Crown: A History of Royal Weddings, 1066–2011*, which she coauthored with Sarah Gristwood, Alison Weir, and Kate Williams. She lives in London with her daughter.

ABOUT THE TYPE

This book was set in Monotype Dante, a typeface designed by Giovanni Mardersteig (1892–1977). Conceived as a private type for the Officina Bodoni in Verona, Italy, Dante was originally cut only for hand composition by Charles Malin, the famous Parisian punch cutter, between 1946 and 1952. Its first use was in an edition of Boccaccio's *Trattatello in laude di Dante* that appeared in 1954. The Monotype Corporation's version of Dante followed in 1957. Though modeled on the Aldine type used for Pietro Cardinal Bembo's treatise *De Aetna* in 1495, Dante is a thoroughly modern interpretation of that venerable face.